Business Model Generation

Business Model Generation

A Handbook for Visionaries, Game Changers, and Challengers

Written by
Alexander Osterwalder and Yves Pigneur

Design
Alan Smith, The Movement

Editor and Contributing Co-Author
Tim Clark

Production
Patrick van der Pijl

Co-created by an amazing crowd of
470 practitioners from 45 countries

WILEY

John Wiley & Sons, Inc.

Co-created by:

Ellen Di Resta
Michael Anton Dila
Remko Vochteloo
Victor Lombardi
Jeremy Hayes
Alf Rehn
Jeff De Cagna
Andrea Mason
Jan Ondrus
Simon Evenblij
Chris Walters
Caspar van Rijnbach
benmlih
Rodrigo Miranda
Saul Kaplan
Lars Geisel
Simon Scott
Dimitri Lévita
Johan fflñrneblad
Craig Sadler
Praveen Singh
Livia Labate
Kristian Salvesen
Daniel Egger
Diogo Carmo
Marcel Ott
Guilhem Bertholet
Thibault Estier
Stephane Rey
Chris Peasner
Jonathan Lin
Cesar Picos
Florian
Armando Maldonado
Eduardo Míguez
Anouar Hamidouche
Francisco Perez
Nicky Smyth
Bob Dunn
Carlo Arioli

Matthew Milan
Ralf Beuker
Sander Smit
Norbert Herman
Atanas Zaprianov
Linus Malmberg
Deborah Mills-Scofield
Peter Knol
Jess McMullin
Marianela Ledezma
Ray Guyot
Martin Andres Giorgetti
Geert van Vlijmen
Rasmus Rønholt
Tim Clark
Richard Bell
Erwin Blom
Frédéric Sidler
John LM Kiggundu
Robert Elm
Ziv Baida
Andra Larin-van der Pijl
Eirik V Johnsen
Boris Fritscher
Mike Lachapelle
Albert Meige
Pablo M. Ramírez
Jean-Loup
Colin Pons
Vacherand
Guillermo Jose Aguilar
Adriel Haeni
Lukas Prochazka
Kim Korn
Abdullah Nadeem
Rory O'Connor
Hubert de Candé
Frans Wittenberg
Jonas Lindelöf
Gordon Gray

Karen Hembrough
Ronald Pilot
Yves Claude Aubert
Wim Saly
Woutergort
Fanco Ivan Santos Negrelli
Amee Shah
Lars Mårtensson
Kevin Donaldson
JD Stein
Ralf de Graaf
Lars Norrman
Sergey Trikhachev
Thomas
Alfred Herman
Bert Spangenberg
Robert van Kooten
Hans Suter
Wolf Schumacher
Bill Welter
Michele Leidi
Asim J. Ranjha
Peter Troxler
Ola Dagberg
Wouter van der Burg
Artur Schmidt
Slabber
Peter Jones
Sebastian Ullrich
Andrew Pope
Fredrik Eliasson
Bruce MacVarish
Göran Hagert
Markus Gander
Marc Castricum
Nicholas K. Niemann
Christian Labezin
Claudio D'Ipolitto
Aurel Hosennen
Adrian Zaugg

Frank Camille Lagerveld
Andres Alcalde
Alvaro Villalobos M
Bernard Racine
Pekka Matilainen
Bas van Oosterhout
Gillian Hunt
Bart Boone
Michael Moriarty
Mike
Design for Innovation
Tom Corcoran
Ari Wurmann
Antonio Robert
Wibe van der Pol
paola valeri
Michael Sommers
Nicolas Fleury
Gert Steens
Jose Sebastian Palazuelos Lopez
jorge zavala
Harry Heijligers
Armand Dickey
Jason King
Kjartan Mjoesund
Louis Rosenfeld
Ivo Georgiev
Donald Chapin
Annie Shum
Valentin Crettaz
Dave Crowther
Chris J Davis
Frank Della Rosa
Christian Schüller
Luis Eduardo de Carvalho
Patrik Ekström
Greg Krauska
Giorgio Casoni
Stef Silvis

Peter Froberg
Lino Piani
Eric Jackson
Indrajit Datta Chaudhuri
Martin Fanghanel
Michael Sandfær
Niall Casey
John McGuire
Vivian Vendeirinho
Martèl Bakker Schut
Stefano Mastrogiacoo
Mark Hickman
Dibrov
Reinhold König
Marcel Jaeggi
John O'Connell
Marije Sluis
David Edwards
Martin Kuplens-Ewart
Jay Goldman
Isckia
Nabil Harfoush
Yannick
Raoef Hussainali
ronald van den hoff
Melbert Visscher
Manfred Fischer
Joe Chao
Carlos Meca
Mario Morales
Paul Johannesson
Rob Griffitts
Marc-Antoine Garrigue
Wassili Bertoen
Bart Pieper
Bruce E. Terry
Michael N. Wilkens
Himikel - TrebeA

Jeroen de Jong
Gertjan Verstoep
Steven Devijver
Jana Thiel
Walter Brand
Stephan Ziegenhorn
Frank Meeuwsen
Colin Henderson
Danilo Tic
Marco Raaijmakers
Marc Sniukas
Khaled Algasem
Jan Pelttari
Yves Sinner
Michael Kinder
Vince Kuraitis
Teofilo Asuan Santiago IV
Ray Lai
Brainstorm Weekly
Huub Raemakers
Peter Salmon
Philippe
Khawaja M.
Jille Sol
Renninger, Wolfgang
Daniel Pandza
Robin Uchida
Pius Bienz
Ivan Torreblanca
Berry Vetjens
David Crow
Helge Hannisdal
Maria Droujkova
Leonard Belanger
Fernando Saenz-Marrero
Susan Foley
Vesela Koleva
Martijn
Eugen Rodel
Edward Giesen

Marc Faltheim
Nicolas De Santis
Antoine Perruchoud
Bernd Nurnberger
Patrick van Abbema
Terje Sand
Leandro Jesus
Karen Davis
Tim Turmelle
Anders Sundelin
Renata Phillippi
Martin Kaczynski
Frank
Bala Vaddi
Andrew Jenkins
Dariush Ghatan
Marcus Ambrosch
Jens Hoffmann
Steve Thomson
Eduardo M Morgado
Rafal Dudkowski
António Lucena de Faria
Knut Petter Nor
Ventenat Vincent
Peter Eckrich
Shridhar Lolla
Jens Larsson
David Sibbet
Mihail Krikunov
Edwin Kruis
Roberto Ortelli
Shana Ferrigan Bourcier
Jeffrey Murphy
Lonnie Sanders III
Arnold Wytenburg
David Hughes
Paul Ferguson
Frontier Service Design,
    LLC
Peter Noteboom

Ricardo Dorado
John Smith
Rod
Eddie
Jeffrey Huang
Terrance Moore
nse_55
Leif-Arne Bakker
Edler Herbert
Björn Kijl
Chris Finlay
Philippe Rousselot
Rob Schokker
Wouter Verwer
Jan Schmiedgen
Ugo Merkli
Jelle
Dave Gray
Rick le Roy
Ravila White
David G Luna Arellano
Joyce Hostyn
Thorwald Westmaas
Jason Theodor
Sandra Pickering
Trond M Fflòvstegaard
Jeaninne Horowitz Gassol
Lukas Feuerstein
Nathalie Magniez
Giorgio Pauletto
Martijn Pater
Gerardo Pagalday Eraña
Haider Raza
Ajay Ailawadhi
Adriana Ieraci
Daniël Giesen
Erik Dejonghe
Tom Winstanley
Heiner P. Kaufmann
Edwin Lee Ming Jin

Stephan Linnenbank
Liliana
Jose Fernando Quintana
Reinhard Prügl
Brian Moore
Gabi
Marko Seppänen
Erwin Fielt
Olivier Glassey
Francisco Conde
    Fernández
Valérie Chanal
Anne McCrossan
Larsen
Fred Collopy
Jana Görs
Patrick Foran
Edward Osborn
Greger Hagström
Alberto Saavedra
Remco de Kramer
Lillian Thompson
Howard Brown
Emil Ansarov
Frank Elbers
Horacio Alvaro Viana
Markus Schroll
Hylke Zeijlstra
Cheenu Srinivasan
Cyril Durand
Jamil Aslam
Oliver Buecken
John Wesner Price
Axel Friese
Gudmundur Kristjansson
Rita Shor
Jesus Villar
Espen Figenschou-
    Skotterud
James Clark

Jose Alfonso Lopez
Eric Schreurs
Donielle Buie
Adilson Chicória
Asanka Warusevitane
Jacob Ravn
Hampus Jakobsson
Adriaan Kik
Julián Domínguez Laperal
Marco W J Derksen
Dr. Karsten Willrodt
Patrick Feiner
Dave Cutherell
    Di Prisco
Darlene Goetzman
Mohan Nadarajah
Fabrice Delaye
Sunil Malhotra
Jasper Bouwsma
Ouke Arts
Alexander Troitzsch
Brett Patching
Clifford Thompson
Jorgen Dahlberg
Christoph Mühlethaler
Ernest Buise
Alfonso Mireles
Richard Zandink
Fraunhofer IAO
Tor Rolfsen Grønsund
David M. Weiss
Kim Peiter Jørgensen
Stephanie Diamond
Stefan Olsson
Anders Stølan
Edward Koops
Prasert Thawat-
    chokethawee
Pablo Azar
Melissa Withers

Edwin Beumer
Dax Denneboom
Mohammed Mushtaq
Gaurav Bhalla
Silvia Adelhelm
Heather McGowan
Phil Sang Yim
Noel Barry
Vishwanath
    Edavayyanamath
Rob Manson
Rafael Figueiredo
Jeroen Mulder
Emilio De Giacomo
Franco Gasperoni
Michael Weiss
Francisco Andrade
Arturo Herrera Sapunar
Vincent de Jong
Kees Groeneveld
Henk Bohlander
Sushil Chatterji
Tim Parsey
Georg E. A. Stampfl
Markus Kreutzer
Iwan Schneider
Michael Schuster
Ingrid Beck
Antti Äkräs
EHJ Peet
Ronald Poulton
Ralf Weidenhammer
Craig Rispin
Nella van Heuven
Ravi Sodhi
Dick Rempt
Rolf Mehnert
Luis Stabile
Enterprise Consulting
Aline Frankfort

Manuel Toscano
John Sutherland
Remo Knops
Juan Marquez
Chris Hopf
Marc Faeh
Urquhart Wood
Lise Tormod
Curtis L. Sippel
Abdul Razak Manaf
George B. Steltman
Karl Burrow
Mark McKeever
Linda Bryant
Jeroen Hinfelaar
Dan Keldsen
Damien
Roger A. Shepherd
Morten Povlsen
Lars Zahl
Elin Mørch Langlo
Xuemei Tian
Harry Verwayen
Riccardo Bonazzi
André Johansen
Colin Bush
Alexander Korbee
J Bartels
Steven Ritchey
Clark Golestani
Leslie Cohen
Amanda Smith
Benjamin De Pauw
Andre Macieira
Wiebe de Jager
Raym Crow
Mark Evans DM
Susan Schaper

Are you an entrepreneurial spirit?

yes ———— no ————

Are you constantly thinking about how to
create value and build new businesses, or how
to improve or transform your organization?

yes ———— no ————

Are you trying to find innovative
ways of doing business to replace
old, outdated ones?

yes ———— no ————

If you've answered "yes" to any of these questions, welcome to our group!

You're holding a handbook for visionaries, game changers, and challengers striving to defy outmoded business models and design tomorrow's enterprises. It's a book for the business model generation.

Today countless innovative business models are emerging. Entirely new industries are forming as old ones crumble. Upstarts are challenging the old guard, some of whom are struggling feverishly to reinvent themselves.

How do you imagine your organization's business model might look two, five, or ten years from now? Will you be among the dominant players? Will you face competitors brandishing formidable new business models?

This book will give you deep insight into the nature of business models. It describes traditional and bleeding-edge models and their dynamics, innovation techniques, how to position your model within an intensely competitive landscape, and how to lead the redesign of your own organization's business model.

Certainly you've noticed that this is not the typical strategy or management book. We designed it to convey the essentials of what you need to know, quickly, simply, and in a visual format. Examples are presented pictorially and the content is complemented with exercises and workshop scenarios you can use immediately. Rather than writing a conventional book about business model innovation, we've tried to design a practical guide for visionaries, game changers, and challengers eager to design or reinvent business models. We've also worked hard to create a beautiful book to enhance the pleasure of your "consumption." We hope you enjoy using it as much as we've enjoyed creating it.

An online community complements this book (and was integral to its creation, as you will discover later). Since business model innovation is a rapidly evolving field, you may want to go beyond the essentials in *Business Model Generation* and discover new tools online. Please consider joining our worldwide community of business practitioners and researchers who have co-created this book. On the Hub you can participate in discussions about business models, learn from others' insights, and try out new tools provided by the authors. Visit the Business Model Hub at www.BusinessModelGeneration.com/hub.

Business model innovation is hardly new. When the founders of Diners Club introduced the credit card in 1950, they were practicing business model innovation. The same goes for Xerox, when it introduced photocopier leasing and the per-copy payment system in 1959. In fact, we might trace business model innovation all the way back to the fifteenth century, when Johannes Gutenberg sought applications for the mechanical printing device he had invented.

But the scale and speed at which innovative business models are transforming industry landscapes today is unprecedented. For entrepreneurs, executives, consultants, and academics, it is high time to understand the impact of this extraordinary evolution. Now is the time to understand and to methodically address the challenge of business model innovation.

Ultimately, business model innovation is about creating value, for companies, customers, and society. It is about replacing outdated models. With its iPod digital media player and iTunes.com online store, Apple created an innovative new business model that transformed the company into the dominant force in online music. Skype brought us dirt-cheap global calling rates and free Skype-to-Skype calls with an innovative business model built on so-called peer-to-peer technology. It is now the world's largest carrier of international voice traffic. Zipcar frees city dwellers from automobile ownership by offering hourly or daily on-demand car rentals under a fee-based membership system. It's a business model response to emerging user needs and pressing environmental concerns. Grameen Bank is helping alleviate poverty through an innovative business model that popularized microlending to the poor.

But how can we systematically invent, design, and implement these powerful new business models? How can we question, challenge, and transform old, outmoded ones? How can we turn visionary ideas into game-changing business models that challenge the establishment—or rejuvenate it if we ourselves are the incumbents? *Business Model Generation* aims to give you the answers.

Since practicing is better than preaching, we adopted a new model for writing this book. Four hundred and seventy members of the Business Model Innovation Hub contributed cases, examples, and critical comments to the manuscript—and we took their feedback to heart. Read more about our experience in the final chapter of *Business Model Generation*.

Seven Faces of Business Model Innovation

The Senior Executive

Jean-Pierre Cuoni,
Chairman / EFG International

Focus: Establish a new business model in an old industry

Jean-Pierre Cuoni is chairman of EFG International, a private bank with what may be the industry's most innovative business model. With EFG he is profoundly transforming the traditional relationships between bank, clients, and client relationship managers. Envisioning, crafting, and executing an innovative business model in a conservative industry with established players is an art, and one that has placed EFG International among the fastest growing banks in its sector.

The Intrapreneur

Dagfinn Myhre,
Head of R&I Business Models / Telenor

Focus: Help exploit the latest techno-logical developments with the right business models

Dagfinn leads a business model unit at Telenor, one of the world's ten larg-est mobile telephone operators. The telecom sector demands continuous innovation, and Dagfinn's initiatives help Telenor identify and understand sustainable models that exploit the potential of the latest technological developments. Through deep analysis of key industry trends, and by develop-ing and using leading-edge analytical tools, Dagfinn's team explores new business concepts and opportunities.

The Entrepreneur

Mariëlle Sijgers,
Entrepreneur / CDEF Holding BV

Focus: Address unsatisfied customer needs and build new business models around them

Marielle Sijgers is a full-fledged entrepreneur. Together with her business partner, Ronald van den Hoff, she's shaking up the meeting, congress, and hospitality industry with innovative business models. Led by unsatisfied customer needs, the pair has invented new concepts such as Seats2meet.com, which allows on-the-fly booking of meetings in untraditional locations. Together, Sijgers and van den Hoff constantly play with new business model ideas and launch the most promising concepts as new ventures.

The Investor

Gert Steens, *President & Investment Analyst / Oblonski BV*

Focus: Invest in companies with the most competitive business models

Gert makes a living by identifying the best business models. Investing in the wrong company with the wrong model could cost his clients millions of euros and him his reputation. Understanding new and innovative business models has become a crucial part of his work. He goes far beyond the usual financial analytics and compares business models to spot strategic differences that may impart a competitive edge. Gert is constantly seeking business model innovations.

The Consultant

Bas van Oosterhout, Senior *Consultant / Capgemini Consulting*

Focus: Help clients question their business models, and envision and build new ones

Bas is part of Capgemini's Business Innovation Team. Together with his clients, he is passionate about boosting performance and renewing competitiveness through innovation. Business Model Innovation is now a core component of his work because of its high relevance to client projects. His aim is to inspire and assist clients with new business models, from ideation to implementation. To achieve this, Bas draws on his understanding of the most powerful business models, regardless of industry.

The Designer

Trish Papadakos, *Sole Proprietor / The Institute of You*

Focus: Find the right business model to launch an innovative product

Trish is a talented young designer who is particularly skilled at grasping an idea's essence and weaving it into client communications. Currently she's working on one of her own ideas, a service that helps people who are transitioning between careers. After weeks of in-depth research, she's now tackling the design. Trish knows she'll have to figure out the right business model to bring her service to market. She understands the client-facing part—that's what she works on daily as a designer. But, since she lacks formal business education, she needs the vocabulary and tools to take on the big picture.

The Conscientious Entrepreneur

Iqbal Quadir, *Social Entrepreneur / Founder of Grameen Phone*

Focus: Bring about positive social and economic change through innovative business models

Iqbal is constantly on the lookout for innovative business models with the potential for profound social impact. His transformative model brought telephone service to over 100 million Bangladeshis, utilizing Grameen Bank's microcredit network. He is now searching for a new model for bringing affordable electricity to the poor. As the head of MIT's Legatum Center, he promotes technological empowerment through innovative businesses as a path to economic and social development.

Table of Contents

The book is divided into five sections: ❶ The Business Model Canvas, a tool for describing, analyzing, and designing business models, ❷ Business Model Patterns, based on concepts from leading business thinkers, ❸ Techniques to help you design business models, ❹ Re-interpreting strategy through the business model lens, and ❺ A generic process to help you design innovative business models, tying together all the concepts, techniques, and tools in *Business Model Generation*. ⬤ The last section offers an outlook on five business model topics for future exploration. ◯ Finally, the afterword provides a peek into "the making of" *Business Model Generation*.

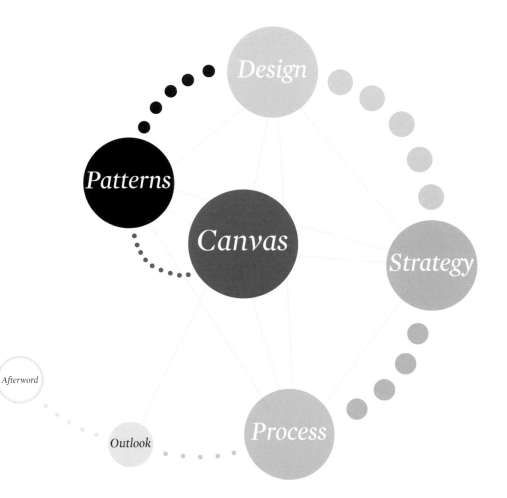

The Business Model Canvas

A shared language for describing, visualizing, assessing, and changing business models

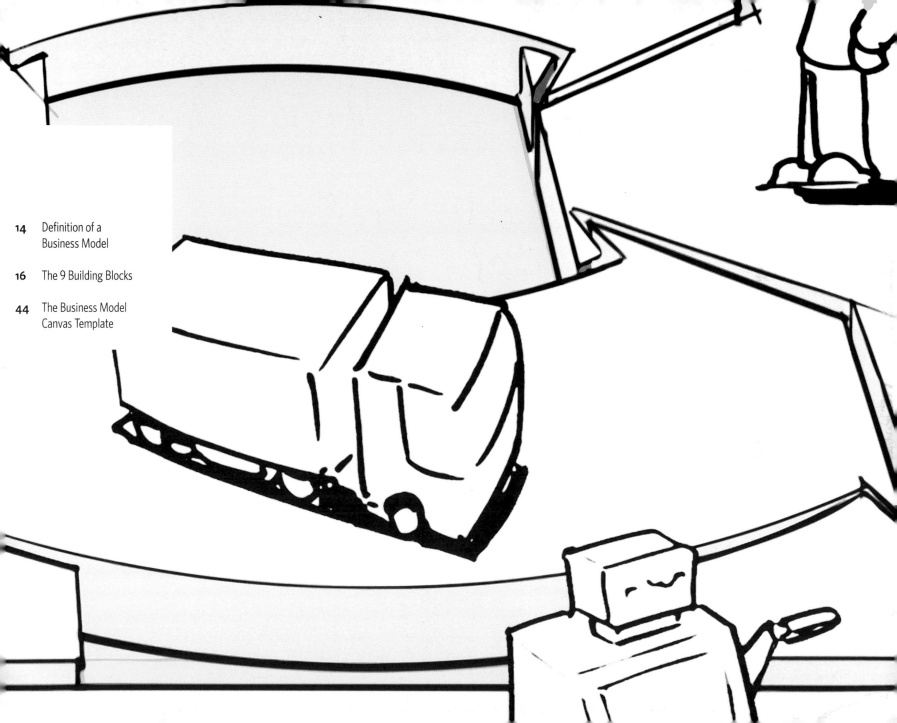

Def_Business Model

A business model describes the rationale of how an organization creates, delivers, and captures value

The starting point for any good discussion, meeting, or workshop on business model innovation should be a shared understanding of what a business model actually is. We need a business model concept that everybody understands: one that facilitates description and discussion. We need to start from the same point and talk about the same thing. The challenge is that the concept must be simple, relevant, and intuitively understandable, while not oversimplifying the complexities of how enterprises function.

In the following pages we offer a concept that allows you to describe and think through the business model of your organization, your competitors, or any other enterprise. This concept has been applied and tested around the world and is already used in organizations such as IBM, Ericsson, Deloitte, the Public Works and Government Services of Canada, and many more.

This concept can become a shared language that allows you to easily describe and manipulate business models to create new strategic alternatives. Without such a shared language it is difficult to systematically challenge assumptions about one's business model and innovate successfully.

We believe a business model can best be described through nine basic building blocks that show the logic of how a company intends to make money. The nine blocks cover the four main areas of a business: customers, offer, infrastructure, and financial viability. The business model is like a blueprint for a strategy to be implemented through organizational structures, processes, and systems.

The 9 Building Blocks

CS

1 Customer Segments

An organization serves one or several Customer Segments.

VP

2 Value Propositions

It seeks to solve customer problems and satisfy customer needs with value propositions.

CH

3 Channels

Value propositions are delivered to customers through communication, distribution, and sales Channels.

CR

4 Customer Relationships

Customer relationships are established and maintained with each Customer Segment.

5 Revenue Streams

Revenue streams result from value propositions successfully offered to customers.

6 Key Resources

Key resources are the assets required to offer and deliver the previously described elements ...

7 Key Activities

... by performing a number of Key Activities.

8 Key Partnerships

Some activities are outsourced and some resources are acquired outside the enterprise.

9 Cost Structure

The business model elements result in the cost structure.

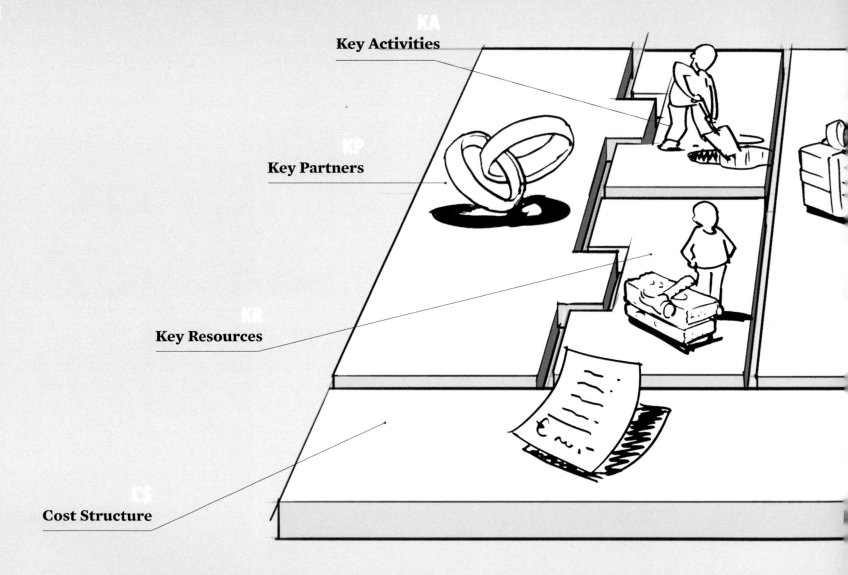

KA
Key Activities

KP
Key Partners

KR
Key Resources

CS
Cost Structure

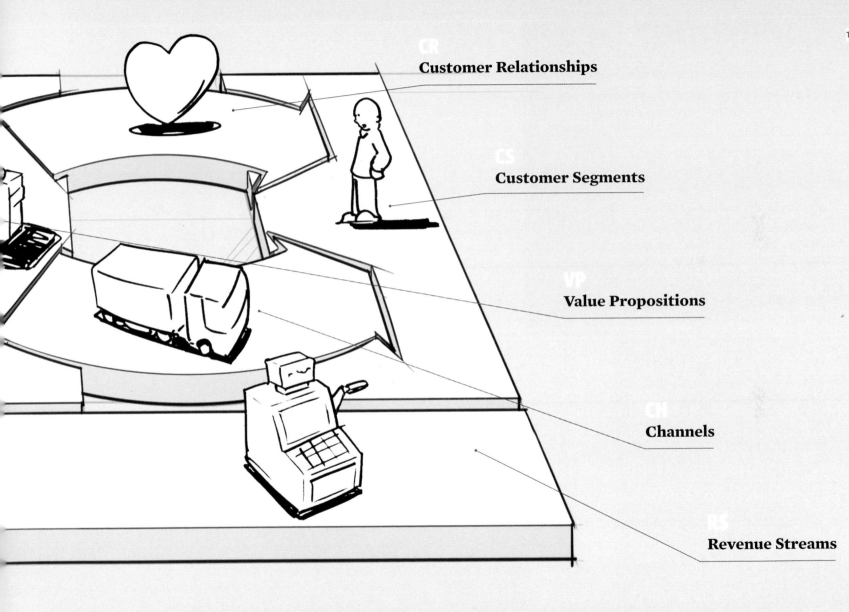

CR **Customer Relationships**

CS **Customer Segments**

VP **Value Propositions**

CH **Channels**

R$ **Revenue Streams**

1 *Customer Segments*

The Customer Segments Building Block defines the different groups of people or organizations an enterprise aims to reach and serve

Customers comprise the heart of any business model. Without (profitable) customers, no company can survive for long. In order to better satisfy customers, a company may group them into distinct segments with common needs, common behaviors, or other attributes. A business model may define one or several large or small Customer Segments. An organization must make a conscious decision about which segments to serve and which segments to ignore. Once this decision is made, a business model can be carefully designed around a strong understanding of specific customer needs.

Customer groups represent separate segments if:
- *Their needs require and justify a distinct offer*
- *They are reached through different Distribution Channels*
- *They require different types of relationships*
- *They have substantially different profitabilities*
- *They are willing to pay for different aspects of the offer*

For whom are we creating value?
Who are our most important customers?

There are different types of Customer Segments. Here are some examples:

Mass market

Business models focused on mass markets don't distinguish between different Customer Segments. The Value Propositions, Distribution Channels, and Customer Relationships all focus on one large group of customers with broadly similar needs and problems. This type of business model is often found in the consumer electronics sector.

Niche market

Business models targeting niche markets cater to specific, specialized Customer Segments. The Value Propositions, Distribution Channels, and Customer Relationships are all tailored to the specific requirements of a niche market. Such business models are often found in supplier-buyer relationships. For example, many car part manufacturers depend heavily on purchases from major automobile manufacturers.

Segmented

Some business models distinguish between market segments with slightly different needs and problems. The retail arm of a bank like Credit Suisse, for example, may distinguish between a large group of customers, each possessing assets of up to U.S. $100,000, and a smaller group of affluent clients, each of whose net worth exceeds U.S. $500,000. Both segments have similar but varying needs and problems. This has implications for the other building blocks of Credit Suisse's business model, such as the Value Proposition, Distribution Channels, Customer Relationships, and Revenue streams. Consider Micro Precision Systems, which specializes in providing outsourced micromechanical design and manufacturing solutions. It serves three different Customer Segments—the watch industry, the medical industry, and the industrial automation sector—and offers each slightly different Value Propositions.

Diversified

An organization with a diversified customer business model serves two unrelated Customer Segments with very different needs and problems. For example, in 2006 Amazon.com decided to diversify its retail business by selling "cloud computing" services: online storage space and on-demand server usage. Thus it started catering to a totally different Customer Segment—Web companies—with a totally different Value Proposition. The strategic rationale behind this diversification can be found in Amazon.com's powerful IT infrastructure, which can be shared by its retail sales operations and the new cloud computing service unit.

Multi-sided platforms (or multi-sided markets)

Some organizations serve two or more interdependent Customer Segments. A credit card company, for example, needs a large base of credit card holders and a large base of merchants who accept those credit cards. Similarly, an enterprise offering a free newspaper needs a large reader base to attract advertisers. On the other hand, it also needs advertisers to finance production and distribution. Both segments are required to make the business model work (read more about multi-sided platforms on p. 76).

2

Value Propositions

The Value Propositions Building Block describes the bundle of products and services that create value for a specific Customer Segment

The Value Proposition is the reason why customers turn to one company over another. It solves a customer problem or satisfies a customer need. Each Value Proposition consists of a selected bundle of products and/or services that caters to the requirements of a specific Customer Segment. In this sense, the Value Proposition is an aggregation, or bundle, of benefits that a company offers customers.

Some Value Propositions may be innovative and represent a new or disruptive offer. Others may be similar to existing market offers, but with added features and attributes.

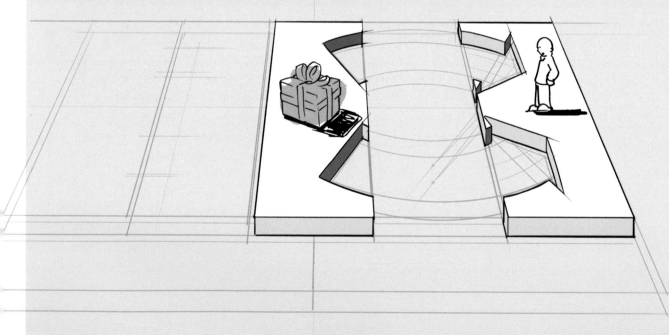

What value do we deliver to the customer? Which one of our customer's problems are we helping to solve? Which customer needs are we satisfying? What bundles of products and services are we offering to each Customer Segment?

A Value Proposition creates value for a Customer Segment through a distinct mix of elements catering to that segment's needs. Values may be quantitative (e.g. price, speed of service) or qualitative (e.g. design, customer experience).

Elements from the following non-exhaustive list can contribute to customer value creation.

Newness

Some Value Propositions satisfy an entirely new set of needs that customers previously didn't perceive because there was no similar offering. This is often, but not always, technology related. Cell phones, for instance, created a whole new industry around mobile telecommunication. On the other hand, products such as ethical investment funds have little to do with new technology.

Performance

Improving product or service performance has traditionally been a common way to create value. The PC sector has traditionally relied on this factor by bringing more powerful machines to market. But improved performance has its limits. In recent years, for example, faster PCs, more disk storage space, and better graphics have failed to produce corresponding growth in customer demand.

Customization

Tailoring products and services to the specific needs of individual customers or Customer Segments creates value. In recent years, the concepts of mass customization and customer co-creation have gained importance. This approach allows for customized products and services, while still taking advantage of economies of scale.

"Getting the job done"

Value can be created simply by helping a customer get certain jobs done. Rolls-Royce understands this very well: its airline customers rely entirely on Rolls-Royce to manufacture and service their jet engines. This arrangement allows customers to focus on running their airlines. In return, the airlines pay Rolls-Royce a fee for every hour an engine runs.

Design

Design is an important but difficult element to measure. A product may stand out because of superior design. In the fashion and consumer electronics industries, design can be a particularly important part of the Value Proposition.

Brand/Status

Customers may find value in the simple act of using and displaying a specific brand. Wearing a Rolex watch signifies wealth, for example. On the other end of the spectrum, skateboarders may wear the latest "underground" brands to show that they are "in."

Price

Offering similar value at a lower price is a common way to satisfy the needs of price-sensitive Customer Segments. But low-price Value Propositions have important implications for the rest of a business model. No frills airlines, such as Southwest, easyJet, and Ryanair have designed entire business models specifically to enable low cost air travel. Another example of a price-based Value Proposition can be seen in the Nano, a new car designed and manufactured by the Indian conglomerate Tata. Its surprisingly low price makes the automobile affordable to a whole new segment of the Indian population. Increasingly, free offers are starting to permeate various industries. Free offers range from free newspapers to free e-mail, free mobile phone services, and more (see p. 88 for more on FREE).

Cost reduction

Helping customers reduce costs is an important way to create value. Salesforce.com, for example, sells a hosted Customer Relationship management (CRM) application. This relieves buyers from the expense and trouble of having to buy, install, and manage CRM software themselves.

Risk reduction

Customers value reducing the risks they incur when purchasing products or services. For a used car buyer, a one-year service guarantee reduces the risk of post-purchase breakdowns and repairs. A service-level guarantee partially reduces the risk undertaken by a purchaser of outsourced IT services.

Accessibility

Making products and services available to customers who previously lacked access to them is another way to create value. This can result from business model innovation, new technologies, or a combination of both. NetJets, for instance, popularized the concept of fractional private jet ownership. Using an innovative business model, NetJets offers individuals and corporations access to private jets, a service previously unaffordable to most customers. Mutual funds provide another example of value creation through increased accessibility. This innovative financial product made it possible even for those with modest wealth to build diversified investment portfolios.

Convenience/Usability

Making things more convenient or easier to use can create substantial value. With iPod and iTunes, Apple offered customers unprecedented convenience searching, buying, downloading, and listening to digital music. It now dominates the market.

3 *Channels*

The Channels Building Block describes how a company communicates with and reaches its Customer Segments to deliver a Value Proposition

Communication, distribution, and sales Channels comprise a company's interface with customers. Channels are customer touch points that play an important role in the customer experience. Channels serve several functions, including:

- *Raising awareness among customers about a company's products and services*
- *Helping customers evaluate a company's Value Proposition*
- *Allowing customers to purchase specific products and services*
- *Delivering a Value Proposition to customers*
- *Providing post-purchase customer support*

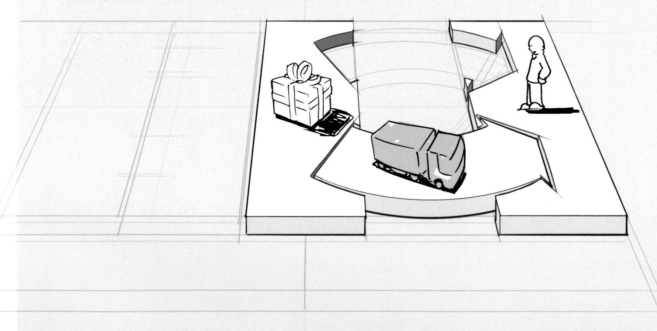

Through which Channels do our Customer Segments want to be reached? How are we reaching them now? How are our Channels integrated? Which ones work best? Which ones are most cost-efficient? How are we integrating them with customer routines?

Channels have five distinct phases. Each channel can cover some or all of these phases. We can distinguish between direct Channels and indirect ones, as well as between owned Channels and partner Channels.

Finding the right mix of Channels to satisfy how customers want to be reached is crucial in bringing a Value Proposition to market. An organization can choose between reaching its customers through its own Channels, through partner Channels, or through a mix of both. Owned Channels can be direct, such as an in-house sales force or a Web site, or they can be indirect, such as retail stores owned or operated by the organization. Partner Channels are indirect and span a whole range of options, such as wholesale distribution, retail, or partner-owned Web sites.

Partner Channels lead to lower margins, but they allow an organization to expand its reach and benefit from partner strengths. Owned Channels and particularly direct ones have higher margins, but can be costly to put in place and to operate. The trick is to find the right balance between the different types of Channels, to integrate them in a way to create a great customer experience, and to maximize revenues.

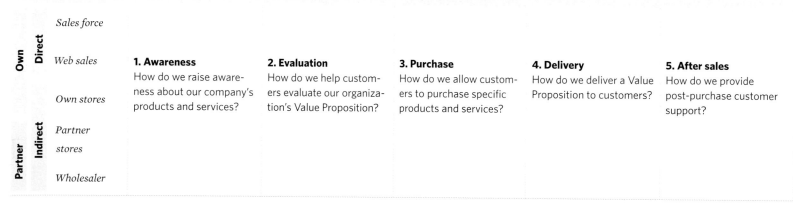

Channel Types

Own
Direct
- Sales force
- Web sales
- Own stores

Partner
Indirect
- Partner stores
- Wholesaler

Channel Phases

1. Awareness
How do we raise awareness about our company's products and services?

2. Evaluation
How do we help customers evaluate our organization's Value Proposition?

3. Purchase
How do we allow customers to purchase specific products and services?

4. Delivery
How do we deliver a Value Proposition to customers?

5. After sales
How do we provide post-purchase customer support?

4 | *Customer Relationships*

The Customer Relationships Building Block describes the types of relationships a company establishes with specific Customer Segments

A company should clarify the type of relationship it wants to establish with each Customer Segment. Relationships can range from personal to automated. Customer relationships may be driven by the following motivations:

- *Customer acquisition*
- *Customer retention*
- *Boosting sales (upselling)*

In the early days, for example, mobile network operator Customer Relationships were driven by aggressive acquisition strategies involving free mobile phones. When the market became saturated, operators switched to focusing on customer retention and increasing average revenue per customer.

The Customer Relationships called for by a company's business model deeply influence the overall customer experience.

What type of relationship does each of our Customer Segments expect us to establish and maintain with them? Which ones have we established? How costly are they? How are they integrated with the rest of our business model?

We can distinguish between several categories of Customer Relationships, which may co-exist in a company's relationship with a particular Customer Segment:

Personal assistance

This relationship is based on human interaction. The customer can communicate with a real customer representative to get help during the sales process or after the purchase is complete. This may happen on-site at the point of sale, through call centers, by e-mail, or through other means.

Dedicated personal assistance

This relationship involves dedicating a customer representative specifically to an individual client. It represents the deepest and most intimate type of relationship and normally develops over a long period of time. In private banking services, for example, dedicated bankers serve high net worth individuals. Similar relationships can be found in other businesses in the form of key account managers who maintain personal relationships with important customers.

Self-service

In this type of relationship, a company maintains no direct relationship with customers. It provides all the necessary means for customers to help themselves.

Automated services

This type of relationship mixes a more sophisticated form of customer self-service with automated processes. For example, personal online profiles give customers access to customized services. Automated services can recognize individual customers and their characteristics, and offer information related to orders or transactions. At their best, automated services can simulate a personal relationship (e.g. offering book or movie recommendations).

Communities

Increasingly, companies are utilizing user communities to become more involved with customers/prospects and to facilitate connections between community members. Many companies maintain online communities that allow users to exchange knowledge and solve each other's problems. Communities can also help companies better understand their customers. Pharmaceutical giant GlaxoSmithKline launched a private online community when it introduced *alli*, a new prescription-free weight-loss product.

GlaxoSmithKline wanted to increase its understanding of the challenges faced by overweight adults, and thereby learn to better manage customer expectations.

Co-creation

More companies are going beyond the traditional customer-vendor relationship to co-create value with customers. Amazon.com invites customers to write reviews and thus create value for other book lovers. Some companies engage customers to assist with the design of new and innovative products. Others, such as YouTube.com, solicit customers to create content for public consumption.

5 | *Revenue Streams*

The Revenue Streams Building Block represents the cash a company generates from each Customer Segment (costs must be subtracted from revenues to create earnings)

If customers comprise the heart of a business model, Revenue Streams are its arteries. A company must ask itself, For what value is each Customer Segment truly willing to pay? Successfully answering that question allows the firm to generate one or more Revenue Streams from each Customer Segment. Each Revenue Stream may have different pricing mechanisms, such as fixed list prices, bargaining, auctioning, market dependent, volume dependent, or yield management.

A business model can involve two different types of Revenue Streams:

1. *Transaction revenues resulting from one-time customer payments*
2. *Recurring revenues resulting from ongoing payments to either deliver a Value Proposition to customers or provide post-purchase customer support*

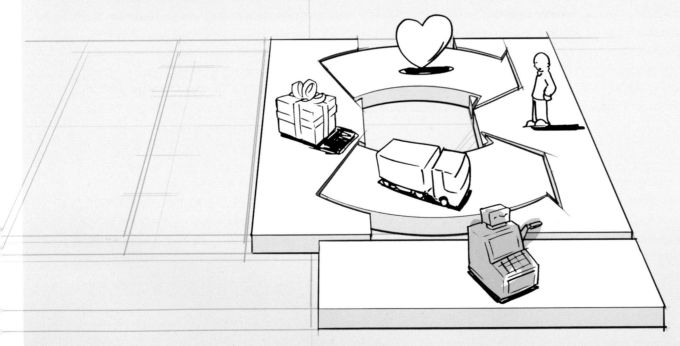

For what value are our customers really willing to pay? For what do they currently pay? How are they currently paying? How would they prefer to pay? How much does each Revenue Stream contribute to overall revenues?

There are several ways to generate Revenue Streams:

Asset sale

The most widely understood Revenue Stream derives from selling ownership rights to a physical product. Amazon.com sells books, music, consumer electronics, and more online. Fiat sells automobiles, which buyers are free to drive, resell, or even destroy.

Usage fee

This Revenue Stream is generated by the use of a particular service. The more a service is used, the more the customer pays. A telecom operator may charge customers for the number of minutes spent on the phone. A hotel charges customers for the number of nights rooms are used. A package delivery service charges customers for the delivery of a parcel from one location to another.

Subscription fees

This Revenue Stream is generated by selling continuous access to a service. A gym sells its members monthly or yearly subscriptions in exchange for access to its exercise facilities. World of Warcraft Online, a Web-based computer game, allows users to play its online game in exchange for a monthly subscription fee. Nokia's Comes with Music service gives users access to a music library for a subscription fee.

Lending/Renting/Leasing

This Revenue Stream is created by temporarily granting someone the exclusive right to use a particular asset for a fixed period in return for a fee. For the lender this provides the advantage of recurring revenues. Renters or lessees, on the other hand, enjoy the benefits of incurring expenses for only a limited time rather than bearing the full costs of ownership. Zipcar.com provides a good illustration. The company allows customers to rent cars by the hour in North American cities. Zipcar.com's service has led many people to decide to rent rather than purchase automobiles.

Licensing

This Revenue Stream is generated by giving customers permission to use protected intellectual property in exchange for licensing fees. Licensing allows rightsholders to generate revenues from their property without having to manufacture a product or commercialize a service. Licensing is common in the media industry, where content owners retain copyright while selling usage licenses to third parties. Similarly, in technology sectors, patentholders grant other companies the right to use a patented technology in return for a license fee.

Brokerage fees

This Revenue Stream derives from intermediation services performed on behalf of two or more parties. Credit card providers, for example, earn revenues by taking a percentage of the value of each sales transaction executed between credit card merchants and customers. Brokers and real estate agents earn a commission each time they successfully match a buyer and seller.

Advertising

This Revenue Stream results from fees for advertising a particular product, service, or brand. Traditionally, the media industry and event organizers relied heavily on revenues from advertising. In recent years other sectors, including software and services, have started relying more heavily on advertising revenues.

Each Revenue Stream might have different pricing mechanisms. The type of pricing mechanism chosen can make a big difference in terms of revenues generated. There are two main types of pricing mechanism: fixed and dynamic pricing.

Pricing Mechanisms

Fixed Menu Pricing Predefined prices are based on static variables		**Dynamic Pricing** Prices change based on market conditions	
List price	Fixed prices for individual products, services, or other Value Propositions	*Negotiation (bargaining)*	Price negotiated between two or more partners depending on negotiation power and/or negotiation skills
Product feature dependent	Price depends on the number or quality of Value Proposition features	*Yield management*	Price depends on inventory and time of purchase (normally used for perishable resources such as hotel rooms or airline seats)
Customer segment dependent	Price depends on the type and characteristic of a Customer Segment	*Real-time-market*	Price is established dynamically based on supply and demand
Volume dependent	Price as a function of the quantity purchased	*Auctions*	Price determined by outcome of competitive bidding

6 *Key Resources*

**The Key Resources Building Block describes
the most important assets required to make a
business model work**

Every business model requires Key Resources. These resources
allow an enterprise to create and offer a Value Proposition, reach
markets, maintain relationships with Customer Segments, and
earn revenues. Different Key Resources are needed depending on
the type of business model. A microchip manufacturer requires
capital-intensive production facilities, whereas a microchip designer
focuses more on human resources.

　　Key resources can be physical, financial, intellectual, or human.
Key resources can be owned or leased by the company or acquired
from key partners.

What Key Resources do our Value Propositions require? Our Distribution Channels? Customer Relationships? Revenue Streams?

Key Resources can be categorized as follows:

Physical

This category includes physical assets such as manufacturing facilities, buildings, vehicles, machines, systems, point-of-sales systems, and distribution networks. Retailers like Wal-Mart and Amazon.com rely heavily on physical resources, which are often capital-intensive. The former has an enormous global network of stores and related logistics infrastructure. The latter has an extensive IT, warehouse, and logistics infrastructure.

Intellectual

Intellectual resources such as brands, proprietary knowledge, patents and copyrights, partnerships, and customer databases are increasingly important components of a strong business model. Intellectual resources are difficult to develop but when success-fully created may offer substantial value. Consumer goods companies such as Nike and Sony rely heavily on brand as a Key Resource. Microsoft and SAP depend on software and related intellectual property developed over many years. Qualcomm, a designer and supplier of chipsets for broadband mobile devices, built its business model around patented microchip designs that earn the company substantial licensing fees.

Human

Every enterprise requires human resources, but people are particularly prominent in certain business models. For example, human resources are crucial in knowledge-intensive and creative industries. A phar-maceutical company such as Novartis, for example, relies heavily on human resources: Its business model is predicated on an army of experienced scientists and a large and skilled sales force.

Financial

Some business models call for financial resources and/or financial guarantees, such as cash, lines of credit, or a stock option pool for hiring key employ-ees. Ericsson, the telecom manufacturer, provides an example of financial resource leverage within a business model. Ericsson may opt to borrow funds from banks and capital markets, then use a portion of the proceeds to provide vendor financing to equipment customers, thus ensuring that orders are placed with Ericsson rather than competitors.

7 · Key Activities

The Key Activities Building Block describes the most important things a company must do to make its business model work

Every business model calls for a number of Key Activities. These are the most important actions a company must take to operate successfully. Like Key Resources, they are required to create and offer a Value Proposition, reach markets, maintain Customer Relationships, and earn revenues. And like Key Resources, Key Activities differ depending on business model type. For software maker Microsoft, Key Activities include software development.

For PC manufacturer Dell, Key Activities include supply chain management. For consultancy McKinsey, Key Activities include problem solving.

What Key Activities do our Value Propositions require? Our Distribution Channels? Customer Relationships? Revenue Streams?

Key Activities can be categorized as follows:

Production

These activities relate to designing, making, and delivering a product in substantial quantities and/or of superior quality. Production activity dominates the business models of manufacturing firms.

Problem solving

Key Activities of this type relate to coming up with new solutions to individual customer problems. The operations of consultancies, hospitals, and other service organizations are typically dominated by problem solving activities. Their business models call for activities such as knowledge management and continuous training.

Platform/Network

Business models designed with a platform as a Key Resource are dominated by platform or network-related Key Activities. Networks, matchmaking platforms, software, and even brands can function as a platform. eBay's business model requires that the company continually develop and maintain its platform: the Web site at eBay.com. Visa's business model requires activities related to its Visa® credit card transaction platform for merchants, customers, and banks. Microsoft's business model requires managing the interface between other vendors' software and its Windows® operating system platform. Key Activities in this category relate to platform management, service provisioning, and platform promotion.

8 *Key Partnerships*

The Key Partnerships Building Block describes the network of suppliers and partners that make the business model work

Companies forge partnerships for many reasons, and partnerships are becoming a cornerstone of many business models. Companies create alliances to optimize their business models, reduce risk, or acquire resources.

We can distinguish between four different types of partnerships:

1. *Strategic alliances between non-competitors*
2. *Coopetition: strategic partnerships between competitors*
3. *Joint ventures to develop new businesses*
4. *Buyer-supplier relationships to assure reliable supplies*

Who are our Key Partners? Who are our key suppliers? Which Key Resources are we acquiring from partners? Which Key Activities do partners perform?

It can be useful to distinguish between three motivations for creating partnerships:

Optimization and economy of scale

The most basic form of partnership or buyer-supplier relationship is designed to optimize the allocation of resources and activities. It is illogical for a company to own all resources or perform every activity by itself. Optimization and economy of scale partnerships are usually formed to reduce costs, and often involve outsourcing or sharing infrastructure.

Reduction of risk and uncertainty

Partnerships can help reduce risk in a competitive environment characterized by uncertainty. It is not unusual for competitors to form a strategic alliance in one area while competing in another. Blu-ray, for example, is an optical disc format jointly developed by a group of the world's leading consumer electronics, personal computer, and media manufacturers. The group cooperated to bring Blu-ray technology to market, yet individual members compete in selling their own Blu-ray products.

Acquisition of particular resources and activities

Few companies own all the resources or perform all the activities described by their business models. Rather, they extend their own capabilities by relying on other firms to furnish particular resources or perform certain activities. Such partnerships can be motivated by needs to acquire knowledge, licenses, or access to customers. A mobile phone manufacturer, for example, may license an operating system for its handsets rather than developing one in-house. An insurer may choose to rely on independent brokers to sell its policies rather than develop its own sales force.

9 # Cost Structure

The Cost Structure describes all costs incurred to operate a business model

This building block describes the most important costs incurred while operating under a particular business model. Creating and delivering value, maintaining Customer Relationships, and generating revenue all incur costs. Such costs can be calculated relatively easily after defining Key Resources, Key Activities, and Key Partnerships. Some business models, though, are more cost-driven than others. So-called "no frills" airlines, for instance, have built business models entirely around low Cost Structures.

What are the most important costs inherent in our business model? Which Key Resources are most expensive? Which Key Activities are most expensive?

Naturally enough, costs should be minimized in every business model. But low Cost Structures are more important to some business models than to others. Therefore it can be useful to distinguish between two broad classes of business model Cost Structures: cost-driven and value-driven (many business models fall in between these two extremes):

Cost-driven

Cost-driven business models focus on minimizing costs wherever possible. This approach aims at creating and maintaining the leanest possible Cost Structure, using low price Value Propositions, maximum automation, and extensive outsourcing. No frills airlines, such as Southwest, easyJet, and Ryanair typify cost-driven business models.

Value-driven

Some companies are less concerned with the cost implications of a particular business model design, and instead focus on value creation. Premium Value Propositions and a high degree of personalized service usually characterize value-driven business models. Luxury hotels, with their lavish facilities and exclusive services, fall into this category.

Cost Structures can have the following characteristics:

Fixed costs

Costs that remain the same despite the volume of goods or services produced. Examples include salaries, rents, and physical manufacturing facilities. Some businesses, such as manufacturing companies, are characterized by a high proportion of fixed costs.

Variable costs

Costs that vary proportionally with the volume of goods or services produced. Some businesses, such as music festivals, are characterized by a high proportion of variable costs.

Economies of scale

Cost advantages that a business enjoys as its output expands. Larger companies, for instance, benefit from lower bulk purchase rates. This and other factors cause average cost per unit to fall as output rises.

Economies of scope

Cost advantages that a business enjoys due to a larger scope of operations. In a large enterprise, for example, the same marketing activities or Distribution Channels may support multiple products.

The nine business model Building Blocks form the basis for a handy tool, which we call the *Business Model Canvas.*

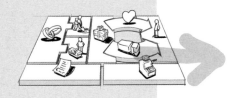

The Business Model Canvas

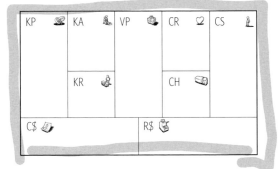

This tool resembles a painter's canvas—preformatted with the nine blocks—which allows you to paint pictures of new or existing business models. *The Business Model Canvas works best when printed out on a large surface so groups of people can jointly start sketching and discussing business model elements* with Post-it® notes or board markers. It is a hands-on tool that fosters understanding, discussion, creativity, and analysis.

The Business Model Canvas

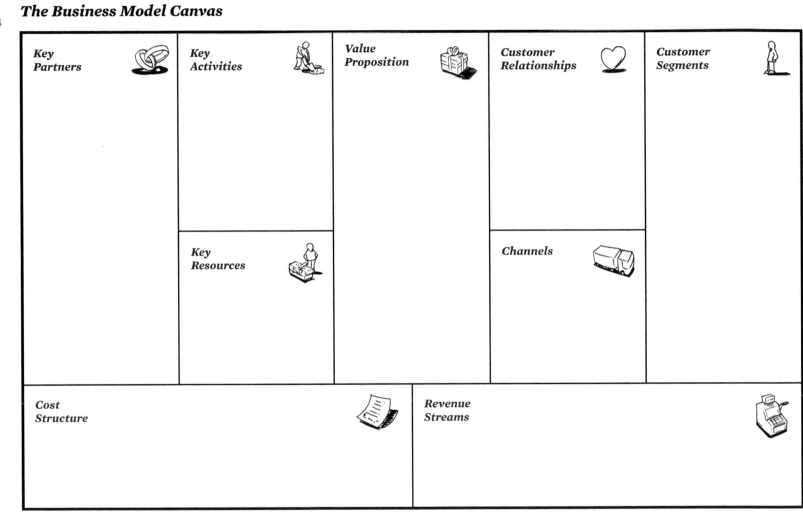

Key Partners	Key Activities	Value Proposition	Customer Relationships	Customer Segments
	Key Resources		Channels	

Cost Structure	Revenue Streams

For a large poster-size version of The Business Model Canvas, visit www.businessmodelgeneration.com.

① Plot the canvas on a poster

② Put the poster on the wall

③ Sketch out your business model

46

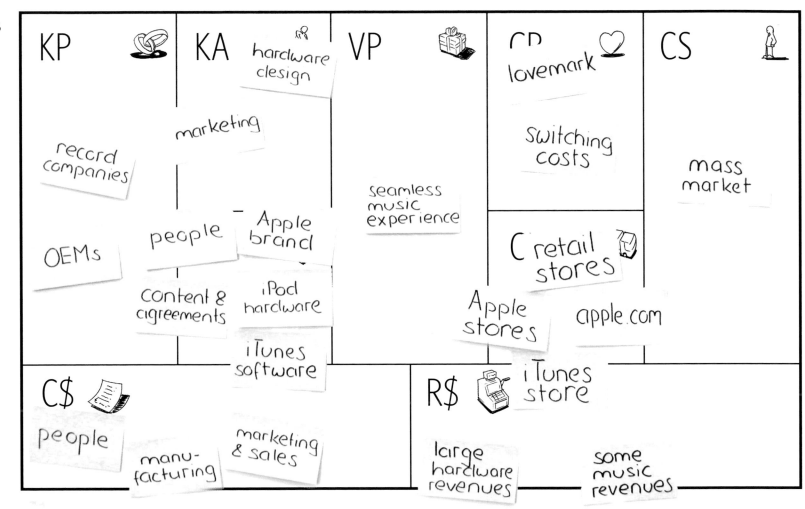

KP

record companies

OEMs

KA

hardware design

marketing

people

Apple brand

content & agreements

iPod hardware

iTunes software

VP

seamless music experience

RP

lovemark

switching costs

C retail stores

Apple stores

apple.com

CS

mass market

C$

people

manu-facturing

marketing & sales

R$

iTunes store

large hardware revenues

some music revenues

Example: Apple iPod/iTunes Business Model

In 2001 Apple launched its iconic iPod brand of portable media player. The device works in conjunction with iTunes software that enables users to transfer music and other content from the iPod to a computer. The software also provides a seamless connection to Apple's online store so users can purchase and download content.

This potent combination of device, software, and online store quickly disrupted the music industry and gave Apple a dominant market position. Yet Apple was not the first company to bring a portable media player to market. Competitors such as Diamond Multimedia, with its Rio brand of portable media players, were successful until they were outpaced by Apple.

How did Apple achieve such dominance? Because it competed with a better business model. On the one hand, it offered users a seamless music experience by combining its distinctively designed iPod devices with iTunes software and the iTunes online store. Apple's Value Proposition is to allow customers to easily search, buy, and enjoy digital music. On the other hand, to make this Value Proposition possible, Apple had to negotiate deals with all the major record companies to create the world's largest online music library.

The twist? Apple earns most of its music-related revenues from selling iPods, while using integration with the online music store to protect itself from competitors.

LEFT BRAIN
logic

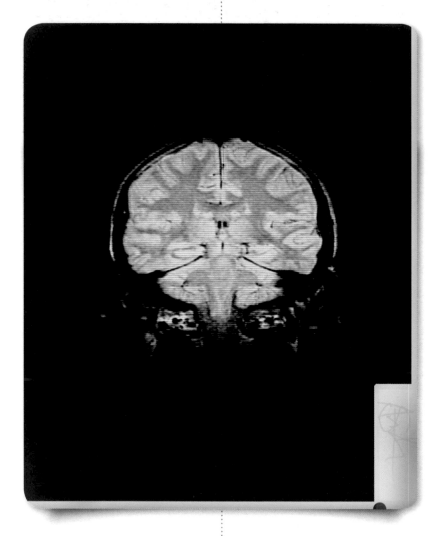

RIGHT BRAIN
emotion

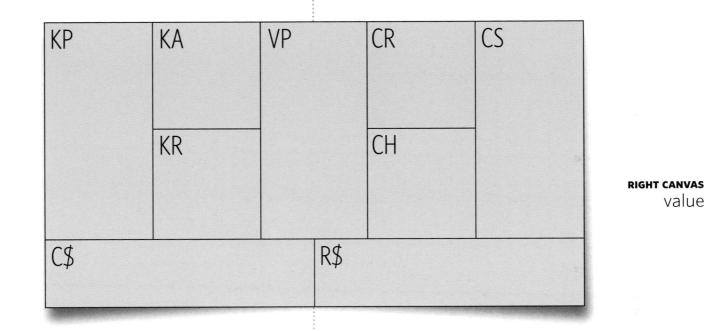

HOW DO YOU USE THE CANVAS?

The public sector is often challenged to implement private sector principles. I have used the Canvas to help a department view itself as a service-oriented business,

establishing externalized as-is and to-be business models.

It has created a whole new conversation around describing and innovating the business.

Mike Lachapelle, Canada

I consult with small companies on using the freemium business model. This model involves giving core products away for free, which is very counterintuitive to most businesspeople. Thanks to the Business Model Canvas, I can

easily illustrate how it makes financial sense.

Peter Froberg, Denmark

I help business owners plan their transition and exit from their companies. Success depends on sustaining long-term company viability and growth. Key to this is a business model innovation program. The Canvas helps us identify and innovate their business models.

Nicholas K. Niemann, United States

I'm using the Business Model Canvas in Brazil to help artists, cultural producers, and game designers to envision innovative business models for the Cultural and Creative Industries. I apply it in the Cultural Production MBA at FGV and in the Innovation Games Lab at COPPE/UFRJ Business Incubator.

Claudio D'Ipolitto, Brazil

When you typically think of a business model, the conclusion is that it is a 'for profit' business. However, I found that the Canvas is also very effective in the non-profit sector. We used it to

DESIGN + ALIGN

members of the leadership team during the formation of a new non-profit program. The Canvas was flexible enough to take into account the goals of this social entrepreneurial venture, and bring clarity to the true Value Proposition of the business and how to make it sustainable.

Kevin Donaldson, United States

I wish I had known the Canvas years ago! With a particular tough and complicated print-to-digital project within the publishing industry it would have been so helpful to

show all project members in this visual way both the big picture, their (important) own roles in it and the interdependencies.

Hours of explaining, arguing, and misunderstanding could have been saved.

Jille Sol, Netherlands

A close friend was looking for a new job. **I used the Business Model Canvas in order to assess her personal business model.** Her core competences and Value Proposition were outstanding but she failed to leverage her strategic partners and develop appropriate Customer Relationships. This adjusted focus opened new opportunities.

Daniel Pandza, Mexico

Imagine 60 first-year students, knowing nothing about entrepreneurship. In less than five days, thanks to the Business Model Canvas, they were able to pitch a viable idea with conviction and clarity. They used it as a tool to cover all the startup-building dimensions.

Guilhem Bertholet, France

I use the Business Model Canvas to teach early stage entrepreneurs across a wide range of industries as a much better way to

TRANSLATE THEIR BUSINESS **PLANS** INTO THE BUSINESS **PROCESSES**

that they (will) need to operate their businesses and to ensure that they are focused properly on being customer-centric in a way that makes the business as highly profitable as it can be.

Bob Dunn, United States

I have used the Canvas with a co-founder to **design a business plan** for a national level contest held by *The Economic Times, India*. The Canvas enabled me to think through all the aspects of the startup and put together a plan that VCs might find well thought out and attractive to fund.

Praveen Singh, India

We were asked to redesign the language service of an international NGO. The Business Model Canvas was especially helpful to **show the links between the needs of people's day-to-day work and a service** that was felt too specialized, considered only as an afterthought, and far away from their priorities.

Paola Valeri, Spain

As a startup coach I support teams to create new products and design their businesses. The Business Model Canvas does a great job assisting me to

remind the teams to think holistically about their business and prevents them from getting stuck on details. This helps to

make their new venture a success.

Christian Schüller, Germany

The Business Model Canvas has allowed me to establish a common language and framework with colleagues.

I've used the Canvas to explore new growth opportunities, assess uses of new business models by competitors, and to communicate across the organization how we could accelerate technology, market, and business model innovations.

Bruce MacVarish, United States

The Business Model Canvas has helped several health care organizations in the Netherlands to **make the move from a budget driven governmental institution to an entrepreneurial value-adding organization.**

Huub Raemakers, Netherlands

I used the Canvas with senior managers of a public company to help them restructure their value chain due to changes in sector regulation. The key success factor was to understand which new Value Propositions could be offered to their clients and then translated into internal operations.

Leandro Jesus, Brazil

WE USED 15,000 POST-ITS AND MORE THAN 100 METERS OF BROWN PAPER

to design a future organizational structure in a global manufacturing company. The key of all activities was, however, the Business Model Canvas. It convinced us by its practical applicability, simplicity, and logical cause-and-effect relationships.

Daniel Egger, Brazil

I used the Canvas to do a

REALITY CHECK

for my new startup Mupps, a platform where artists can make their own music apps for iPhone and Android phones in minutes. You know what? The Canvas made me even surer of the possible success! So I gotta go, work to do!

Erwin Blom, Netherlands

The Business Model Canvas has proven to be a very useful tool for capturing ideas and solutions for e-commerce projects. Most of my clients are SMEs and the Canvas helps them to

clarify their current business models and

understand and focus on the impact of e-commerce on their organizations.

Marc Castricum, Netherlands

I applied the Canvas to help a company align key staff in order to determine shared goals and strategic priorities, which were used during the planning process and incorporated with the BSC. It also ensured that the chosen initiatives were clearly driven by the new strategic priorities.

Martin Fanghanel, Bolivia

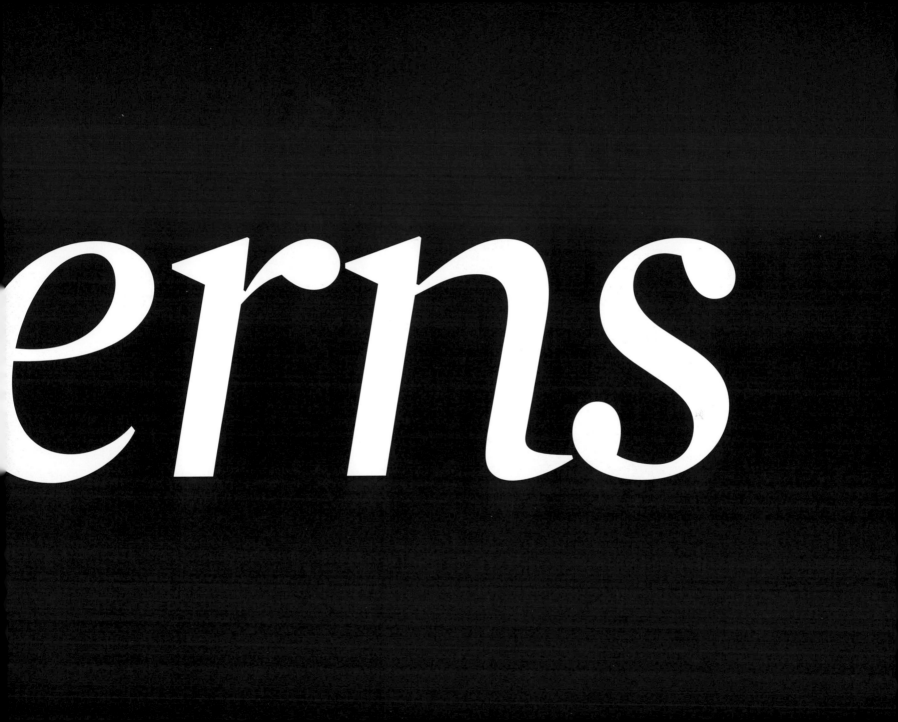

"Pattern in architecture is the idea of capturing architectural design ideas as archetypal and reusable descriptions."

Christopher Alexander, Architect

This section describes business models with similar characteristics, similar arrangements of business model Building Blocks, or similar behaviors. We call these similarities business model patterns. The patterns described in the following pages should help you understand business model dynamics and serve as a source of inspiration for your own work with business models.

We've sketched out five business model patterns built on important concepts in the business literature. We've "translated" these into the language of the Business Model Canvas to make the concepts comparable, easy to understand, and applicable. A single business model can incorporate several of these patterns.

Concepts upon which our patterns are based include Unbundling, the Long Tail, Multi-Sided Platforms, FREE, and Open Business Models. New patterns based on other business concepts will certainly emerge over time.

Our goal in defining and describing these business model patterns is to recast well-known business concepts in a standardized format—the Business Model Canvas—so that they are immediately useful in your own work around business model design or invention.

Patterns

Un-Bundling Business Models

Def_Pattern No. 1

The concept of the "unbundled" corporation holds that there are three fundamentally different types of businesses: Customer Relationship businesses, product innovation businesses, and infrastructure businesses. • Each type has different economic, competitive, and cultural imperatives. • The three types may co-exist within a single corporation, but ideally they are "unbundled" into separate entities in order to avoid conflicts or undesirable trade-offs.

[REF·ER·ENCES]

1 • "Unbundling the Corporation." *Harvard Business Review.* Hagel, John, Singer, Marc. March–April 1999.

2 • *The Discipline of Market Leaders: Choose Your Customers, Narrow Your Focus, Dominate Your Market.* Treacy, Michael, Wiersema, Fred. 1995.

[EX·AM·PLES]

mobile telecom industry, private banking industry

1 John Hagel and Marc Singer, who coined the term "unbundled corporation," believe that companies are composed of three very different types of businesses with different economic, competitive, and cultural imperatives: Customer Relationship businesses, product innovation businesses, and infrastructure businesses. Similarly, Treacy and Wiersema suggest that companies should focus on one of three value disciplines: operational excellence, product leadership, or customer intimacy.

Bundled

2 Hagel and Singer describe the role of Customer Relationship businesses as finding and acquiring customers and building relationships with them. Similarly, the role of product innovation businesses is to develop new and attractive products and services, while the role of infrastructure businesses is to build and manage platforms for high volume, repetitive tasks. Hagel and Singer argue that companies should separate these businesses and focus on only one of the three internally. Because each type of business is driven by different factors, they can conflict with each other or produce undesirable trade-offs within the same organization.

Unbundling

3 On the following pages we show how the idea of unbundling applies to business models. In the first example, we describe the conflicts and undesirable trade-offs created by a "bundled" business model within the private banking industry. In the second example we show how mobile telecom operators are unbundling and focusing on new core businesses.

Unbundled!

THREE CORE BUSINESS TYPES

	Product Innovation	Customer Relationship Management	Infrastructure Management
Economics	Early market entry enables charging premium prices and acquiring large market share; speed is key	High cost of customer acquisition makes it imperative to gain large wallet share; economies of scope are key	High fixed costs make large volumes essential to achieve low unit costs; economies of scale are key
Competition	Battle for talent; low barriers to entry; many small players thrive	Battle for scope; rapid consolidation; a few big players dominate	Battle for scale; rapid consolidation; a few big players dominate
Culture	Employee centered; coddling the creative stars	Highly service oriented; customer-comes-first mentality	Cost focused; stresses standardization, predictability, and efficiency

Source: Hagel and Singer, 1999.

Private Banking: Three Businesses in One

Swiss private banking, the business of providing banking services to the very wealthy, was long known as a sleepy, conservative industry. Yet over the last decade the face of the Swiss private banking industry changed considerably. Traditionally, private banking institutions were vertically integrated and performed tasks ranging from wealth management to brokerage to financial product design. There were sound reasons for this tight vertical integration. Outsourcing was costly, and private banks preferred keeping everything in-house due to secrecy and confidentiality concerns.

But the environment changed. Secrecy became less of an issue with the demise of the mystique surrounding Swiss banking practices, and outsourcing became attractive with the breakup of the banking value chain due to the emergence of specialty service providers such as transaction banks and financial product boutiques. The former focus exclusively on handling banking transactions, while the latter concentrate solely on designing new financial products.

Zurich-based private banking institution Maerki Baumann is an example of a bank that has unbundled its business model. It spun off its transaction-oriented platform business into a separate entity called Incore Bank, which offers banking services to other banks and securities dealers. Maerki Baumann now focuses solely on building Customer Relationships and advising clients.

On the other hand, Geneva-based Pictet, the largest Swiss private bank, has preferred to remain integrated. This 200-year-old institution develops deep Customer Relationships, handles many client transactions, and designs its own financial products. Though the bank has been successful with this model, it has to carefully manage trade-offs between three fundamentally different types of businesses.

The figure opposite depicts the traditional private banking model, describes trade-offs, and unbundles it into three basic businesses: relationship management, product innovation, and infrastructure management.

Trade Offs

1 The bank serves two different markets with very different dynamics. Advising the wealthy is a long-term, relationship-based business. Selling financial products to private banks is a dynamic, fast-changing business.

2 The bank aims to sell its products to competing banks in order to increase revenues—but this creates a conflict of interest.

3 The bank's product division pressures advisors to sell the bank's own products to clients. This conflicts with client interest in neutral advice. Clients want to invest in the best products on the market, regardless of origin.

4 The cost- and efficiency-focused transaction platform business conflicts with the remuneration-intensive advisory and financial products business, which needs to attract costly talent.

5 The transaction platform business requires scale to drive down costs, which is difficult to achieve within a single bank.

6 The product innovation business is driven by speed and quick market entry, which is at odds with the long-term business of advising the wealthy.

The Private Banking Model

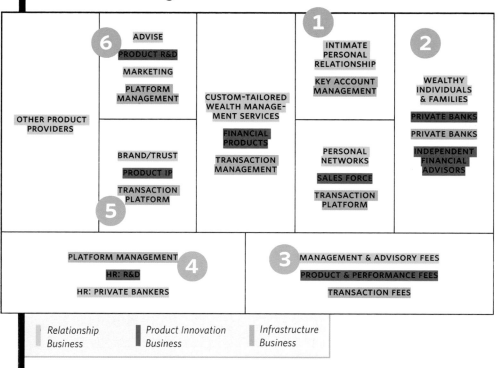

Unbundling the Mobile Telco

Mobile telecommunication firms have started unbundling their businesses. Traditionally they competed on network quality, but now they are striking network sharing deals with competitors or outsourcing network operations altogether to equipment manufacturers. Why? Because they realize that their key asset is no longer the network—it is their brand and their Customer Relationships.

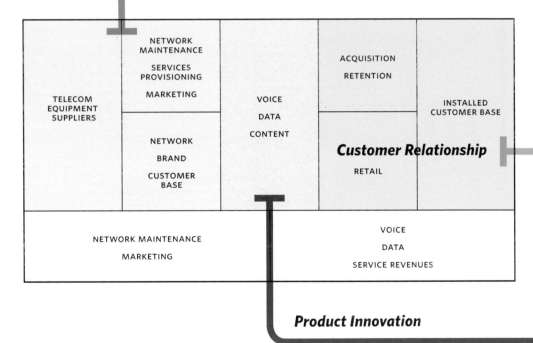

Infrastructure Management

| TELECOM EQUIPMENT SUPPLIERS | NETWORK MAINTENANCE / SERVICES PROVISIONING / MARKETING | | VOICE DATA CONTENT | ACQUISITION / RETENTION | INSTALLED CUSTOMER BASE |

NETWORK BRAND CUSTOMER BASE

Customer Relationship

RETAIL

NETWORK MAINTENANCE
MARKETING

VOICE
DATA
SERVICE REVENUES

Product Innovation

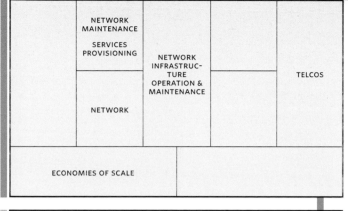

Equipment Manufacturers

Telcos such as France Telecom, KPN, and Vodafone have outsourced operation and maintenance of some of their networks to equipment manufacturers such as Nokia Siemens Networks, Alcatel-Lucent, and Ericsson. Equipment manufacturers can run the networks at lower cost because they service several telcos at a time and thus benefit from economies of scale.

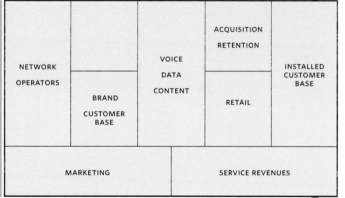

Unbundled Telco

After unbundling its infrastructure business, a telco can sharpen its focus on branding and segmenting customers and services. Customer relationships comprise its key asset and its core business. By concentrating on customers and increasing share of wallet with current subscribers, it can leverage investments made over the years acquiring and retaining customers. One of the first mobile telcos to pursue strategic unbundling was Bharti Airtel, now one of India's leading telcos. It outsourced network operations to Ericsson and Nokia Siemens Networks and IT infrastructure to IBM, allowing the company to focus on its core competency: building Customer Relationships.

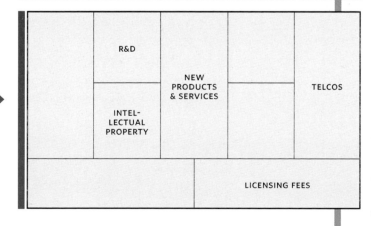

Content Providers

For product and service innovation, the unbundled telco can turn to smaller, creative firms. Innovation requires creative talent, which smaller and more dynamic organizations typically do a better job of attracting. Telcos work with multiple third-parties that assure a constant supply of new technologies, services, and media content such as mapping, games, video, and music. Two examples are Mobilizy of Austria and Sweden's tat. Mobilizy focuses on location-based service solutions for smartphones (it developed a popular mobile travel guide), and tat concentrates on creating advanced mobile user interfaces.

Unbundled Patterns ×3

Everything in this model is tailored to understanding and serving customers, or building strong Customer Relationships

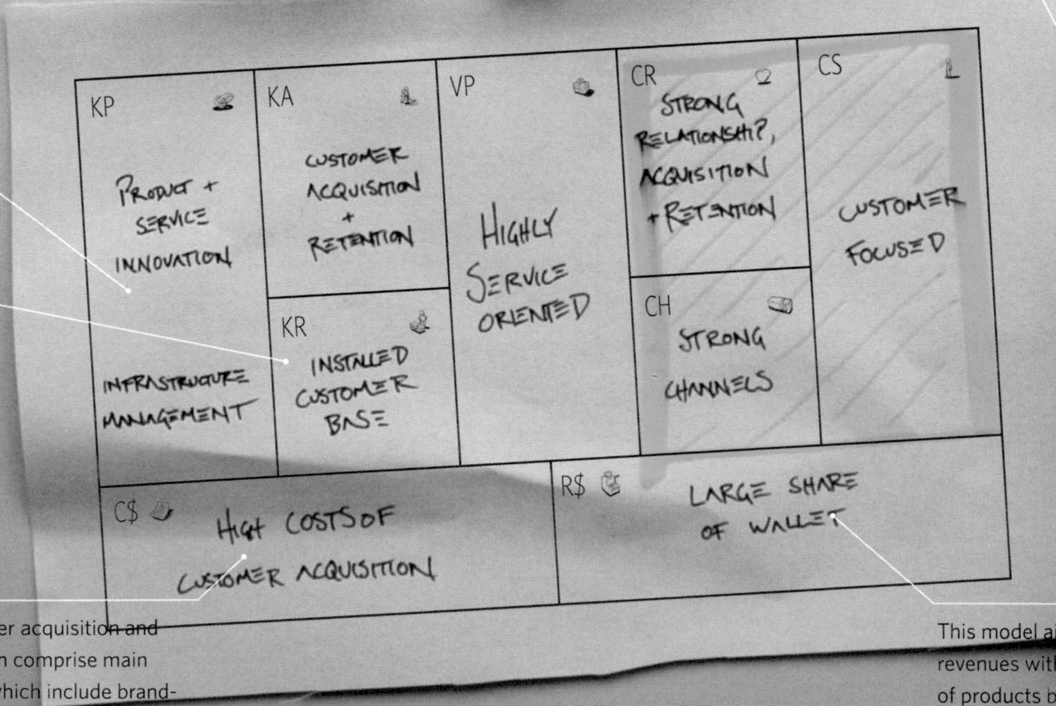

Product and service innovation, infrastructure acquired from THIRD PARTIES

KEY ASSETS and RESOURCES are the customer base and subscriber trust acquired over time

KP	KA	VP	CR	CS
PRODUCT + SERVICE INNOVATION	CUSTOMER ACQUISITION + RETENTION	HIGHLY SERVICE ORIENTED	STRONG RELATIONSHIP, ACQUISITION + RETENTION	CUSTOMER FOCUSED
INFRASTRUCTURE MANAGEMENT	KR — INSTALLED CUSTOMER BASE		CH — STRONG CHANNELS	

C$	R$
HIGH COSTS OF CUSTOMER ACQUISITION	LARGE SHARE OF WALLET

KP

C$

Customer acquisition and retention comprise main COSTS, which include branding and marketing expenses

This model aims at generating revenues with a broad scope of products built upon customer trust—the goal is to win a large "share of wallet"

ACTIVITY is focused on leveraging research and development to bring new products and services to market

Products and services can be brought to market directly, but are usually delivered through B2B intermediaries focused on CUSTOMER RELATIONSHIPS

The ACTIVITIES and offer are focused on delivering infrastructure services

Services are usually delivered to BUSINESS CUSTOMERS

High COST base due to the battle over creative talent, the KEY RESOURCE in this model

High PREMIUM CHARGEABLE because of novelty factor

Platform is characterized by HIGH FIXED COSTS, which are leveraged through scale and large volume

REVENUES are based on low margins and high volume

The
Long
Tail

Def_Pattern No. 2

LONG TAIL BUSINESS MODELS are about selling less of more: They focus on offering a large number of niche products, each of which sells relatively infrequently. • Aggregate sales of niche items can be as lucrative as the traditional model whereby a small number of bestsellers account for most revenues. • Long Tail business models require low inventory costs and strong platforms to make niche content readily available to interested buyers.

[REF·ER·ENCES]

1 • *The Long Tail: Why the Future of Business Is Selling Less of More.* Anderson, Chris. 2006.

2 • "The Long Tail." *Wired Magazine.* Anderson, Chris. October 2004.

[EX·AM·PLES]

Netflix, eBay, YouTube, Facebook, Lulu.com

# of Sales

TOP
20%

Focus on a small
number of products,
each selling in high volume

The
Long
Tail
concept
was coined by
Chris Anderson
to describe a shift in
the media business from
selling a small number of "hit"
items in large volumes toward
selling a very large number of niche
items, each in relatively small quantities.
Anderson described how many infrequent sales
can produce aggregate revenues equivalent to or
even exceeding revenues produced by focusing on
"hit" products.

Anderson believes three economic triggers gave
rise to this phenomenon in the media industry:

1. Democratization of tools of production: Falling
technology costs gave individuals access to tools
that were prohibitively expensive just a few years
ago. Millions of passionate amateurs can now
record music, produce short films, and design

simple
software
with professional
results.

2. Democratization of distribution: The Internet
has made digital content distribution a commodity, and dramatically lowered inventory, communications, and transaction costs, opening up new
markets for niche products.

3. Falling search costs to connect supply with
demand: The real challenge of selling niche content
is finding interested potential buyers. Powerful
search and recommendation engines, user ratings,
and communities of interest have made this
much easier.

LONG TAIL Focus on a large number of products, each selling in low volumes

Anderson's research focuses primarily on the media industry. For example, he showed how online video rental company Netflix moved toward licensing a large number of niche movies. While each niche movie is rented relatively infrequently, aggregate revenue from Netflix's vast niche film catalog rivals that from the rental of blockbuster movies.

But Anderson demonstrates that the Long Tail concept applies outside the media industry as well. The success of online auction site eBay is based on a huge army of auctioneers selling and buying small quantities of "non-hit" items.

# of Products

The Transformation of the Book Publishing Industry

Old Model

We've all heard about aspiring authors who carefully craft and submit manuscripts to publishing houses in the hope of seeing their work in print—and face constant rejection. This stereotypical image of publishers and authors holds much truth. The traditional book publishing model is built on a process of selection whereby publishers screen many authors and manuscripts and select those that seem most likely to achieve minimum sales targets. Less promising authors and their titles are rejected because it would be unprofitable to copyedit, design, print, and promote books that sell poorly. Publishers are most interested in books they can print in quantity for sale to large audiences.

-	CONTENT ACQUISITION PUBLISHING SALES	BROAD CONTENT (IDEALLY "HITS")	-	BROAD AUDIENCE
	PUBLISHING KNOWLEDGE CONTENT		RETAIL NETWORK	
PUBLISHING / MARKETING			WHOLESALE REVENUES	

A New Model

Lulu.com turned the traditional bestseller-centric publishing model on its head by enabling anyone to publish. Lulu.com's business model is based on helping niche and amateur authors bring their work to market. It eliminates traditional entry barriers by providing authors the tools to craft, print, and distribute their work through an online marketplace. This contrasts strongly with the traditional model of selecting "market-worthy" work. In fact, the more authors Lulu.com attracts, the more it succeeds, because authors become customers. In a nutshell, Lulu.com is a multi-sided platform (see p. 76) that serves and connects authors and readers with a Long Tail of user-generated niche content. Thousands of authors use Lulu.com's self-service tools to publish and sell their books. This works because books are printed only in response to actual orders. The failure of a particular title to sell is irrelevant to Lulu.com, because such a failure incurs no costs.

-	PLATFORM DEVELOPMENT LOGISTICS	SELF-PUBLISH-ING SERVICES	COMMUNITIES OF INTEREST ONLINE PROFILE	NICHE AUTHORS
	PLATFORM PRINT-ON-DEMAND INFRASTRUC-TURE	MARKETPLACE FOR NICHE CONTENT	LULU.COM	NICHE AUDIENCES
PLATFORM MANAGEMENT & DEVELOPMENT			SALES COMMISSIONS (LOW) PUBLISHING SERVICE FEES	

LEGO®'s New Long Tail

The Danish toy company LEGO started manufacturing its now famous interlocking bricks in 1949. Generations of children have played with them, and LEGO has released thousands of kits around a variety of themes, including space stations, pirates, and the Middle Ages. But over time, intensifying competition in the toy industry forced LEGO to seek innovative new paths to growth. It started licensing the rights to use characters from blockbuster movies such as *Star Wars*, *Batman*, and *Indiana Jones*. While such licensing is expensive, it proved to be an impressive revenue generator.

In 2005 LEGO started experimenting with user-generated content. It introduced LEGO Factory, which allows customers to assemble their very own LEGO kits and order them online. Using software called LEGO Digital Designer, customers can invent and design their own buildings, vehicles, themes, and characters, choosing from thousands of components and dozens of colors. Customers can even design the box containing the customized kit. With LEGO Factory, LEGO turned passive users into active participants in the LEGO design experience.

This requires transforming the supply chain infrastructure, and because of low volumes LEGO has not yet fully adapted its support infrastructure to the new LEGO Factory model. Instead, it simply tweaked existing resources and activities.

In terms of a business model, though, LEGO took a step beyond mass customization by entering Long Tail territory. In addition to helping users design their own LEGO sets, LEGO Factory now sells user-designed sets online. Some sell well; some sell poorly or not at all. What's important for LEGO is that the user-designed sets expand a product line previously focused on a limited number of best-selling kits. Today this aspect of LEGO's business accounts for only a small portion of total revenue, but it is a first step towards implementing a Long Tail model as a complement—or even alternative—to a traditional mass-market model.

LEGO

+

LEGO users can make
their own designs
and order them online

=

LEGO Factory

+

LEGO allows users
to post and sell their
designs online

=

LEGO Users Catalog

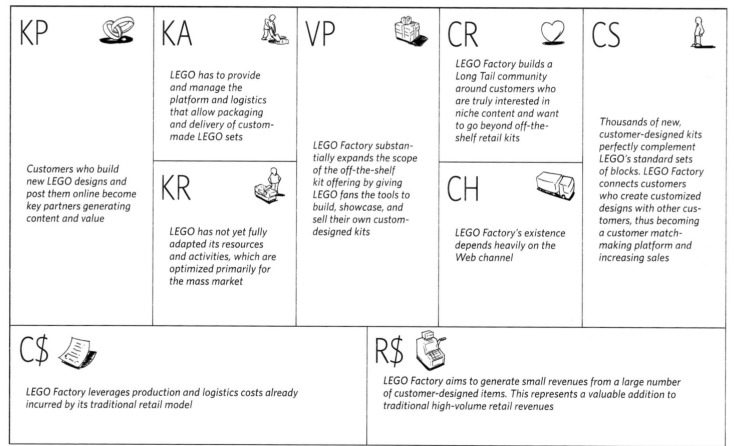

LEGO Factory: Customer-Designed Kits

KP

Customers who build new LEGO designs and post them online become key partners generating content and value

KA

LEGO has to provide and manage the platform and logistics that allow packaging and delivery of custom-made LEGO sets

KR

LEGO has not yet fully adapted its resources and activities, which are optimized primarily for the mass market

VP

LEGO Factory substantially expands the scope of the off-the-shelf kit offering by giving LEGO fans the tools to build, showcase, and sell their own custom-designed kits

CR

LEGO Factory builds a Long Tail community around customers who are truly interested in niche content and want to go beyond off-the-shelf retail kits

CH

LEGO Factory's existence depends heavily on the Web channel

CS

Thousands of new, customer-designed kits perfectly complement LEGO's standard sets of blocks. LEGO Factory connects customers who create customized designs with other customers, thus becoming a customer match-making platform and increasing sales

C$

LEGO Factory leverages production and logistics costs already incurred by its traditional retail model

R$

LEGO Factory aims to generate small revenues from a large number of customer-designed items. This represents a valuable addition to traditional high-volume retail revenues

Long Tail Pattern

Niche content providers (professional and/or user-generated) are the KEY PARTNERS in this pattern.

The VALUE PROPOSITION of a Long Tail business model is characterized by offering a wide scope of "non-hit" items that may co-exist with "hit" products. Long Tail business models may also facilitate and build on user-generated content.

Long Tail business models focus on niche CUSTOMERS.

A Long Tail business model can serve both professional and amateur content producers, and may create a multi-sided platform (see p. 76) catering to users and producers alike.

The KEY RESOURCE is the platform; KEY ACTIVITIES include platform development and maintenance and niche content acquisition and production.

Business Model Canvas — handwritten:

- KP: NICHE CONTENT PROVIDERS
- KA: PLATFORM MANAGEMENT / SERVICE PROVISIONING / PLATFORM PROMOTION
- KR: USER GENERATED CONTENT / PLATFORM
- VP: LARGE SCOPE OF NICHE CONTENT / CONTENT PRODUCTION TOOLS
- CR: (blank)
- CH: INTERNET
- CS: MANY NICHE SEGMENTS / NICHE CONTENT PROVIDERS
- C$: PLATFORM MANAGEMENT + DEVELOPMENT
- R$: SELLING LESS OF MORE

The main COSTS incurred cover platform development and maintenance

This model is based on aggregating small revenues from a large number of items. REVENUE STREAMS vary; they may come from advertising, product sales, or subscriptions.

Long Tail business models usually rely on the Internet as a CUSTOMER RELATIONSHIP and/or TRANSACTION CHANNEL.

Multi-Sided Platforms

Def_Pattern No. 3

MULTI-SIDED PLATFORMS bring together two or more distinct but interdependent groups of customers. • Such platforms are of value to one group of customers *only* if the other groups of customers are also present. • The platform creates value by *facilitating interactions* between the different groups. • A multi-sided platform grows in value to the extent that it attracts more users, a phenomenon known as the *network effect.*

[REF·ER·ENCES]

1 • "Strategies for Two-Sided Markets." *Harvard Business Review*. Eisenmann, Parker, Van Alstyne. October 2006.

2 • *Invisible Engines: How Software Platforms Drive Innovation and Transform Industries.* Evans, Hagiu, Schmalensee. 2006.

3 • "Managing the Maze of Multisided Markets." *Strategy & Business.* Evans, David. Fall 2003.

[EX·AM·PLES]

Visa, Google, eBay, Microsoft Windows, *Financial Times*

Multi-sided platforms, known by economists as multi-sided markets, are an important business phenomenon. They have existed for a long time, but proliferated with the rise of information technology. The Visa credit card, the Microsoft Windows operating system, the *Financial Times*, Google, the Wii game console, and Facebook are just a few examples of successful multi-sided platforms. We address them here because they represent an increasingly important business model pattern.

What exactly are multi-sided platforms? They are platforms that bring together two or more distinct but interdependent groups of customers. They create value as intermediaries by connecting these groups. Credit cards, for example, link merchants with cardholders; computer operating systems link hardware manufacturers, application developers, and users; newspapers link readers and advertisers; video gaming consoles link game developers with players. The key is that the platform must attract and serve all groups simultane-ously in order to create value. The platform's value for a particular user group depends substantially on the number of users on the platform's "other sides." A video game console will only attract buyers if enough games are available for the platform. On the other hand, game developers will develop games for a new video console only if a substantial number of gamers already use it. Hence multi-sided platforms often face a "chicken and egg" dilemma.

One way multi-sided platforms solve this problem is by subsidizing a Customer Segment. Though a platform operator incurs costs by serving all customer groups, it often decides to lure one segment to the platform with an inexpensive or free Value Proposition in order to subsequently attract users of the platform's "other side." One difficulty multi-sided platform operators face is understanding which side to subsidize and how to price correctly to attract customers.

Segments ≥ 2

Customer
Segment A

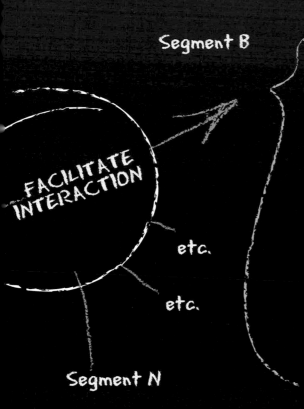

Segment B

FACILITATE INTERACTION

etc.

etc.

Segment N

One example is *Metro*, the free daily newspaper that originated in Stockholm and can now be found in many large cities worldwide. It launched in 1995 and immediately attracted a large readership because it was distributed free of charge to urban commuters in train and bus stations throughout Stockholm. This allowed it to attract advertisers and rapidly become profitable. Another example is Microsoft, which gave its Windows software development kit (SDK) away for free to encourage development of new applications for its operating system. The larger number of applications attracted more users to the Windows platform and increased Microsoft's revenues. Sony's Playstation 3 game console, on the other hand, is an example of a multi-sided platform strategy that backfired. Sony subsidized each console purchased in hopes of later collecting more game royalties. This strategy performed poorly because fewer Playstation 3 games sold than Sony initially estimated.

Operators of multi-sided platforms must ask themselves several key questions: Can we attract sufficient numbers of customers for each side of the platform? Which side is more price sensitive? Can that side be enticed by a subsidized offer? Will the other side of the platform generate sufficient revenues to cover the subsidies?

The following pages outline three examples of multi-sided platform patterns. First, we sketch Google's multi-sided platform business model. Then we show how Nintendo, Sony, and Microsoft compete with slightly different multi-sided platform patterns. Finally, we describe how Apple has slowly evolved into an operator of a powerful multi-sided platform.

Google's Business Model

The heart of Google's business model is its Value Proposition of providing extremely targeted text advertising globally over the Web. Through a service called AdWords, advertisers can publish advertisements and sponsored links on Google's search pages (and on an affiliated content network as we will later see). The ads are displayed alongside search results when people use the Google search engine. Google ensures that only ads relevant to the search term are displayed. The service is attractive to advertisers because it allows them to tailor online campaigns to specific searches and particular demographic targets. The model only works, though, if many people use Google's search engine. The more people Google reaches, the more ads it can display and the greater the value created for advertisers.

Google's Value Proposition to advertisers depends heavily on the number of customers it attracts to its Web site. So Google caters to this second group of consumer customers with a powerful search engine and a growing number of tools such as Gmail (Web based e-mail), Google maps, and Picasa (an online photo album) among others. To extend its reach even further, Google designed a third service that enables its ads to be displayed on other, non-Google Web sites. This service, called AdSense, allows third parties to earn a portion of Google's advertising revenue by showing Google ads on their own sites. AdSense automatically analyzes a participating Web site's content and displays relevant text and image ads to visitors. The Value Proposition to these third party Web site owners, Google's third Customer Segment, is to enable them to earn money from their content.

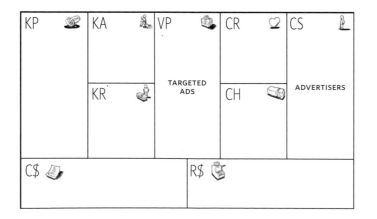

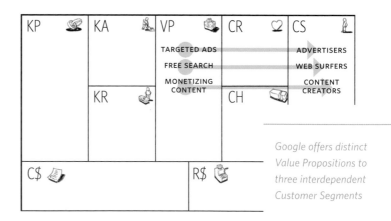

Google offers distinct Value Propositions to three interdependent Customer Segments

As a multi-sided platform Google has a very distinct revenue model. It makes money from one Customer Segment, advertisers, while subsidizing free offers to two other segments: Web surfers and content owners. This is logical because the more ads it displays to Web surfers, the more it earns from advertisers. Increased advertising earnings, in turn, motivates even more content owners to become AdSense partners. Advertisers don't directly buy advertising space from Google. They bid on ad-related keywords associated with either search terms or content on third party Web sites. The bidding occurs through an AdWords auction service: the more popular a keyword, the more an advertiser has to pay for it. The substantial revenue that Google earns from AdWords allows it to continuously improve its free offers to search engine and AdSense users.

Google's Key Resource is its search platform, which powers three different services: Web search (Google.com), advertising (AdWords), and third-party content monetization (AdSense). These services are based on highly complex proprietary search and matchmaking algorithms supported by an extensive IT infrastructure. Google's three Key Activities can be defined as follows: (1) building and maintaining the search infrastructure, (2) managing the three main services, and (3) promoting the platform to new users, content owners, and advertisers.

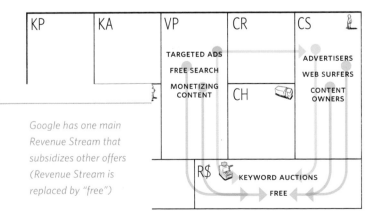

Google has one main Revenue Stream that subsidizes other offers (Revenue Stream is replaced by "free")

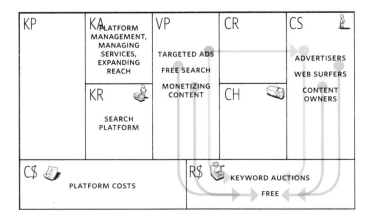

Wii versus PSP/Xbox
Same Pattern, Different Focus

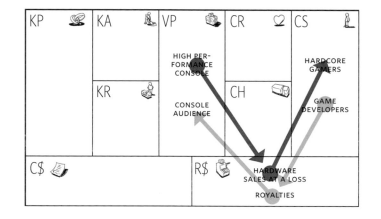

PSP/Xbox Focus

Video game consoles, today a multi-billion dollar business, provide good examples of double-sided platforms. On one hand, a console manufacturer has to draw as many players as possible to attract game developers. On the other hand, players only buy the hardware if there is a sufficient number of interesting games available for that console. In the game industry, this has led to a fierce battle between three main competitors and their respective devices: the Sony Playstation series, the Microsoft Xbox series, and the Nintendo Wii. All three are based on double-sided platforms, but there are substantial differences between the Sony/Microsoft business model and Nintendo's approach, demonstrating that there is no "proven" solution for a given market.

Sony and Microsoft dominated the game console market until Nintendo's Wii swept the sector with a fresh approach to technology and an astonishingly different business model. Before launching the Wii, Nintendo was spiraling downward, rapidly losing market share, and teetering on the edge of bankruptcy. The Wii console changed all that and catapulted the company to the market leader position.

Traditionally, video console manufacturers targeted avid gamers and competed on console price and performance. For this audience of "hardcore gamers" graphics and game quality and processor speed were the main selection criteria. As a consequence, manufacturers developed extremely sophisticated and expensive consoles and sold them at a loss for years, subsidizing the hardware with two other revenue sources.

First, they developed and sold their own games for their own consoles. Second, they earned royalties from third party developers who paid for the right to create games for specific consoles. This is the typical pattern of a double-sided platform business model: one side, the consumer, is heavily subsidized to deliver as many consoles as possible to the market. Money is then earned from the other side of the platform: game developers.

*Same pattern, but
different business model:
Nintendo's Wii*

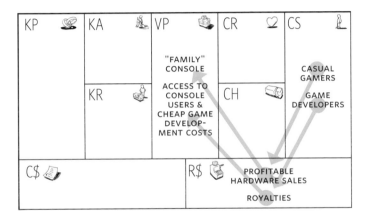

Wii Focus

Nintendo's Wii changed all this. Like its competitors, the Wii is based on a double-sided platform business, but with substantially different elements. Nintendo aimed its consoles at the huge audience of casual gamers rather than the smaller "traditional" market of avid gamers. It won the hearts of casual gamers with relatively inexpensive machines equipped with a special remote control device that allows players to control the action with physical gestures. The novelty and fun of motion-controlled games such as Wii Sports, Wii Music, and Wii Fit attracted enormous numbers of casual gamers. This differentiator is also the basis for the new type of double-sided platform that Nintendo created.

Sony and Microsoft competed with costly, proprietary, state-of-the-art technology aimed at avid gamers and subsidized it in order to gain market share and keep hardware prices affordable. Nintendo, on the other hand, focused on a market segment that was far less sensitive to technological performance. Instead, it lured customers with its motion-controlled "fun factor." This was a much cheaper technological innovation compared to new, more powerful chipsets. Thus, the Nintendo Wii was less costly to produce, allowing the company to forego commercialization subsidies. This is the main difference between Nintendo and rivals Sony and Microsoft: Nintendo earns money from both sides of its double-sided Wii platform. It generates profits on each console sold to consumers and pockets royalties from game developers.

To summarize, three interlinked business model factors explain the commercial success of the Wii: (1) low-cost differentiation of the product (motion control), (2) focus on a new, untapped market that cares less about technology (casual gamers), and (3) a double-sided platform pattern that generates revenues from both "sides" of the Wii. All three represent clean breaks from past game sector traditions.

Apple's Evolution into a Platform Operator

The evolution of Apple's product line from the iPod to the iPhone highlights the company's transition to a powerful platform business model pattern. The iPod was initially a stand-alone device. The iPhone, on the contrary, evolved into a powerful multi-sided platform for which Apple controls third party applications through its App Store.

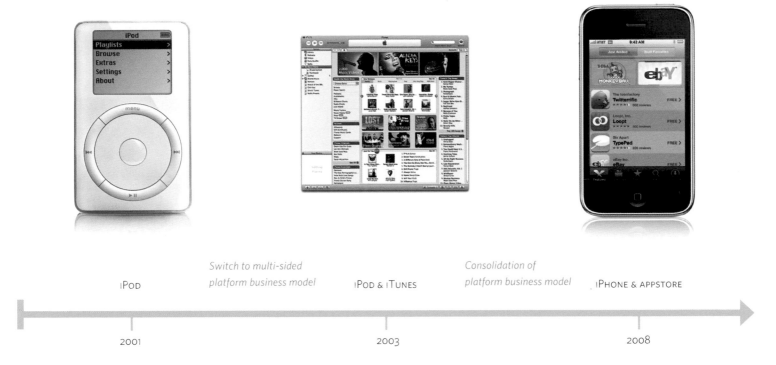

Switch to multi-sided
platform business model

Consolidation of
platform business model

iPOD   iPOD & iTUNES   iPHONE & APPSTORE

2001   2003   2008

Apple introduced the iPod in 2001 as a stand-alone product. Users could copy their CDs and download music from the Internet onto the device. The iPod represented a technology platform for storing music from various sources. At this point, though, Apple was not exploiting the platform aspect of the iPod in its business model.

In 2003 Apple introduced the iTunes Music Store, which was closely integrated with the iPod. The store allowed users to buy and download digital music in an extremely convenient way. The store was Apple's first attempt at exploiting platform effects. iTunes essentially connected "music rightsholders" directly with buyers. This strategy catapulted Apple to its position today as the world's largest online music retailer.

In 2008 Apple consolidated its platform strategy by launching its App Store for the highly popular iPhone. The App Store allows users to browse, buy, and download applications directly from the iTunes Store and install them on their iPhones. Application developers must channel sales of all applications through the App Store, with Apple collecting a 30 percent royalty on each application sold.

Multi-Sided Platform Pattern

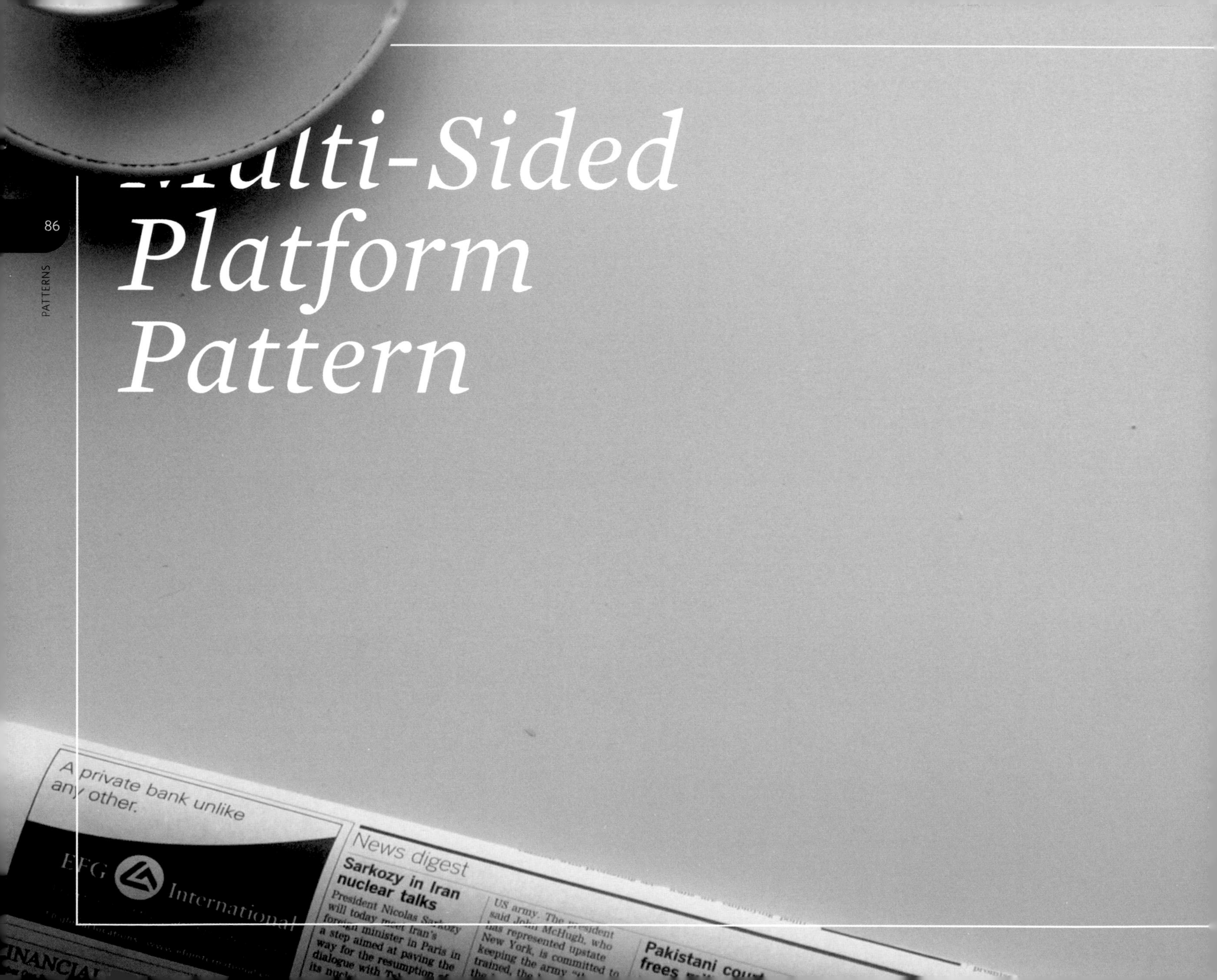

The VALUE PROPOSITION usually creates value in three main areas: First, attracting user groups (i.e. Customer Segments); Second, matchmaking between Customer Segments; Third, reducing costs by channeling transactions through the platform.

Business models with a multi-sided platform pattern have a distinct structure. They have two or more CUSTOMER SEGMENTS, each of which has its own Value Proposition and associated Revenue Stream. Moreover, one Customer Segment cannot exist without the others.

The KEY RESOURCE required for this business model pattern is the platform. The three Key Activities are usually platform management, service provisioning, and platform promotion.

Each Customer Segment produces a different REVENUE STREAM. One or more segments may enjoy free offers or reduced prices subsidized by revenues from other Customer Segments. Choosing which segment to subsidize can be a crucial pricing decision that determines the success of a multi-sided platform business model.

The main COSTS incurred under this pattern relate to maintaining and developing the platform.

KP · KA PLATFORM MANAGEMENT · SERVICE PROVISIONING · PLATFORM PROMOTION · VP VALUE PROPOSITION 1 · VALUE PROPOSITION 2 · ETC... · CR · CS CUSTOMER SEGMENT 1 · CUSTOMER SEGMENT 2 · ETC... · KR PLATFORM · CH · C$ PLATFORM MANAGEMENT + DEVELOPMENT · POSSIBLE REVENUE FLOW · SUBSIDY · R$ REVENUE FLOW 1 · REVENUE FLOW 2 · ETC...

FREE as a Business Model

Def_Pattern No. 4

FREE • In the *FREE* business model *at least one* substantial Customer Segment is able to *continuously benefit* from a free-of-charge offer. • *Different patterns* make the free offer possible. • Non-paying customers are financed by another part of the business model or by another Customer Segment.

[REF·ER·ENCES]

1 • "Free! Why $0.00 is the Future of Business." *Wired Magazine.* Anderson, Chris. February 2008.

2 • "How about Free? The Price Point That Is Turning Industries on Their Heads." *Knowledge@ Wharton.* March 2009.

3 • *Free: The Future of a Radical Price.* Anderson, Chris. 2008.

[EX·AM·PLES]

Metro (free paper), Flickr, Open Source, Skype, Google, Free Mobile Phones

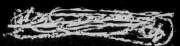

Receiving something free of charge has always
been an attractive Value Proposition. Any marketer or
economist will confirm that the demand generated at a price of zero
is many times higher than the demand generated at one cent or any other price
point. In recent years free offers have exploded, particularly over the Internet. The question, of course, is how can you systematically offer something for free and still earn substantial
revenues? Part of the answer is that the cost of producing certain giveaways, such as online data storage
capacity, has fallen dramatically. Yet to make a profit, an organization offering free products or services must
still generate revenues somehow.

There are several patterns that make integrating free products and services into a business model possible. Some of the traditional FREE patterns are well known, such as advertising, which is based on the previously discussed pattern of multi-sided
platforms (see p. 76). Others, such as the so-called freemium model, which provides basic services free of charge and premium
services for a fee, have become popular in step with the increasing digitization of goods and services offered via the Web.

Chris Anderson, whose Long Tail concept we discussed previously (see p. 66), has helped the concept of FREE gain widespread
recognition. Anderson shows that the rise of new free-of-charge offers is closely related to the fundamentally different economics of digital products and services. For example, creating and recording a song costs an artist time and money, but the cost of
digitally replicating and distributing the work over the Internet is close to zero. Hence, an artist can promote and deliver music
to a global audience over the Web, as long as he or she finds other Revenue Streams, such as concerts and merchandis-
ing, to cover costs. Bands and artists who have experimented successfully with free music include Radiohead and Trent
Reznor of Nine Inch Nails.

In this section we look at three different patterns that make FREE a viable business model option. Each
has different underlying economics, but all share a common trait: at least one Customer Segment
continuously benefits from the free-of-charge offer. The three patterns are (1) free offer based
on multi-sided platforms (advertising-based), (2) free basic services with optional
premium services (the so-called "freemium" model), (3) and the "bait &
hook" model whereby a free or inexpensive initial offer lures
customers into repeat purchases.

(How) can you set it free?

Advertising: A Multi-Sided Platform Model

Advertising is a well-established revenue source that enables free offers. We recognize it on television, radio, the Web, and in one of its most sophisticated forms, in targeted Google ads. In business model terms, FREE based on advertising is a particular form of the multi-sided platform pattern (see p. 76). One side of the platform is designed to attract users with free content, products, or services. Another side of the platform generates revenue by selling space to advertisers.

One striking example of this pattern is *Metro*, the free newspaper that started in Stockholm and is now available in dozens of cities around the world. The genius of *Metro* lies in how it modified the traditional daily newspaper model. First, it offered the paper for free. Second, it focused on distributing in high-traffic commuter zones and public transport networks by hand and with self-service racks. This required *Metro* to develop its own distribution network, but enabled the company to quickly achieve broad circulation. Third, it cut editorial costs to produce a paper just good enough to entertain younger commuters during their short rides

to and from work. Competitors using the same model soon followed, but *Metro* kept them at bay with a couple of smart moves. For example, it controlled many of the news racks at train and bus stations, forcing rivals to resort to costly hand distribution in important areas.

Minimizes costs by cutting editorial team to produce a daily paper just "good enough" for a commute read

Assures high circulation through free offer and by focusing on distributing in high-traffic commuter zones and public transport networks

Metro

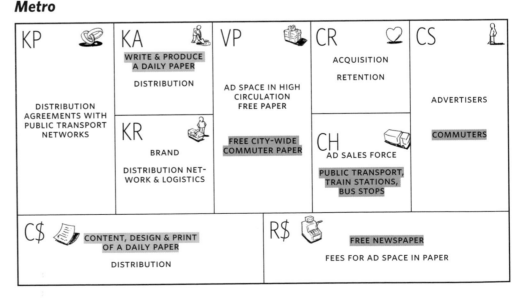

Mass ≠ automatic ad $

A large number of users does not automatically translate into an El Dorado of advertising revenues, as the social networking service Facebook has demonstrated. The company claimed over 200 million active users as of May 2009, and said more than 100 million log on to its site daily. Those figures make Facebook the world's largest social network. Yet users are less responsive to Facebook advertising than to traditional Web ads, according to industry experts. While advertising is only one of several potential Revenue Streams for Facebook, clearly a mass of users does not guarantee huge advertising revenues. At this writing, privately held Facebook did not disclose revenue data.

Facebook

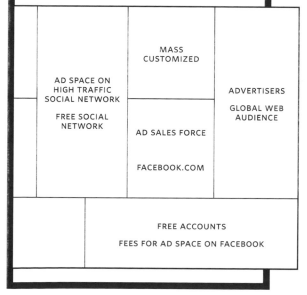

Newspapers: Free or Not Free?

One industry crumbling under the impact of FREE is newspaper publishing. Sandwiched between freely available Internet content and free newspapers, several traditional papers have already filed for bankruptcy. The U.S. news industry reached a tipping point in 2008 when the number of people obtaining news online for free outstripped those paying for newspapers or news magazines, according to a study by the Pew Research Center.

Traditionally, newspapers and magazines relied on revenues from three sources: newsstand sales, subscription fees, and advertising. The first two are rapidly declining and the third is not increasing quickly enough. Though many newspapers have increased online readership, they've failed to achieve correspondingly greater advertising revenues. Meanwhile, the high fixed costs that guarantee good journalism—news gathering and editorial teams—remained unchanged.

Several newspapers have experimented with paid online subscriptions, with mixed results. It is difficult to charge for articles when readers can view similar content for free on Web sites such as CNN.com or MSNBC.com. Few newspapers have succeeded in motivating readers to pay for access to premium content online.

On the print side, traditional newspapers are under attack from free publications such as *Metro*. Though *Metro* offers a completely different format and journalistic quality and focuses primarily on young readers who previously ignored newspapers, it is ratcheting up the pressure on fee-for-service news providers. Charging money for news is an increasingly difficult proposition.

Some news entrepreneurs are experimenting with novel formats focused on the online space. For example, news provider True/Slant (trueslant.com) aggregates on one site the work of over 60 journalists, each an expert in a specific field. The writers are paid a share of the advertising and sponsorship revenues generated by True/Slant. For a fee, advertisers can publish their own material in pages paralleling the news content.

Free Advertising: Pattern of Multi-Sided Platforms

With the right PRODUCT OR SERVICE and high traffic, the platform becomes interesting to advertisers, which in turn allows CHARGING fees to subsidize free products and services.

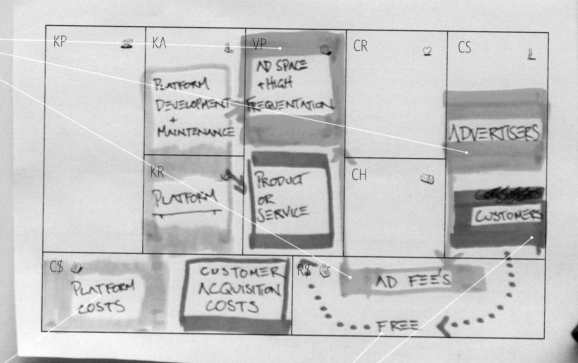

KP	KA	VP	CR	CS
	PLATFORM DEVELOPMENT + MAINTENANCE	AD SPACE + HIGH FREQUENTATION		ADVERTISERS
	KR	PRODUCT OR SERVICE	CH	CUSTOMERS
	PLATFORM			

C$		R$	
PLATFORM COSTS	CUSTOMER ACQUISITION COSTS	AD FEES	
			FREE

Main COSTS relate to developing and maintaining the platform; traffic-generation and retention costs may also arise.

Free products or services generate high platform traffic and increase attractiveness to advertisers.

Freemium: Get the Basics for Free, Pay for More

The term "freemium" was coined by Jarid Lukin and popularized by venture capitalist Fred Wilson on his blog. It stands for business models, mainly Web-based, that blend free basic services with paid premium services. The freemium model is characterized by a large user base benefiting from a free, no-strings-attached offer. Most of these users never become paying customers; only a small portion, usually less than 10 percent of all users, subscribe to the paid premium services. This small base of paying users subsidizes the free users. This is possible because of the low marginal cost of serving additional free users. In a freemium model, the key metrics to watch are (1) the average cost of serving a free user, and (2) the rates at which free users convert to premium (paying) customers.

Flickr, the popular photo-sharing Web site acquired by Yahoo! in 2005, provides a good example of a freemium business model. Flickr users can subscribe for free to a basic account that enables them to upload and share images. The free service has certain constraints, such as limited storage space and a maximum number of uploads per month. For a small annual fee users

can purchase a "pro" account and enjoy unlimited uploads and storage space, plus additional features.

Flickr

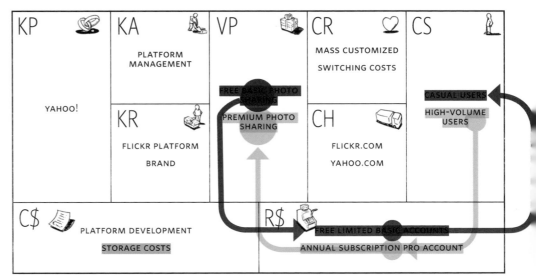

Fixed and sunk costs related to platform development	Variable cost depending on number of photos stored

Large base of basic accounts for casual users	Small base of paying "pro" users

Open Source: Freemium with a Twist

Business models in the enterprise software industry are usually characterized by two traits: First, the high fixed cost of supporting an army of expert software developers who build the product; Second, a revenue model based on selling multiple per-user licenses and regular upgrades of the software.

Red Hat, a U.S. software company, turned this model upside down. Rather than creating software from scratch, it builds its product on top of so-called open source software developed voluntarily by thousands of software engineers around the world. Red Hat understood that companies were interested in robust, licensing fee-free open source software, but were reluctant to adopt it due to concerns that no single entity was legally responsible for providing and maintaining it. Red Hat filled this gap by offering stable, tested, service-ready versions of freely available open source software, particularly Linux.

Each Red Hat release is supported for seven years. Customers benefit from this approach because it allows them to enjoy the cost and stability advantages of open source software,

while protecting them from the uncertainties surrounding a product not officially "owned" by anyone. Red Hat benefits because its software kernel is continuously improved by the open source community free of charge. This substantially reduces Red Hat's development costs.

Naturally, Red Hat also has to earn money. So rather than charging clients for each major new release—the traditional software revenue model—it sells subscriptions. For an annual fee, each client enjoys continuous access to the latest Red Hat release, unlimited service support, and the security of interacting with the legal owner of the product. Companies are willing to pay for these benefits despite the free availability of many versions of Linux and other open source software.

Red Hat

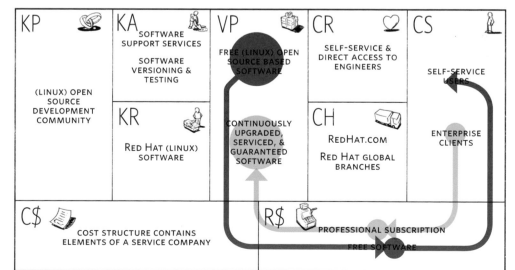

Skype

Skype offers an intriguing example of a freemium pattern that disrupted the telecommunications sector by enabling free calling services via the Internet. Skype developed software by the same name that, when installed on computers or smartphones, enables users to make calls from one device to another free of charge. Skype can offer this because its Cost Structure is completely different from that of a telecom carrier. Free calls are fully routed through the Internet based on so-called peer-to-peer technology that employs user hardware and the Internet as communications infrastructure. Hence, Skype does not have to manage its own network like a telco and incurs only minor costs to support additional users. Skype requires very little of its own infrastructure besides backend software and the servers hosting user accounts.

Users pay only for calling landlines and mobile phones through a premium service called SkypeOut, which offers very low rates. In fact, users are charged only slightly more than the termination costs that Skype itself incurs for calls routed through wholesale carriers such as iBasis and Level 3, which handle the company's network traffic.

Skype

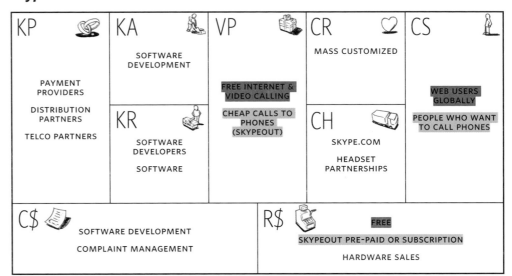

Skype claims it has over 400 million registered users who have made more than 100 billion free calls since the company was founded in 2004. Skype reported revenues of U.S. $550 million in 2008, though the company and its owner, eBay, do not release detailed financial data including information on profitability. We may soon know more as eBay has announced plans to list Skype through an initial public offering (IPO).

Over 90 percent of Skype users subscribe to the free service

Paid SkypeOut calls account for less than 10 percent of total usage

5+ years old
400 million+ users
100 billion+ free
   calls generated
2008 revenues of
   U.S. $550 million

Skype disrupted the telecommunications
industry and helped drive voice communication costs close to zero. Telecom operators
initially didn't understand why Skype would
offer calls for free and didn't take the company
seriously. What's more, only a tiny fraction
of the traditional carriers' customers used
Skype. But over time more and more customers
decided to make their international calls with
Skype, eating into one of the most lucrative
carrier revenue sources. This pattern, typical of
a disruptive business model, severely affected
the traditional voice communication business,
and today Skype is the world's largest provider
of cross-border voice communication services,
according to telecommunications research
firm Telegeography.

Skype versus Telco

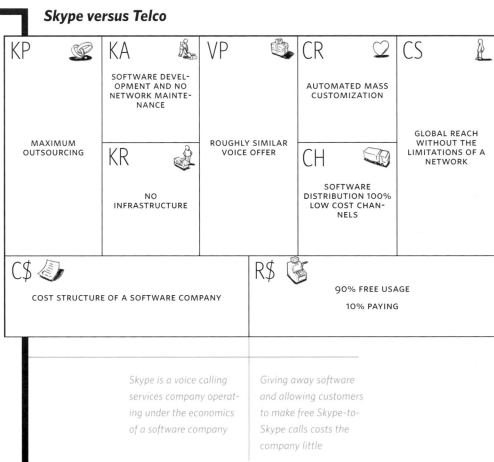

KP	KA	VP	CR	CS
MAXIMUM OUTSOURCING	SOFTWARE DEVELOPMENT AND NO NETWORK MAINTENANCE	ROUGHLY SIMILAR VOICE OFFER	AUTOMATED MASS CUSTOMIZATION	GLOBAL REACH WITHOUT THE LIMITATIONS OF A NETWORK
	KR: NO INFRASTRUCTURE		CH: SOFTWARE DISTRIBUTION 100% LOW COST CHANNELS	

C$ COST STRUCTURE OF A SOFTWARE COMPANY

R$ 90% FREE USAGE 10% PAYING

*Skype is a voice calling
services company operat-
ing under the economics
of a software company*

*Giving away software
and allowing customers
to make free Skype-to-
Skype calls costs the
company little*

The Insurance Model: Freemium Upside Down

In the freemium model a small base of customers paying for a premium service subsidizes a large base of non-paying customers. The insurance model is actually the opposite—it's the freemium model turned on its head. In the insurance model, a large base of customers pay small regular fees to protect themselves from unlikely—but financially devastating—events. In short, a large base of paying customers subsidizes a small group of people with actual claims—but any one of the paying customers could at any time become part of the beneficiary group.

Let's look at REGA as an example. REGA is a Swiss non-profit organization that uses helicopters and airplanes to transport medical staff to the scene of accidents, notably in the mountainous areas of Switzerland. Over two million so-called "patrons" finance the organization. In return, patrons are exempt from paying any costs arising from being rescued by REGA. Mountain rescue operations can be extremely expensive, so REGA patrons find the service attractive in protecting them against the high cost of accidents during skiing vacations, summer hikes, or mountain drives.

REGA

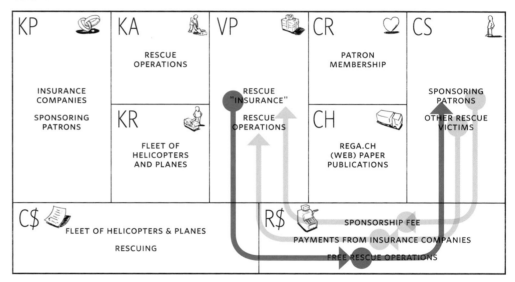

Many paying users cover the costs of a few claims

"Every industry that becomes digital eventually becomes free."

— *Chris Anderson*
Editor-in-Chief, Wired Magazine

"We can no longer stand by and watch others walk off with our work under misguided legal theories."

— *Dean Singleton*
Chairman, Associated Press

"The demand you get at a price of zero is many times higher than the demand you get at a very low price."

— *Kartik Hosanagar*
Assistant Professor, Wharton

"Google's not a real company. It's a house of cards."

— *Steve Ballmer*
CEO, Microsoft

Freemium Pattern

PLATFORM
ENABLES
FREE SERVICE
PAID SERVICE

KP	KA	VP	CR	CS
	INFRASTRUCTURE DEVELOPMENT + MAINTENANCE	FREE BASIC SERVICE	AUTOMATED + MASS CUSTOMIZED.	LARGE BASE OF FREE USERS
	KR		CH	
	PLATFORM	Premium Service		SMALL BASE OF PAYING USERS

C$			R$	
FIXED COSTS	COST OF SERVICE FOR PREMIUM USERS	COST OF SERVICE FOR FREE USERS		FREE BASIC SERVICES
				Paid Premium Services

The platform is the most important ASSET in the freemium pattern, because it allows free basic services to be offered at low marginal cost.

The COST STRUCTURE of this pattern is tripartite: usually with substantial fixed costs, very low marginal costs for services to free accounts, and (separate) costs for premium accounts

CUSTOMER RELATIONSHIP must be automated and low cost in order to handle large numbers of free users.

An IMPORTANT METRIC to follow is the rate at which free accounts convert to premium accounts

USERS describes how many users a company with a freemium business model can attract

FIXED COSTS a company incurs to run its business model (e.g. systems costs)

The freemium model is characterized by a large base of free service users subsidized by a small base of paying users.

Users enjoy a free basic service and can pay for a premium service that offers additional benefits.

COST OF SERVICE
indicates the average cost the company incurs to deliver a free or premium service to a free or premium user.

GROWTH & CHURN RATE
specifies how many users defect/respectively join the user base.

CUSTOMER ACQUISITION COSTS
total expenses a company incurs to acquire new users.

PERCENT OF PREMIUM & FREE USERS
specifies how many of all users are premium paying users or free users.

PRICE OF PREMIUM SERVICE
indicates the average cost the company incurs to deliver a premium service to a premium paying user.

operating profit period	income	cost of service	fixed costs	customer acquisition costs	operating profit
month 1	$2,116,125	$391,500	$1,100,000	$650,000	−$2
month 2	$2,151,041	$397,960	$1,100,000	$650,000	$3,081
month 3	$2,186,533	$404,526	$1,100,000	$650,000	$32,007
month 4	$2,222,611	$411,201	$1,100,000	$650,000	$6
month 5	$2,259,284	$417,986	$1,100,000	$650,000	
month 6	$2,296,562	$424,882	$1,100,000	$650,000	
month 7	$2,334,456	$431,893			
month 8	$2,372,974				
month 9	$2				

cost of service period	users	% of free users	cost of service free users	users	% of premium users	cost of service premium users	cost of service to all users
month 1	9,000,000	0.95	$0.03	9,000,000	0.05	$0.30	$391,500
	9,148,500	0.95	$0.03	9,148,500	0.05	$0.30	$397,960
			$0.03	9,299,450	0.05	$0.30	$404,526
					0.05	$0.30	$411,201
					0.05		$417,986

income period	users	% of premium users	price of premium service/month	growth rate	churn rate	income
month 1	9,000,000	0.05	$4.95	1.07	0.95	$2,116,125
month 2	9,148,500	0.05	$4.95	1.07	0.95	$2,151,041
month 3	9,299,450	0.05	$4.95	1.07	0.95	$2,186,533
month 4	9,452,891	0.05	$4.95	1.07	0.95	$2,222,611
month 5	9,608,864	0.05	$4.95	1.07	0.95	$2,259,284
month 6	9,767,410	0.05	$4.95	1.07	0.95	$2,296,562
month 7	9,928,572	0.05	$4.95	1.07	0.95	$2,334,456
month 8	10,092,394	0.05	$4.95	1.07	0.95	$2,372,974
	10,258,918	0.05	$4.95	1.07	0.95	$2,412,128
	191	0.05	$4.95	1.07	0.95	$2,451,928
		0.05	$4.95	1.07	0.95	$2,492,385
			$4.95	1.07	0.95	$2,533,509

$$\text{INCOME} = \left\{ \text{USERS} \times \frac{\%\ OF}{\text{PREMIUM USERS}} \times \frac{\text{PRICE OF}}{\text{PREMIUM SERVICE}} \right\} \times \text{GROWTH RATE} \times \text{CHURN RATE}$$

$$\text{COST OF SERVICE} = \left\{ \text{USERS} \times \frac{\%\ OF}{\text{FREE USERS}} \times \frac{\text{COST OF SERVICE TO FREE USERS}}{} \right\} + \left\{ \text{USERS} \times \frac{\%\ OF}{\text{PREMIUM USERS}} \times \frac{\text{COST OF SERVICE TO PREMIUM USERS}}{} \right\}$$

$$\text{OPERATING PROFIT} = \text{INCOME} - \text{COST OF SERVICE} - \text{FIXED COSTS} - \text{CUSTOMER ACQUISITION COSTS}$$

Bait & Hook

"Bait & hook" refers to a business model pattern characterized by an attractive, inexpensive, or free initial offer that encourages continuing future purchases of related products or services. This pattern is also known as the "loss leader" or "razor & blades" model. "Loss leader" refers to a subsidized, even money-losing initial offer with the intention of generating profits from subsequent purchases. "Razor & blades" refers to a business model popularized by an American businessman, King C. Gillette, inventor of the disposable razor blade (see p. 105). We use the term bait & hook pattern to describe the general idea of luring customers with an initial offering, while earning from follow-up sales.

The mobile telecommunications industry provides a good illustration of the bait & hook pattern with a free offer. It is now standard practice for mobile network operators to offer free telephone handsets bundled with service subscriptions. Operators initially lose money by giving away mobile phones for free, but they easily cover the loss through subsequent monthly service fees. Operators provide instant gratification with a free offer that later generates recurring income.

Bait & Hook of Free Mobile Phones

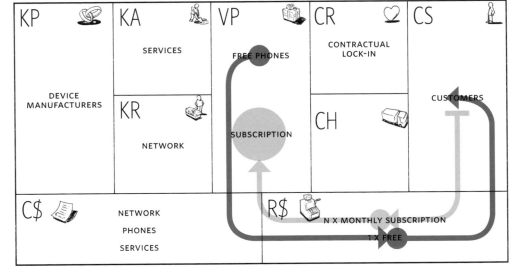

The form of the bait & hook pattern known as the razor and blades model derives from the way the first disposable razors were sold. In 1904 King C. Gillette, who commercialized the first disposable razor blade system, decided to sell razor handles at a steep discount or even give them away with other products in order to create demand for his disposable blades. Today Gillette is still the preeminent brand in shaving products. The key to this model is the close link between the inexpensive or free initial product and the follow-up item—usually disposable—on which the company earns a high margin. Controlling the "lock-in" is crucial to this pattern's success. Through blocking patents, Gillette ensured that competitors couldn't offer cheaper blades for the Gillette razor handles. In fact, today razors are among the world's most heavily patented consumer products, with more than 1,000 patents covering everything from lubricating strips to cartridge-loading systems.

Razor & Blades : Gillette

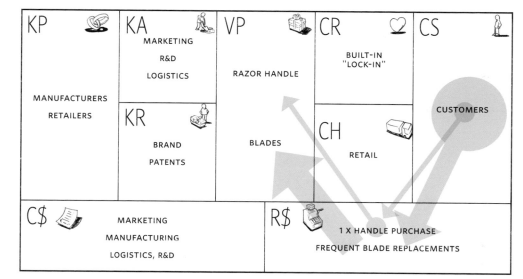

This pattern is popular in the business world and has been applied in many sectors, including inkjet printers. Manufacturers such as HP, Epson, and Canon typically sell printers at very low prices, but they generate healthy margins on subsequent sales of ink cartridges.

Bait & Hook Pattern

Cheap or free "bait" LURES customers—and is closely linked to a (disposable) follow-up item or service.

This pattern is characterized by a tight link or "LOCK-IN" between the initial product and the follow-up products or services.

CUSTOMERS are attracted by the instant gratification of a cheap or free initial product or service.

The initial one-time purchase generates little or no REVENUE, but is made up for through repeat follow-up purchases of high-margin products or services.

Focuses on DELIVERY of follow-up products or services.

Bait & hook patterns usually require a strong BRAND.

Important COST STRUCTURE elements include subsidization of the initial product and the costs of producing follow-up products or services.

KP	KA	VP	CR	CS
	PRODUCTION AND/OR SERVICE DELIVERY.	"BAIT" PRODUCT	"LOCK IN"	CUSTOMER SEGMENT
	KR PATENTS BRAND	"HOOK" PRODUCT OR SERVICE	CH	

C$ PRODUCTION + SERVICES SUBSIDIZING OF "BAIT" PRODUCT	R$ 1 x PURCHASE OF "BAIT" REPEAT PURCHASE OF "HOOK" PRODUCTS OR SERVICES

Open
Business
Models

Def_Pattern No. 5

OPEN BUSINESS MODELS can be used by companies to create and capture value by systematically *collaborating with outside partners.* • This may happen from the *"outside-in"* by exploiting external ideas within the firm, or from the *"inside-out"* by providing external parties with ideas or assets lying idle within the firm.

[REF·ER·ENCES]

1 • *Open Business Models: How to Thrive in the New Innovation Landscape.* Chesbrough, Henry. 2006.

2 • "The Era of Open Innovation." *MIT Sloan Management Review.* Chesbrough, Henry. Nº 3, 2003.

[EX·AM·PLES]

P&G, GlaxoSmithKilne, Innocentive

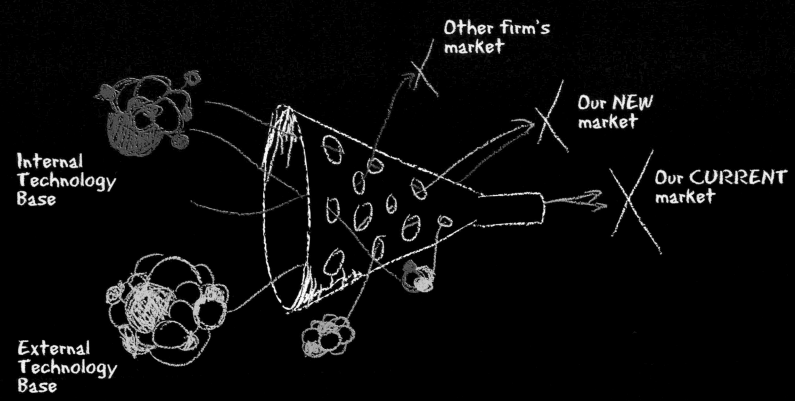

Internal
Technology
Base

External
Technology
Base

Other firm's
market

Our NEW
market

Our CURRENT
market

Open innovation and open business models are two terms coined by Henry Chesbrough. They refer to opening up a company's research process to outside parties. Chesbrough argues that in a world characterized by distributed knowledge, organizations can create more value and better exploit their own research by integrating outside knowledge, intellectual property, and products into their innovation processes. In addition, Chesbrough shows that products, technologies, knowledge, and intellectual property lying idle inside a company can be monetized by making them available to outside parties through licensing, joint ventures, or spin-offs. Chesbrough distinguishes between "outside-in" innovation and "inside-out" innovation. "Outside-in" innovation occurs when an organization brings external ideas, technology, or intellectual property into its development and commercialization processes. The table opposite illustrates how companies increasingly rely on outside sources of technology to strengthen their business models. "Inside-out" innovation occurs when organizations license or sell their intellectual property or technologies, particularly unused assets. In this section we describe the business model patterns of firms that practice open innovation.

PRINCIPLES OF INNOVATION

Closed	Open
The smart people in our field work for us.	We need to work with smart people both inside and outside our company.
To profit from research and development (R&D), we must discover it, develop it, and ship it ourselves.	External R&D can create significant value; internal R&D is needed to claim some portion of that value.
If we conduct most of the best research in the industry, we will win.	We don't have to originate the research to benefit from it.
If we create the most or the best ideas in the industry, we will win.	If we make the best use of internal and external ideas, we will win.
We should control our innovation process, so that competitors don't profit from our ideas.	We should profit from others' use of our innovations, and we should buy others' intellectual property (IP) whenever it advances our own interests.

Source: Adapted from Chesbrough, 2003 and Wikipedia, 2009.

Procter & Gamble: Connect & Develop

In June of 2000, amid a continuing slide in Procter & Gamble's share price, longtime P&G executive A.G. Lafley got the call to become the consumer product giant's new CEO. To rejuvenate P&G, Lafley resolved to put innovation back at the company's core. But instead of boosting R&D spending, he focused on structuring a new innovation culture: one that moved from an internally focused R&D approach to an open R&D process. A key element was a "Connect & Develop" strategy aimed at exploiting internal research through outside partnerships. Lafley set an ambitious goal: create 50 percent of P&G's innovations with outside partners at a time when that figure was closer to 15 percent. The company surpassed that goal in 2007. Meanwhile, R&D productivity had soared 85 percent, even though R&D spending was only modestly higher compared to when Lafley took over as CEO.

In order to link its internal resources and R&D activities with the outside world, Procter & Gamble built three "bridges" into its business model: technology entrepreneurs, Internet platforms, and retirees.

Outside-In

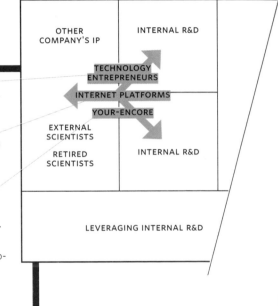

❶ Technology entrepreneurs are senior scientists from P&G business units who systematically develop relationships with researchers at universities and other companies. They also act as "hunters" who scan the outside world for solutions to internal P&G challenges.

❷ Through Internet platforms, P&G connects with expert problem-solvers around the world. Platforms such as InnoCentives (see p. 114) allow P&G to expose some of its research problems to non-P&G scientists around the globe. Respondents earn cash prizes for developing successful solutions.

❸ P&G solicits knowledge from retirees through YourEncore.com, a platform the company launched specifically to serve as an open innovation "bridge" to the outside world.

GlaxoSmithKline's Patent Pools

The inside-out approach to open innovation ordinarily focuses on monetizing unused internal assets, primarily patents and technology. In the case of GlaxoSmithKline's "patent pool" research strategy, though, the motivation was slightly different. The company's goal was to make drugs more accessible in the world's poorest countries and to facilitate research into understudied diseases. One way to achieve this was to place intellectual property rights relevant to developing drugs for such diseases into a patent pool open to exploration by other researchers. Since pharmaceutical companies focus mainly on developing blockbuster drugs, intellectual property related to less-studied diseases often lies idle. Patent pools aggregate intellectual property from different rights-holders and makes it more accessible. This helps prevent R&D advances from being blocked by a single rights-holder.

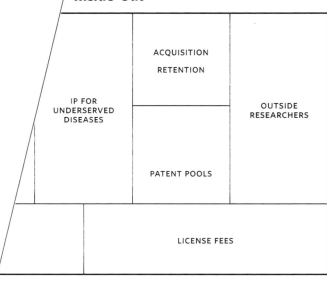

Inside-Out

IP FOR UNDERSERVED DISEASES

ACQUISITION RETENTION

OUTSIDE RESEARCHERS

PATENT POOLS

LICENSE FEES

Unused internal ideas, R&D, and intellectual property related to diseases in poor nations have substantial value when "pooled"

The Connector: Innocentive

Innocentive

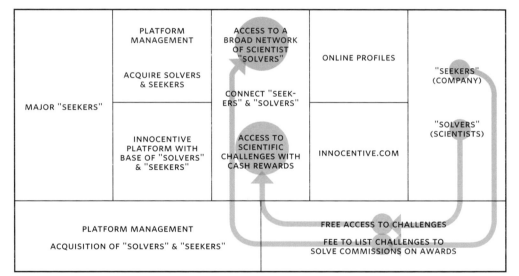

Companies seeking insights from external researchers incur substantial costs when trying to attract people or organizations with knowledge that could solve their problems. On the other hand, researchers who want to apply their knowledge outside their own organizations also incur search costs when seeking attractive opportunities. That is where a company called InnoCentive saw opportunity.

InnoCentive provides connections between organizations with research problems to solve and researchers from around the world who are eager to solve challenging problems. Originally part of drug maker Eli Lilly, InnoCentive now functions as an independent intermediary listing non-profits, government agencies, and commercial organizations such as Procter & Gamble, Solvay, and the Rockefeller Foundation. Companies who post their innovation challenges on InnoCentive's Web site are called "seekers." They reward successful problem-solvers with cash prizes that can range from $5,000 to $1,000,000. Scientists who attempt to find solutions to listed problems are called "solvers." InnoCentive's Value Proposition lies

in aggregating and connecting "seekers" and "solvers." You may recognize these qualities as characteristic of the multi-sided platform business model pattern (see p. 76). Companies with open business model patterns often build on such platforms to reduce search costs.

"Open Innovation is fundamentally about operating in a world of abundant knowledge, where not all the smart people work for you, so you better go find them, connect to them, and build upon what they can do."

— Henry Chesbrough
Executive Director, Center for Open Innovation
Haas School of Business, UC Berkeley

"Long known for a preference to do everything in-house, we began to seek out innovation from any and all sources, inside, outside the company."

— A.G. Lafley
Chairman & CEO, P&G

"Nestlé clearly recognizes that to achieve its growth objective it must extend its internal capabilities to establish a large number of strategic partnering relationships. It has embraced open innovation and works aggressively with strategic partners to co-create significant new market and product opportunities."

— Helmut Traitler
Head of Innovation Partnerships, Nestlé

Outside-In Pattern

EXTERNAL ORGANIZATIONS, sometimes from completely different industries, may be able to offer valuable insights, knowledge, patents, or ready-made products to internal R&D groups.

Building on external knowledge requires dedicated **ACTIVITIES** that connect external entities with internal business processes and R&D groups.

Taking advantage of outside innovation requires specific **RESOURCES** to build gateways to external networks.

It **COSTS** money to acquire innovation from outside sources. But by building on externally-created knowledge and advanced research programs, a company can shorten time-to-market and increase its internal R&D productivity.

Established companies with strong brands, strong Distribution Channels, and strong Customer Relationships are well suited to an outside-in open business model. They can leverage existing Customer Relationships by building on outside sources of innovation.

Inside-Out Pattern

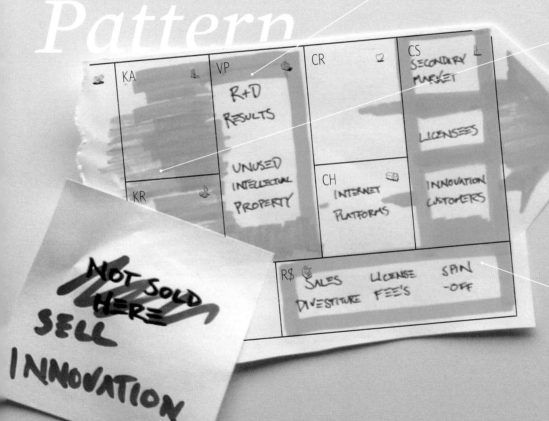

Some R&D outputs that are unusable internally—for strategic or operational reasons—may be of high VALUE to organizations in other industries.

Organizations with substantial internal R&D operations typically possess much unutilized knowledge, technology, and intellectual property. Due to sharp focus on core businesses, some of these otherwise valuable intellectual assets sit idle. Such businesses are good candidates for an "inside-out" open business model.

By enabling others to exploit unused internal ideas, a company adds "easy" additional REVENUE STREAMS.

Patterns
Overview

	Unbundling Business Models	*The Long Tail*
CONTEXT (BEFORE)	An integrated model combines infrastructure management, product innovation, and Customer Relationships under one roof.	The Value Proposition targets only the most profitable clients.
CHALLENGE	Costs are too high. Several conflicting organizational cultures are combined in a single entity, resulting in undesirable trade-offs.	Targeting less profitable segments with specific Value Propositions is too costly.
SOLUTION (AFTER)	The business is unbundled into three separate but complementary models dealing with • Infrastructure management • Product innovation • Customer relationships	The new or additional Value Proposition targets a large number of historically less profitable, niche Customer Segments—which in aggregate are profitable.
RATIONALE	IT and management tool improvements allow separating and coordinating different business models at lower cost, thus eliminating undesirable trade-offs.	IT and operations management improvements allow delivering tailored Value Propositions to a very large number of new customers at low cost.
EXAMPLES	Private Banking Mobile Telco	Publishing Industry (Lulu.com) LEGO

Multi-Sided Platforms	FREE as a Business Model	Open Business Models
One Value Proposition targets one Customer Segment.	A high-value, high-cost Value Proposition is offered to paying customers only.	R&D Resources and Key Activities are concentrated in-house: • Ideas are invented "inside" only • Results are exploited "inside" only
Enterprise fails to acquire potential new customers who are interested in gaining access to a company's existing customer base (e.g. game developers who want to reach console users)	The high price dissuades customers.	R&D is costly and/or productivity is falling.
A Value Proposition "giving access" to a company's existing Customer Segment is added (e.g. a game console manufacturer provides software developers with access to its users)	Several Value Propositions are offered to different Customer Segments with different Revenue Streams, one of them being free-of-charge (or very low cost).	Internal R&D Resources and Activities are leveraged by utilizing outside partners. Internal R&D results are transformed into a Value Proposition and offered to interested Customer Segments.
An intermediary operating a platform between two or more Customer Segments adds Revenue Streams to the initial model.	Non-paying Customer Segments are subsidized by paying customers in order to attract the maximum number of users.	Acquiring R&D from external sources can be less expensive, resulting in faster time-to-market. Unexploited innovations have the potential to bring in more revenue when sold outside.
Google Video game consoles from Nintendo, Sony, Microsoft Apple iPod, iTunes, iPhone	Advertising and newspapers *Metro* Flickr Open Source Red Hat Skype (versus Telco) Gillette Razor and blades	Procter & Gamble GlaxoSmithKline Innocentive

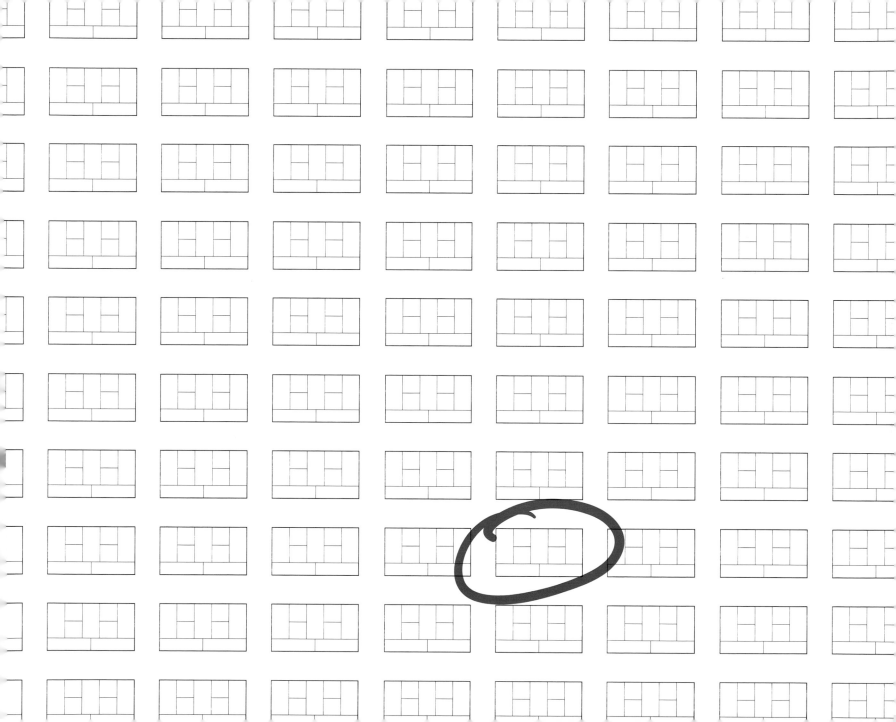

"Businesspeople don't just need to understand designers better; they need to become designers."

Roger Martin, Dean, Rotman School of Management

This section describes a number of techniques and tools from the world of design that can help you design better and more innovative business models. A designer's business involves relentless inquiry into the best possible way to create the new, discover the unexplored, or achieve the functional. A designer's job is to extend the boundaries of thought, to generate new options, and, ultimately, to create value for users. This requires the ability to imagine "that which does not exist." We are convinced that the tools and attitude of the design profession are prerequisites for success in the business model generation.

Businesspeople unknowingly practice design every day. We design organizations, strategies, business models, processes, and projects. To do this, we must take into account a complex web of factors, such as competitors, technology, the legal environment, and more. Increasingly, we must do so in unfamiliar, uncharted territory. This is precisely what design is about. What businesspeople lack are design tools that complement their business skills.

The following pages explore six business model design techniques: Customer Insights, Ideation, Visual Thinking, Prototyping, Storytelling, and Scenarios. We introduce each technique with a story, then demonstrate how the technique applies to business model design. Here and there we've added exercises and suggestions for workshop activities that show you specifically how the design technique can be applied. Book references are provided at the end for those interested in exploring each technique in more depth.

Design

Customer Insights

Outside an office building on the outskirts of Oslo, four Norwegian teenagers wearing American-style "letter" jackets and baseball caps are engaged in a lively discussion with a man in his 50s...

... The teenagers are young, hip snowboarders answering questions posed by Richard Ling, a senior sociologist working for Telenor, the world's seventh largest mobile operator. Ling is interviewing the group as part of a study to gain insights into the use of photos and photo sharing over social networks. Now that nearly every mobile phone sports a camera, photo sharing is of keen interest to cellular operators. Ling's research will help Telenor capture the "big picture" of photo sharing. He focuses not just on existing and potential new mobile photo sharing services, but on broader issues, such as the role photo-sharing plays with respect to trust, secrecy, group identity, and the social fabric linking these young men. Ultimately, his work will enable Telenor to design and deliver better services.

Building Business Models on Customer Insights

—

Companies invest heavily in market research, yet often wind up neglecting the customer perspective when designing products, services—and business models. Good business model design avoids this error. It views the business model through customers' eyes, an approach that can lead to the discovery of completely new opportunities. This does not mean that customer thinking is the only place from which to start an innovation initiative, but it does mean that we should include the customer perspective when evaluating a business model. Successful innovation requires a deep understanding of customers, including environment, daily routines, concerns, and aspirations.

Apple's iPod media player provides an example. Apple understood that people were uninterested in digital media players per se. The company perceived that consumers wanted a seamless way to search, find, download, and listen to digital content, including music, and were willing to pay for a successful solution. Apple's view was unique at a time when illegal downloading was rampant and most companies argued that nobody would be willing to pay for digital music online. Apple dismissed these views and created a seamless music experience for customers, integrating the iTunes music and media software, the iTunes online store, and the iPod media player. With this Value Proposition as the kernel of its business model, Apple went on to dominate the online digital music market

The challenge is to develop a sound understanding of customers on which to base business model design choices. In the field of product and service design, several leading companies work with social scientists to achieve this understanding. At Intel, Nokia, and Telenor, teams of anthropologists and sociologists work to develop new and better products and services. The same approach can lead to new or better business models.

Many leading consumer companies organize field trips for senior executives to meet customers, talk to sales teams, or visit outlets. In other industries, particularly those involving heavy capital investments, talking to customers is part of the daily routine. But the challenge of innovation is developing a deeper understanding of customers rather than just asking them what they want.

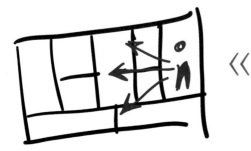

《 *Adopting the customer perspective is a guiding principle for the entire business model design process. Customer perspectives should inform our choices regarding Value Propositions, Distribution Channels, Customer Relationships, and Revenue Streams.*

As pioneering automaker Henry Ford once said, "If I had asked my customers what they wanted, they would have told me 'a faster horse.'"

Another challenge lies in knowing which customers to heed and which customers to ignore. Sometimes tomorrow's growth segments wait at the periphery of today's cash cows. Therefore business model innovators should avoid focusing exclusively on existing Customer Segments and set their sights on new or unreached segments. A number of business model innovations have succeeded precisely because they satisfied the unmet needs of new customers. For example, Stelios Haji-Ioannou's easyJet made air travel available to lower- and middle-income customers who rarely flew. And Zipcar allowed city dwellers to eliminate the hassles of metropolitan car ownership. Instead, customers who pay an annual fee can rent automobiles by the hour. Both are examples of new business models built on Customer Segments located at the periphery under incumbent models: traditional air travel and traditional car rentals.

YOU
Organization-centric business model design

What can we sell customers?

How can we reach customers most efficiently?

What relationships do we need to establish with customers?

How can we make money from our customers?

THEM!
Customer-centric business model design

What job(s) do(es) our customer need to get done and how can we help? What are our customer's aspirations and how can we help him live up to them?

How do our customers prefer to be addressed? How do we, as an enterprise, best fit into their routines?

What relationship do our customers expect us to establish with them?

For what value(s) are customers truly willing to pay?

SHIFTING YOUR PERSPECTIVE

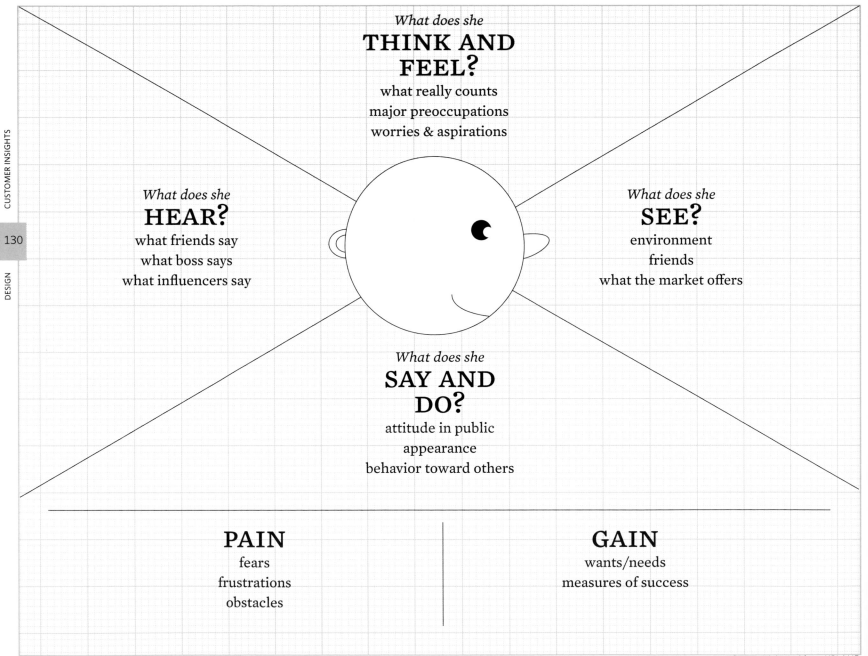

What does she
THINK AND FEEL?
what really counts
major preoccupations
worries & aspirations

What does she
HEAR?
what friends say
what boss says
what influencers say

What does she
SEE?
environment
friends
what the market offers

What does she
SAY AND DO?
attitude in public
appearance
behavior toward others

PAIN
fears
frustrations
obstacles

GAIN
wants/needs
measures of success

Source : Adapted from XPLANE

The Empathy Map

Few of us enjoy the services of a full team of social scientists, but anybody examining a business model can sketch profiles of the Customer Segments addressed therein. A good way to start is by using the Empathy Map, a tool developed by visual thinking company XPLANE. This tool, which we also like to call the "really simple customer profiler," helps you go beyond a customer's demographic characteristics and develop a better understanding of environment, behavior, concerns, and aspirations. Doing so allows you to devise a stronger business model, because a customer profile guides the design of better Value Propositions, more convenient ways to reach customers, and more appropriate Customer Relationships. Ultimately it allows you to better understand what a customer is truly willing to pay for.

How to Use the (Customer) Empathy Map

Here's how it works. First, brainstorm to come up with all the possible Customer Segments that you might want to serve using your business model. Choose three promising candidates, and select one for your first profiling exercise.

Start by giving this customer a name and some demographic characteristics, such as income, marital status, and so forth. Then, referring to the diagram on the opposite page, use a flipchart or whiteboard to build a profile for your newly-named customer by asking and answering the following six questions:

1

WHAT DOES SHE SEE?

DESCRIBE WHAT THE CUSTOMER SEES IN HER ENVIRONMENT

- *What does it look like?*
- *Who surrounds her?*
- *Who are her friends?*
- *What types of offers is she exposed to daily (as opposed to all market offers)?*
- *What problems does she encounter?*

2

WHAT DOES SHE HEAR?

DESCRIBE HOW THE ENVIRONMENT INFLU- ENCES THE CUSTOMER

- *What do her friends say? Her spouse?*
- *Who really influences her, and how?*
- *Which media Channels are influential?*

3

WHAT DOES SHE REALLY THINK AND FEEL?

TRY TO SKETCH OUT WHAT GOES ON IN YOUR CUSTOMER'S MIND

- *What is really important to her (which she might not say publicly)?*
- *Imagine her emotions. What moves her?*
- *What might keep her up at night?*
- *Try describing her dreams and aspirations.*

4

WHAT DOES SHE SAY AND DO?

IMAGINE WHAT THE CUSTOMER MIGHT SAY, OR HOW SHE MIGHT BEHAVE IN PUBLIC

- *What is her attitude?*
- *What could she be telling others?*
- *Pay particular attention to potential conflicts between what a customer might say and what she may truly think or feel.*

5

WHAT IS THE CUSTOMER'S PAIN?

- *What are her biggest frustrations?*
- *What obstacles stand between her and what she wants or needs to achieve?*
- *Which risks might she fear taking?*

6

WHAT DOES THE CUSTOMER GAIN?

- *What does she truly want or need to achieve?*
- *How does she measure success?*
- *Think of some strategies she might use to achieve her goals.*

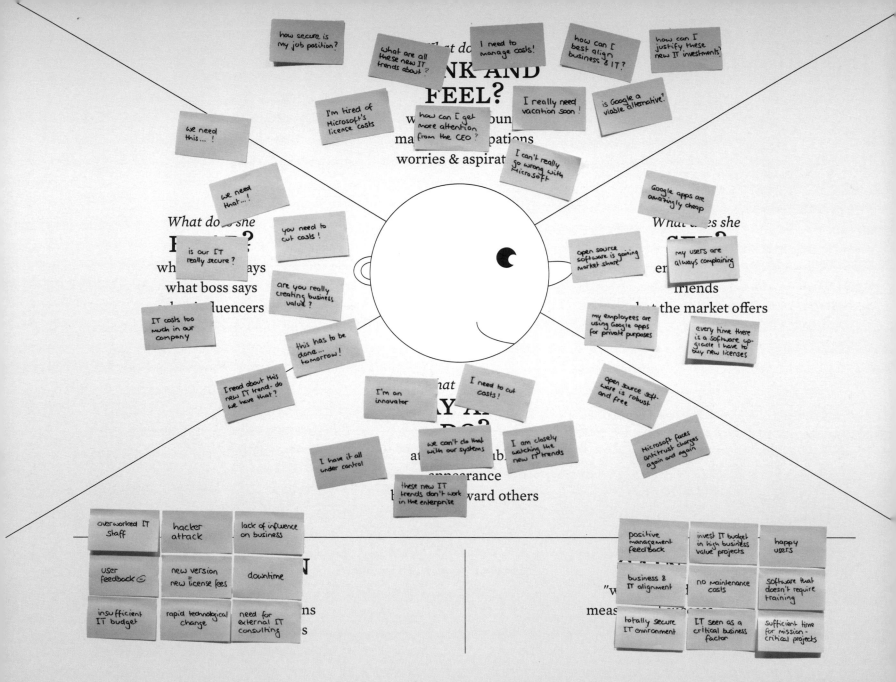

Source : Adapted from XPLANE

Understanding a B2B customer using the Empathy Map

In October 2008, Microsoft announced plans to provide its entire suite of Office applications online. According to the announcement, customers will eventually be able to use Word, Excel, and all other Office applications through browsers. This will require Microsoft to significantly reengineer its business model. One starting point for this business model renovation could be to create a customer profile for a key buying segment: chief information officers (CIO), who define IT strategy and make overarching purchasing decisions. What might a CIO customer profile look like?

The goal is to create a customer viewpoint for continuously questioning your business model assumptions. Customer profiling enables you to generate better answers to questions such as: Does this Value Proposition solve real customer problems? Would she really be willing to pay for this? How would she like to be reached?

Technique_No. 2

Ideation

*Elmar Mock is
listening carefully
as Peter elaborates
excitedly on an idea
amid a sea of Post-it™
notes smothering
the walls…*

… Peter works for a pharmaceutical group that has hired Elmar's innovation consultancy, Creaholic, to help with a breakthrough product. The two men are part of a six-person innovation team holding a three-day offsite meeting.

The group is deliberately heterogeneous, a pastiche of different experience levels and backgrounds. Though all members are accomplished specialists, they joined the group not as technicians, but as consumers unsatisfied with the current state of affairs. Creaholic instructed them to leave their expertise at the door and carry it with them only as a "backpack" of distant memories.

For three days the six form a consumer microcosm and unleash their imaginations to dream up potential breakthrough solutions to a problem, unbridled by technical or financial constraints. Ideas collide and new thinking emerges, and only after generating a multitude of potential solutions are they asked to recall their expertise and pin down the three most promising candidates.

Elmar Mock boasts a long track record of breakthrough innovation. He is one of two inventors of the legendary Swatch watch. Since then, he and his team at Creaholic have helped companies such as BMW, Nestlé, Mikron, and Givaudan innovate successfully.

Elmar knows how difficult it is for established companies to innovate. Such firms require predictability, job descriptions, and financial projections. Yet real innovations emerge from something better described as systematic chaos. Creaholic has found a way to master that chaos. Elmar and his team are obsessed by innovation.

Generating New
Business Model Ideas

—

Mapping an existing business model is one thing; designing a new and innovative business model is another. What's needed is a creative process for generating a large number of business model ideas and successfully isolating the best ones. This process is called ideation. Mastering the art of ideation is crucial when it comes to designing viable new business models.

Traditionally, most industries were characterized by a dominant business model. This has changed radically. Today we enjoy many more choices when designing new business models. Today, different business models compete in the same markets, and boundaries between industries are blurring—or disappearing altogether.

One challenge we face when trying to create new business model options is ignoring the status quo and suspending concerns over operational issues so that we can generate truly new ideas.

Business model innovation is not about looking back, because the past indicates little about what is possible in terms of future business models. Business model innovation is not about looking to competitors, since business model innovation is not about copying or benchmarking, but about creating new mechanisms to create value and derive revenues. Rather, business model innovation is about challenging orthodoxies to design original models that meet unsatisfied, new, or hidden customer needs.

To come up with new or better options, you must dream up a grab bag of ideas before narrowing them down to a short list of conceivable options. Thus, ideation has two main phases: idea generation, where quantity matters, and synthesis, in which ideas are discussed, combined, and narrowed down to a small number of viable options. Options do not necessarily have to represent disruptive business models. They may be innovations that expand the boundaries of your current business model to improve competitiveness.

You can generate ideas for innovative business models from several different starting points. We will look at two: epicenters of business model innovation using the Business Model Canvas, and "what if" questions.

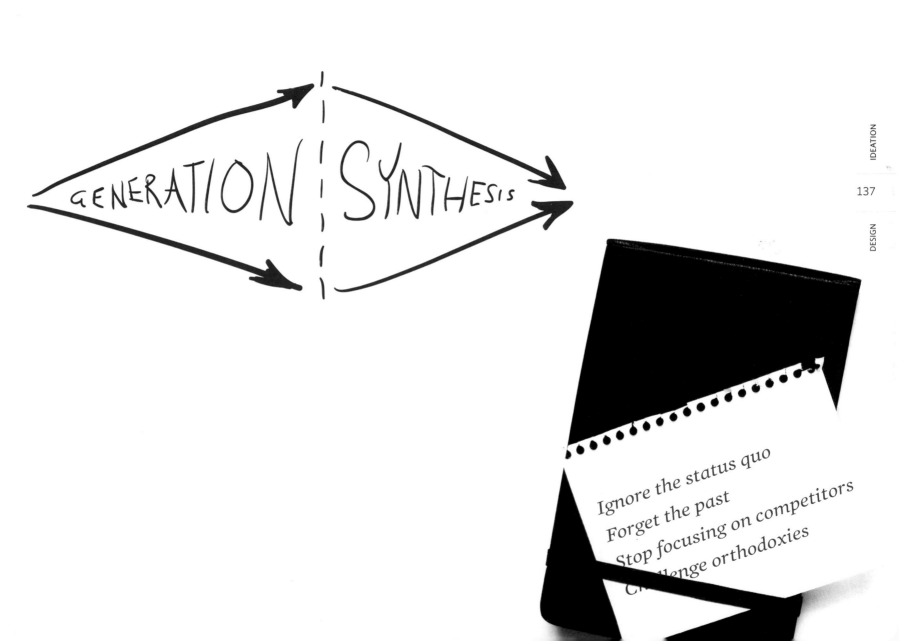

GENERATION | SYNTHESIS

Ignore the status quo
Forget the past
Stop focusing on competitors
Challenge orthodoxies

Epicenters of Business Model Innovation

Ideas for business model innovation can come from anywhere, and each of the nine business model building blocks can be a starting point. Transformative business model innovations affect multiple building blocks. We can distinguish four epicenters of business model innovation: *resource-driven, offer-driven, customer-driven, and finance-driven.*

Each of the four epicenters can serve as the starting point for a major business model change, and each can have a powerful impact on the other eight building blocks. Sometimes, business model innovation can emerge from several epicenters. Also, change often originates in areas identified through a SWOT analysis: an investigation of a business model's strengths, weaknesses, opportunities, and threats (see p. 216).

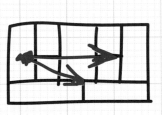

RESOURCE-DRIVEN

RESOURCE-DRIVEN INNOVATIONS ORIGINATE FROM AN ORGANIZATION'S EXISTING INFRASTRUCTURE OR PARTNERSHIPS TO EXPAND OR TRANSFORM THE BUSINESS MODEL.

Example: Amazon Web Services was built on top of Amazon.com's retail infrastructure to offer server capacity and data storage space to other companies.

OFFER-DRIVEN

OFFER-DRIVEN INNOVATIONS CREATE NEW VALUE PROPOSITIONS THAT AFFECT OTHER BUSINESS MODEL BUILDING BLOCKS.

Example: When Cemex, a Mexican cement maker, promised to deliver poured cement to job sites within four hours rather than the 48 hour industry standard, it had to transform its business model. This innovation helped change Cemex from a regional Mexican player into the world's second largest cement producer.

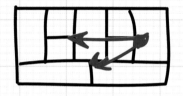

CUSTOMER-DRIVEN

CUSTOMER-DRIVEN INNOVATIONS ARE BASED ON CUSTOMER NEEDS, FACILITATED ACCESS, OR INCREASED CONVENIENCE. LIKE ALL INNOVATIONS EMERGING FROM A SINGLE EPICENTER, THEY AFFECT OTHER BUSINESS MODEL BUILDING BLOCKS.

FINANCE-DRIVEN

INNOVATIONS DRIVEN BY NEW REVENUE STREAMS, PRICING MECHANISMS, OR REDUCED COST STRUCTURES THAT AFFECT OTHER BUSINESS MODEL BUILDING BLOCKS.

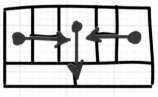

MULTIPLE-EPICENTER DRIVEN

INNOVATIONS DRIVEN BY MULTIPLE EPICENTERS CAN HAVE SIGNIFICANT IMPACT ON SEVERAL OTHER BUILDING BLOCKS.

Example: 23andMe brought personalized DNA testing to individual clients—an offer previously available exclusively to health professionals and researchers, This had substantial implications for both the Value Proposition and the delivery of test results, which 23andMe accomplishes through mass-customized Web profiles.

Example: When Xerox invented the Xerox 914 in 1958—one of the first plain paper copiers—it was priced too high for the market. So Xerox developed a new business model. It leased the machines at $95 per month, including 2,000 free copies, plus five cents per additional copy. Clients acquired the new machines and started making thousands of copies each month.

Example: Hilti, the global manufacturer of professional construction tools, moved away from selling tools outright and toward renting sets of tools to customers. This was a substantial change in Hitli's Value Proposition, but also in its Revenue Streams, which shifted from one-time product revenues to recurring service revenues.

The Power of "What If" Questions

We often have trouble conceiving innovative business models because we are held back in our thinking by the status quo. The status quo stifles imagination. One way to overcome this problem is to challenge conventional assumptions with "what if" questions. With the right business model ingredients, what we think of as impossible might be just doable. "What if" questions help us break free of constraints imposed by current models. They should provoke us and challenge our thinking. They should disturb us as intriguing, difficult-to-execute propositions.

Managers of a daily newspaper might ask themselves: What if we stopped our print edition and went to entirely digital distribution, through Amazon's Kindle e-book reader or through the Web? This would allow the newspaper to drastically reduce production and logistics costs, but would require making up lost print advertising revenues and transitioning readers to digital Channels.

"What if" questions are merely starting points. They challenge us to discover the business model that could make their suppositions work. Some "what if" questions may remain unanswered because they are too provocative. Some may simply need the right business model to become reality.

... furniture buyers picked up components in flat pack form from a large warehouse and assembled the products themselves in their homes? What is common practice today was unthinkable until IKEA introduced the concept in the 1960s.

... airlines didn't buy engines for their airplanes, but paid for every hour an engine runs? That is how Rolls-Royce transformed itself from a money-losing British manufacturer into a service firm that today is the world's second biggest provider of large jet engines.

... voice calls were free worldwide? In 2003 Skype launched a service that allowed free voice calling via the Internet. After five years Skype had acquired 400 million registered users who collectively had made 100 billion free calls.

... car manufacturers didn't sell cars, but provided mobility services? In 2008 Daimler launched car2go, an experimental business in the German city of Ulm. Car2go's fleet of vehicles allows users to pick up and drop off cars anywhere in the city, paying by-the-minute fees for mobility services.

... individuals could lend money to each other rather than borrowing from banks? In 2005, U.K.-based Zopa launched a peer-to-peer lending platform on the Internet.

... every villager in Bangladesh had access to a telephone? That is what Grameenphone set out to achieve under a partnership with micro-finance institution Grameen Bank. At the time, Bangladesh still had the world's lowest tele-density. Today Grameenphone is Bangladesh's largest taxpayer.

The Ideation Process

The ideation process can take several forms. Here we outline a general approach to producing innovative business model options:

1. TEAM COMPOSITION

KEY QUESTION: IS OUR TEAM SUFFICIENTLY DIVERSE TO GENERATE FRESH BUSINESS MODEL IDEAS?

Assembling the right team is essential to generating effective new business model ideas. Members should be diverse in terms of seniority, age, experience level, business unit represented, customer knowledge, and professional expertise.

2. IMMERSION

KEY QUESTION: WHICH ELEMENTS MUST WE STUDY BEFORE GENERATING BUSINESS MODEL IDEAS?

Ideally the team should go through an immersion phase. which could include general research, studying customers or prospects, scrutinizing new technologies, or assessing existing business models. Immersion could last several weeks or could be as short as a couple of workshop exercises (e.g. the Empathy Map).

3. EXPANDING

KEY QUESTION: WHAT INNOVATIONS CAN WE IMAGINE FOR EACH BUSINESS MODEL BUILDING BLOCK?

During this phase the team expands the range of possible solutions, aiming to generate as many ideas as possible. Each of the nine business model building blocks can serve as a starting point. The goal of this phase is quantity, not quality. Enforcing brainstorming rules will keep people focused on generating ideas rather than on critiquing too early in the process (see p. 144).

4. CRITERIA SELECTION

KEY QUESTION: WHAT ARE THE MOST IMPORTANT CRITERIA FOR PRIORITIZING OUR BUSINESS MODEL IDEAS?

After expanding the range of possible solutions, the team should define criteria for reducing the number of ideas to a manageable few. The criteria will be specific to the context of your business, but could include things such as estimated implementation time, revenue potential, possible customer resistance, and impact on competitive advantage.

5. "PROTOTYPING"

KEY QUESTION: WHAT DOES THE COMPLETE BUSINESS MODEL FOR EACH SHORTLISTED IDEA LOOK LIKE?

With criteria defined, the team should be able to reduce the number of ideas to a prioritized shortlist of three to five potential business model innovations. Use the Business Model Canvas to sketch out and discuss each idea as a business model prototype (see p. 160).

Assemble a Diverse Team

The task of generating new ideas should not be left exclusively to those typically considered to be "creative types." Ideation is a team exercise. In fact, by its very nature business model innovation requires the participation of people from across the entire organization. Business model innovation is about seeking to create value by exploring new business model building blocks and forging innovative links between blocks. This can involve all nine blocks of the canvas, whether Distribution Channels, Revenue Streams, or Key Resources. Thus it requires input and ideas from people representing multiple areas.

That's why assembling the right task force is a critical prerequisite for generating new business model ideas. Thinking about business model innovation should not be confined to the R&D unit or the strategic planning office. Business model innovation teams should have a diverse membership. The diversity will help you generate, discuss, and select new ideas. Consider adding outsiders, or even children. Diversity works. But make sure to teach people how to listen actively, and consider engaging a neutral facilitator for key meetings.

A diverse business model innovation team has members...

- *from various business units*
- *of different ages*
- *with different areas of expertise*
- *of differing levels of seniority*
- *with a mixture of experiences*
- *from different cultural backgrounds*

Brainstorming Rules

*Successful brainstorming requires
following a set of rules. Enforcing
these rules will help you maximize the
number of useful ideas generated.*

Stay focused

Start with a well-honed statement of the problem at hand. Ideally, this should be articulated around a customer need. Don't let the discussion stray too far; always bring it back to the problem statement.

Enforce rules

Clarify the brainstorming rules upfront and enforce them. The most important rules are "defer judgment," "one conversation at a time," "go for quantity," "be visual," and "encourage wild ideas." Facilitators should enforce the rules.

Think visually

Write ideas down or sketch them out on a surface everyone can see. A good way to collect ideas is to jot them down on Post-it™ notes and stick these to a wall. This allows you to move ideas around and regroup them.

Prepare

Prepare for brainstorming with some sort of immersion experience related to the problem at hand. This could be a field trip, discussions with customers, or any other means of immersing the team in issues related to your problem statement.

Adapted from an interview with Tom Kelley of IDEO in *Fast Company* magazine: "Seven Secrets to Good Brainstorming"

Warm-Up:
The Silly Cow Exercise

To get your team's creative juices flowing, it can be helpful to start an ideation session with a warm-up such as the Silly Cow exercise. Here's how it works: Instruct participants to sketch out three different business models using a cow. Ask them to first define some characteristics of a cow (produces milk, eats all day, makes a mooing sound, etc.). Tell them to use those characteristics to come up with an innovative business model based on a cow. Give them three minutes.

Keep in mind that this exercise can backfire, as it is indeed quite silly. But it has been tested with senior executives, accountants, risk managers, and entrepreneurs, and usually is a great success. The goal is to take people out of their day-to-day business routines and show them how readily they can generate ideas by disconnecting from orthodoxies and letting their creativity flow.

Technique_No. 3

Visual Thinking

The meeting room walls are plastered with large posters on which a group of 14 people are assiduously sketching drawings and pasting Post-it™ notes. Though the scene almost has the atmosphere of an art class, it's taking place at the headquarters of Hewlett-Packard, the technology products and services giant …

… The 14 participants hail from throughout HP, but all are involved in information management. They've gathered here for a one-day workshop to literally draw a picture of how a global enterprise should manage information flows.

Dave Gray, founder and chairman of consultancy XPLANE, is facilitating the meeting. XPLANE uses visual thinking tools to help clients clarify problems involving everything from corporate strategy to operational implementations. Together with an XPLANE artist, Dave helps the 14 HP specialists gain a better understanding of the big picture of information sharing in a global enterprise. The group uses the posted sketches to discuss information sharing, to identify relationships between elements, to fill in missing pieces, and to develop a joint understanding of multiple issues.

With a knowing smile, Dave talks about a common misconception: that one shouldn't draw something until one understands it. On the contrary, he explains, sketches—however rudimentary or amateurish—help people better describe, discuss, and understand issues, particularly those of a complex nature. For the 14 Hewlett-Packard collaborators, XPLANE's visualization approach has worked beautifully. They gathered as 14 specialists with deeply individual understandings, but parted with a simple one-page image of how a global enterprise should manage information. XPLANE's client roster, which reads like a who's who of the world's most successful companies, testifies to the growing number of organizations that understand the value of this type of visual thinking.

The Value of Visual Thinking

—

Visual thinking is indispensable to working with business models. By visual thinking we mean using visual tools such as pictures, sketches, diagrams, and Post-it™ notes to construct and discuss meaning. Because business models are complex concepts composed of various building blocks and their interrelationships, it is difficult to truly understand a model without sketching it out.

A business model really is a system where one element influences the other; it only makes sense as a whole. Capturing that big picture without visualizing it is difficult. In fact, by visually depicting a business model, one turns its tacit assumptions into explicit information. This makes the model tangible and allows for clearer discussions and changes. Visual techniques give "life" to a business model and facilitate co-creation.

Sketching a model transforms it into a persistent object and a conceptual anchor to which discussions can always return. This is critical because it shifts discourse from the abstract toward the concrete and greatly improves the quality of debate. Typically, if you aim to improve an existing business model, visually depicting it will unearth logical gaps and facilitate their discussion. Similarly,

if you are designing a completely new business model, drawing it will allow you to discuss different options easily by adding, removing, or moving pictures around.

Businesses already make frequent use of visual techniques such as diagrams and charts. Such elements are used extensively to clarify messages within reports and plans. But visual techniques are used less frequently to discuss, explore, and define business issues. When was the last time you attended a meeting where executives were drawing on the walls? Yet it is in the strategic process where visual thinking can add tremendous value. Visual thinking enhances strategic inquiries by making the abstract concrete, by illuminating relationships between elements, and by simplifying the complex. In this section we describe how visual thinking can help you throughout the process of defining, discussing, and changing business models.

We refer to two techniques: the use of Post-it™ notes and the use of sketches in combination with the Business Model Canvas. We also discuss four processes improved by visual thinking: understanding, dialogue, exploration, and communication.

Visualizing with Post-it™ Notes

A set of Post-it™ notes is an indispensable tool that everyone reflecting on business models should keep handy. Post-it™ notes function like idea containers that can be added, removed, and easily shifted between business model building blocks. This is important because during business model discussions, people frequently do not immediately agree on which elements should appear in a Business Model Canvas or where they should be placed. During exploratory discussions, some elements might be removed and replaced multiple times to explore new ideas.

Here are three simple guidelines: (1) use thick marking pens, (2) write only one element per Post-it™ note, and (3) write only a few words per note to capture the essential point. Using thick markers is more than a detail: it prevents you from putting too much information on a single Post-it™, and makes for easier reading and overview.

Keep in mind, too, that the discussion leading to the final business model picture created by all the Post-it™ notes is just as important as the outcome. Discussion around which notes to place on or remove from the Canvas and debate over how one element influences others give participants a deep understanding of the business model and its dynamics. Consequently, a Post-it™ note becomes more than just a piece of sticky paper representing a business model building block; it becomes a vector for strategic discussion.

Visualizing with Drawings

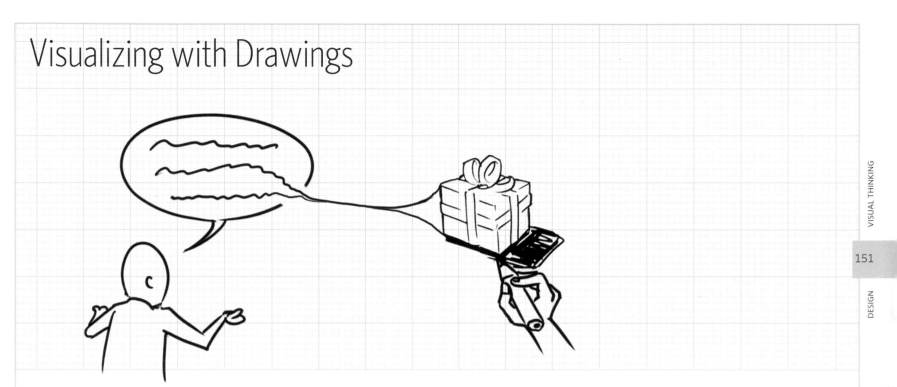

Drawings can be even more powerful than Post-it™ notes because people react more strongly to images than to words. Pictures deliver messages instantly. Simple drawings can express ideas that otherwise require many words.

It's easier than we think. A stick figure with a smiling face conveys emotion. A big bag of money and a small bag of money convey proportions. The problem is that most of us think we can't draw. We're embarrassed lest our sketches appear unsophisticated or childish. The truth is that even crude drawings, sincerely rendered, make things tangible and understandable. People interpret simple stick figures far more easily than abstract concepts expressed in text.

Sketches and drawings can make a difference in several ways. The most obvious one is explaining and communicating your business model based on simple drawings, something we explain how to do at the end of this chapter. Another is sketching out a typical client and her environment to illustrate one of your Customer Segments. This will trigger a more concrete, intensive discussion compared to outlining that person's characteristics in writing. Finally, sketching out a Customer Segment's needs and jobs-to-get-done is a powerful way to exploit visual techniques.

Such drawings will likely trigger constructive discussion from which new business model ideas will emerge. Now let's examine four processes improved by visual thinking.

Understand the Essence

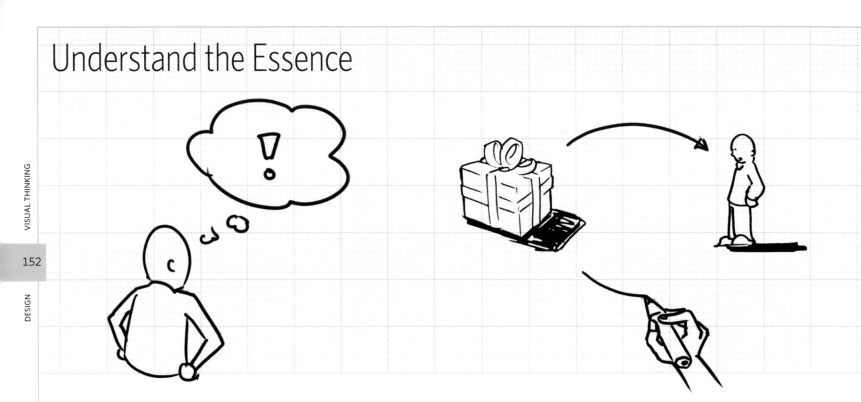

VISUAL GRAMMAR

The Business Model Canvas poster is a conceptual map that functions as a visual language with corresponding grammar. It tells you which pieces of information to insert in the model, and where. It provides a visual and text guide to all the information needed to sketch out a business model.

CAPTURING THE BIG PICTURE

By sketching out all the elements of the Canvas you immediately give viewers the big picture of a business model. A sketch provides just the right amount of information to allow a viewer to grasp the idea, yet not too much detail to distract him. The Business Model Canvas visually simplifies the reality of an enterprise with all its processes, structures, and systems. In a business model like Rolls-Royce's, where jet engine units are leased by the hour rather than sold, it is the big picture, rather than the individual pieces, that is compelling.

SEEING RELATIONSHIPS

Understanding a business model requires not only knowing the compositional elements, but also grasping the interdependencies between elements. This is easier to express visually than through words. This is even more true when several elements and relationships are involved. In describing the business model of a low-cost airline, for example, drawings can effectively show why a homogenous fleet of airplanes is crucial to keeping maintenance and training costs low.

Enhance Dialogue

COLLECTIVE REFERENCE POINT

We all hold tacit assumptions in our heads, and posting an image that turns those implicit assumptions into explicit information is a powerful way to improve dialogue. It makes a business model into a tangible and persistent object, and provides a reference point to which participants can always return. Given that people can hold only a limited number of ideas in short-term memory, visually portraying business models is essential to good discussion. Even the simplest models are composed of several building blocks and interrelationships.

SHARED LANGUAGE

The Business Model Canvas is a shared visual language. It provides not only a reference point, but also a vocabulary and grammar that helps people better understand each other. Once people are familiar with the Canvas, it becomes a powerful enabler of focused discussion about business model elements and how they fit together. This is particularly valuable in organizations with matrix reporting structures where individuals in a working group or task force may know little about each other's functional areas. A shared visual business model language powerfully supports idea exchange and increases team cohesiveness.

JOINT UNDERSTANDING

Visualizing business models as a group is the most effective way to achieve shared understanding. People from different parts of an organization may deeply understand parts of a business model but lack a solid grasp of the whole. When experts jointly draw a business model, everybody involved gains an understanding of the individual components and develops a shared understanding of the relationships between these components.

Explore Ideas

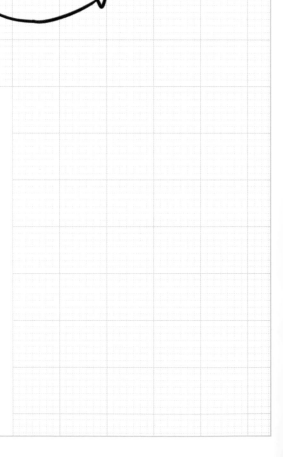

IDEA TRIGGER

The Business Model Canvas is a bit like an artist's canvas. When an artist starts painting, he often has a vague idea—not an exact image—in mind. Rather than starting in one corner of a canvas and executing sequentially, he starts wherever his muse dictates and builds the painting organically. As Pablo Picasso said, "I begin with an idea and then it becomes something else." Picasso saw ideas as nothing more than points of departure. He knew they would evolve into something new during their explication.

Crafting a business model is no different. Ideas placed in the Canvas trigger new ones. The Canvas becomes a tool for facilitating the idea dialogue—for individuals sketching out their ideas and for groups developing ideas together.

PLAY

A visual business model also provides opportunity for play. With the elements of a model visible on a wall in the form of individual Post-it™ notes, you can start discussing what happens when you remove certain elements or insert new ones. For example, what would happen to your business model if you eliminated the least profitable Customer Segment? Could you do that? Or do you need the unprofitable segment to attract profitable customers? Would eliminating unprofitable customers enable you to reduce resources and costs and improve services to profitable customers? A visual model helps you think through the systemic impact of modifying one element or another.

Improve Communication

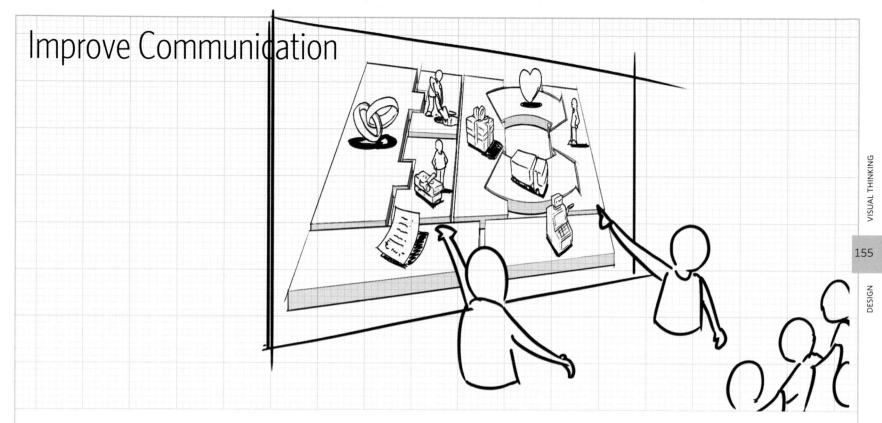

CREATE COMPANY-WIDE UNDERSTANDING

When it comes to communicating a business model and its most important elements, a picture is truly worth a thousand words. Everybody in an organization needs to understand its business model, because everybody can potentially contribute to its improvement. At the very least, employees need a shared understanding of the model so they can move in the same strategic direction. Visual depiction is the best way to create such a shared understanding.

SELLING INTERNALLY

In organizations, ideas and plans often must be "sold" internally at various levels to garner support or obtain funding. A powerful visual story reinforcing your pitch can increase your chances of winning understanding and backing for your idea. Using images rather than just words to tell the story makes your case even stronger, because people identify immediately with images. Good imagery readily communicates your organization's current status, what needs doing, how it can be done, and what the future might look like.

SELLING EXTERNALLY

Just as employees must "sell" ideas internally, entrepreneurs with plans based on new business models must sell them to other parties, such as investors or potential collaborators. Strong visuals substantially increase chances of success.

Different Types of Visualization for Different Needs

Visual representations of business models call for different levels of detail depending on one's goal. The sketch of Skype's business model on the right drives home the key differences between its business model and that of a traditional telecommunications carrier. The goal is to point out the striking differences between Skype's business model building blocks and those of a traditional carrier, even though both offer similar services.

The right-hand page sketch depicting the young Dutch company Sellaband has a different goal and is therefore more detailed. It aims to paint the big picture of a completely new music industry business model: that of a platform enabling crowd-funding of independent musical artists. Sellaband uses the drawing to explain its innovative business model to investors, partners, and employees. Sellaband's combination of images and text has proven to be far more effective than words alone at accomplishing this task.

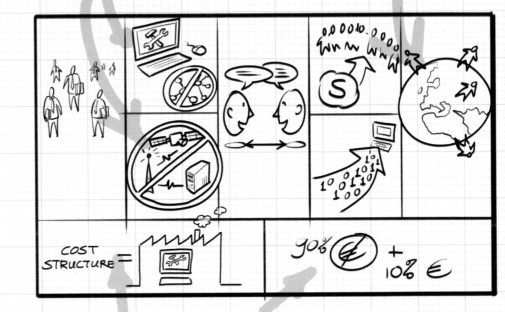

- *Skype's Key Resources and Activities resemble those of a software company, because its service is based on software that uses the Internet to carry calls. Given its 400 million+ user base, the company enjoys very low infrastructure costs. In fact, it does not own or operate a telecommunications network at all.*

- *From day one, Skype was a global voice carrier because its service is delivered through the Internet, unrestricted by traditional telecommunications networks. Its business is highly scalable.*

- *Though it provides a telecommunications service, Skype's business model features the economics of a software company rather than a telecommunications network operator.*

- *Ninety percent of Skype users never pay. Only an estimated 10 percent of users are paying customers. Unlike traditional telecommunication carriers, Skype's Channels and Relationships are highly automated. They require almost no human intervention and are therefore relatively inexpensive.*

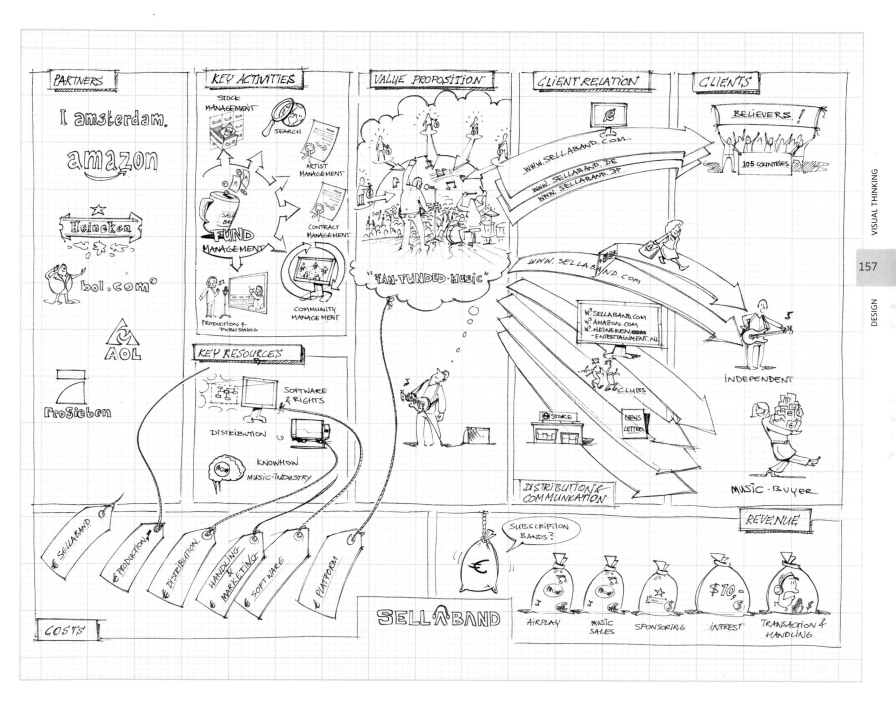

Telling a Visual Story

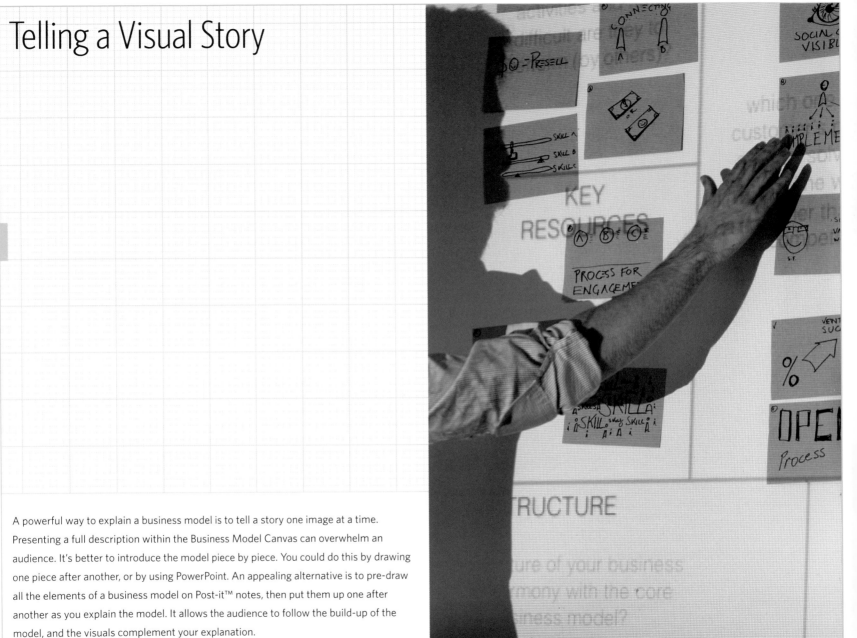

A powerful way to explain a business model is to tell a story one image at a time. Presenting a full description within the Business Model Canvas can overwhelm an audience. It's better to introduce the model piece by piece. You could do this by drawing one piece after another, or by using PowerPoint. An appealing alternative is to pre-draw all the elements of a business model on Post-it™ notes, then put them up one after another as you explain the model. It allows the audience to follow the build-up of the model, and the visuals complement your explanation.

Visual Storytelling Activity

1

MAP YOUR BUSINESS MODEL

- *Begin by mapping out a simple, text-based version of your business model.*

- *Write each business model element on an individual Post-it™ note.*

- *Mapping can be done individually or with a group.*

2

DRAW EACH BUSINESS MODEL ELEMENT

- *One at a time, take each Post-it™ note and replace it with a drawing representing the content.*

- *Keep the images simple: omit detail.*

- *Drawing quality is unimportant as long as the message is conveyed.*

3

DEFINE THE STORYLINE

- *Decide which Post-it™ notes you will put up first when telling your story.*

- *Try different paths. You might start with Customer Segments, or maybe the Value Proposition.*

- *Basically, any starting point is possible if it effectively supports your story.*

4

TELL THE STORY

- *Tell your business model story one drawn Post-it™ picture at a time.*

  Note: Depending on the context and your personal preferences, you may want to use PowerPoint or Keynote. Slideware, though, is unlikely to produce the positive surprise effect of the Post-it™ approach.

Prototyping

With a look bordering on panic, Weatherhead School of Management Professor Richard Boland Jr. watched as Matt Fineout, an architect with Gehry & Associates, casually tore up plans for a new school building …

… Boland and Fineout had been struggling for two full days to remove some 5,500 square feet from the floor plan designed by star architect Frank Gehry, while leaving room needed for meeting spaces and office equipment.

At the end of the marathon planning session, Boland had breathed a sigh of relief. "It's finally done," he thought. But at that very moment, Fineout rose from his chair, ripped the document apart, and tossed the scraps into a trash bin, not bothering to retain a single trace of the pair's hard labor. He responded to Professor Boland's shocked expression with a gentle shrug and a soft remark. "We've shown we *can* do it; now we need to think of *how* we want to do it."

Looking back, Boland describes the incident as an extreme example of the relentless approach to inquiry he experienced while working with the Gehry group on the new Weatherhead building. During the design phase, Gehry and his team made hundreds of models with different materials and of varying sizes, simply to explore new directions. Boland explains that the goal of this prototyping activity was far more than the mere testing or proving of ideas. It was a methodology for exploring different possibilities until a truly good one emerged. He points out that prototyping, as practiced by the Gehry group, is a central part of an inquiry process that helps participants gain a better sense of what is missing in the initial understanding of a situation. This leads to completely new possibilities, among which the right one can be identified. For Professor Boland, the experience with Gehry & Associates was transformative. He now understands how design techniques, including prototyping, contribute to finding better solutions for the entire spectrum of business problems. Together with fellow professor Fred Collopy and other colleagues, Boland is now spearheading the concept of Manage by Designing: the integration of design thinking, skills, and experiences into Weatherhead's MBA curriculum. Here, students use tools of design to sketch alternatives, follow through on problem situations, transcend traditional boundaries, and prototype ideas.

Prototyping's Value

—

Prototyping is a powerful tool for developing new, innovative business models. Like visual thinking, it makes abstract concepts tangible and facilitates the exploration of new ideas. Prototyping comes from the design and engineering disciplines, where it is widely used for product design, architecture, and interaction design. It is less common in business management because of the less tangible nature of organizational behavior and strategy. While prototyping has long played a role at the intersection of business and design, for example in manufactured product design, in recent years it has gained traction in areas such as process design, service design, and even organization and strategy design. Here we show how prototyping can make an important contribution to business model design.

Although they use the same term, product designers, architects, and engineers all have different understandings of what constitutes a "prototype." We see prototypes representing potential future business models: as tools that serve the purpose of discussion, inquiry, or proof of concept. A business model prototype can take the form of a simple sketch, a fully thought-through concept described with the Business Model Canvas, or a spreadsheet that simulates the financial workings of a new business.

It is important to understand that a business model prototype is not necessarily a rough picture of what the actual business model will actually look like. Rather, a prototype is a thinking tool that helps us explore different directions in which we could take our business model. What does it mean for the model if we add another client segment? What are the consequences of removing a costly resource? What if we gave away something for free and replaced that Revenue Stream with something more innovative? Making and manipulating a business model prototype forces us to address issues of structure, relationship, and logic in ways unavailable through mere thought and discussion. To truly understand the pros and cons of different possibilities, and to further our inquiry, we need to construct multiple prototypes of our business model at different levels of refinement. Interaction with prototypes produces ideas far more readily than discussion. Prototype business models may be thought-provoking—even a bit crazy—and thus help push our thinking. When this happens, they become signposts pointing us in as-yet unimagined directions rather than serving as mere representations of to-be-implemented business models. "Inquiry" should signify a relentless search for the best solution. Only after deep inquiry can we effectively pick a prototype to refine and execute—after our design has matured.

Businesspeople are likely to display one of two reactions to this process of business model inquiry. Some might say, "Well, that is a nice idea, if we only had the time to explore different options." Others might say that a market research study would be an equally good way to come up with new business models. Both reactions are based on dangerous preconceptions.

The first supposes that "business as usual" or incremental improvements are sufficient to survive in today's competitive environment. We believe this path leads to mediocrity. Businesses that fail to take the time to develop and prototype new, ground-breaking business model ideas risk being sidelined or overtaken by more dynamic competitors—or by insurgent challengers appearing, seemingly, from nowhere.

The second reaction assumes that data is the most important consideration when designing new strategic options. It is not. Market research is a single input in the long and laborious process of prototyping powerful new business models with the potential to outperform competitors or develop entirely new markets.

Where do you want to be? At the top of the game, because you've taken the time to prototype powerful new business models? Or on the sidelines, because you were too busy sustaining your existing model? We're convinced that new, game-changing business models emerge from deep and relentless inquiry.

Design Attitude

"If you freeze an idea too quickly, you fall in love with it.
If you refine it too quickly, you become attached to it
and it becomes very hard to keep exploring, to keep
looking for better. The crudeness of the early models
in particular is very deliberate."

Jim Glymph, Gehry Partners

As businesspeople, when we see a prototype we tend to focus on its physical form or its representation, viewing it as something that models, or encapsulates the essence of, what we eventually intend to do. We perceive a prototype as something that simply needs to be refined. In the design profession, prototypes do play a role in pre-implementation visualization and testing. But they also play another very important role: that of a tool of inquiry. In this sense they serve as thinking aids for exploring new possibilities. They help us develop a better understanding of what could be.

This same design attitude can be applied to business model innovation. By making a prototype of a business model we can explore particular aspects of an idea: novel Revenue Streams, for example. Participants learn about the elements of a prototype as they construct and discuss

it. As previously discussed , business model prototypes vary in terms of scale and level of refinement. We believe it is important to think through a number of basic business model possibilities before developing a business case for a specific model. This spirit of inquiry is called design attitude, because it is so central to the design professions, as Professor Boland discovered. The attributes of design attitude include a willingness to explore crude ideas, rapidly discard them, then take the time to examine multiple possibilities before choosing to refine a few—and accepting uncertainty until a design direction matures. These things don't come naturally to businesspeople, but they are requirements for generating new business models. Design attitude demands changing one's orientation from making decisions to creating options from which to choose.

Prototypes at Different Scales

In architecture or product design, it is easy to understand what is meant by prototyping at different scales, because we are talking about physical artifacts. Architect Frank Gehry and product designer Philippe Starck construct countless prototypes during a project, ranging from sketches and rough models to elaborate, full-featured prototypes. We can apply the same scale and size variations when prototyping business models, but in a more conceptual way. A business model prototype can be anything from a rough sketch of an idea on a napkin to a detailed Business Model Canvas to a field-testable business model. You may wonder how all of this is any different from simply sketching out business ideas, something any businessperson or entrepreneur does. Why do we need to call it "prototyping"?

There are two answers. First, the mindset is different. Second, the Business Model Canvas provides structure to facilitate exploration.

Business model prototyping is about a mindset we call "design attitude." It stands for an uncompromising commitment to discovering new and better business models by sketching out many prototypes —both rough and detailed—representing many strategic options. It's not about outlining only ideas you really plan to implement. It's about exploring new and perhaps absurd, even impossible ideas by adding and removing elements of each prototype. You can experiment with prototypes at different levels.

NAPKIN SKETCH	ELABORATED CANVAS	BUSINESS CASE	FIELD-TEST
OUTLINE AND PITCH A ROUGH IDEA	**EXPLORE WHAT IT WOULD TAKE TO MAKE THE IDEA WORK**	**EXAMINE THE VIABILITY OF THE IDEA**	**INVESTIGATE CUSTOMER ACCEPTANCE AND FEASIBILITY**
DRAW A SIMPLE BUSINESS MODEL CANVAS. DESCRIBE THE IDEA USING ONLY KEY ELEMENTS.	DEVELOP A MORE ELABORATE CANVAS TO EXPLORE ALL THE ELEMENTS NEEDED TO MAKE THE BUSINESS MODEL WORK.	TURN THE DETAILED CANVAS INTO A SPREADSHEET TO ESTIMATE YOUR MODEL'S EARNING POTENTIAL.	YOU'VE DECIDED ON A POTENTIAL NEW BUSINESS MODEL, AND NOW WANT TO FIELD-TEST SOME ASPECTS.
• *Outline the idea* • *Include the Value Proposition* • *Include the main Revenue Streams*	• *Develop a full Canvas* • *Think through your business logic* • *Estimate the market potential* • *Understand the relationships between Building Blocks* • *Do some basic fact-checking*	• *Create a full Canvas* • *Include key data* • *Calculate costs and revenues* • *Estimate profit potential* • *Run financial scenarios based on different assumptions*	• *Prepare a well-justified business case for the new model* • *Include prospective or actual customers in the field test* • *Test the Value Proposition, Channels, pricing mechanism, and/or other elements in the marketplace*

Eight Business Model Prototypes
for Publishing a Book

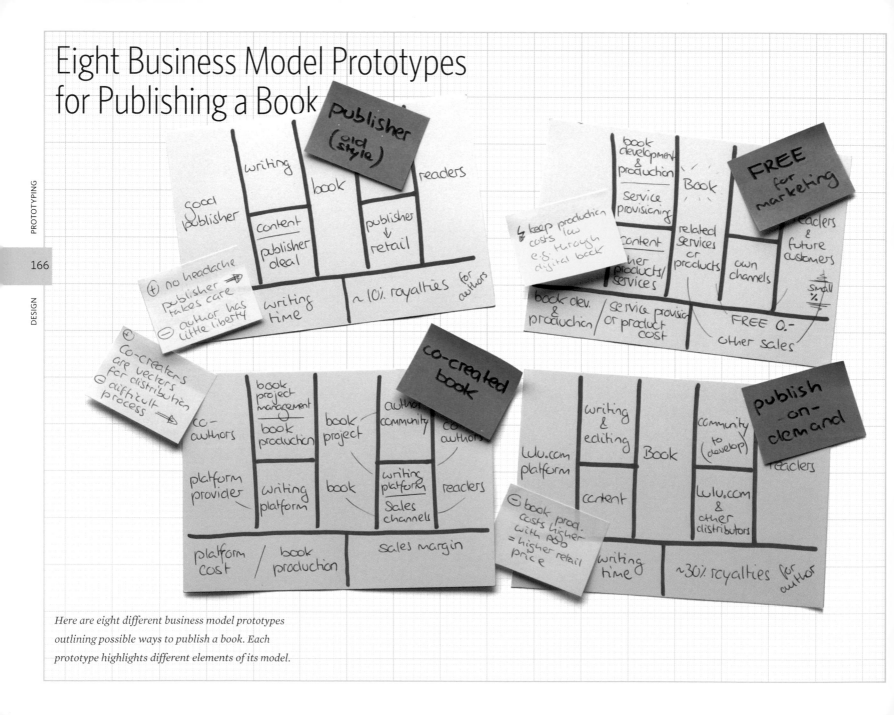

Here are eight different business model prototypes
outlining possible ways to publish a book. Each
prototype highlights different elements of its model.

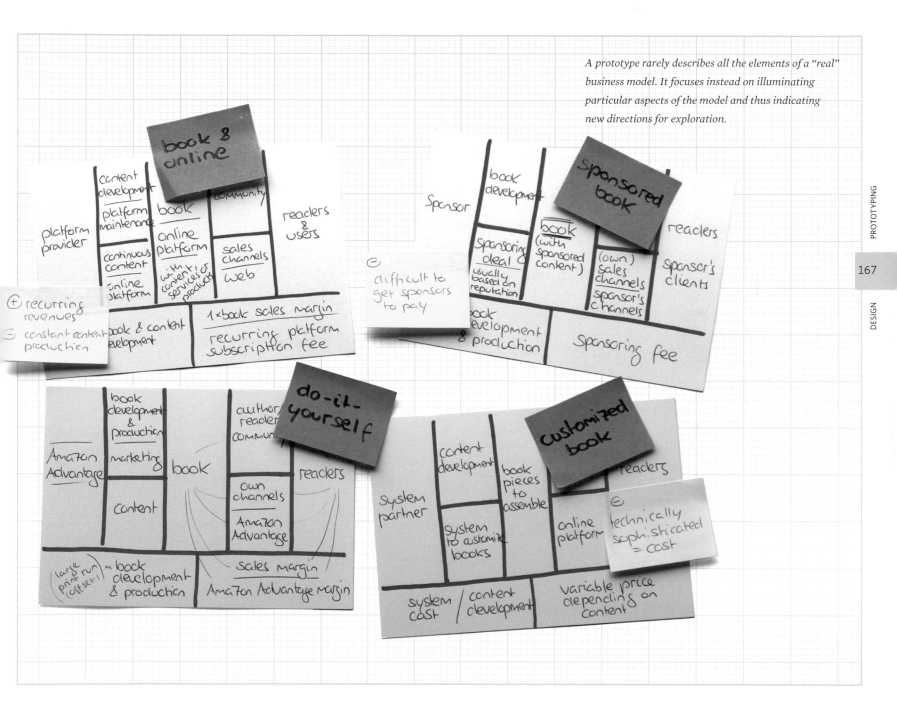

A prototype rarely describes all the elements of a "real" business model. It focuses instead on illuminating particular aspects of the model and thus indicating new directions for exploration.

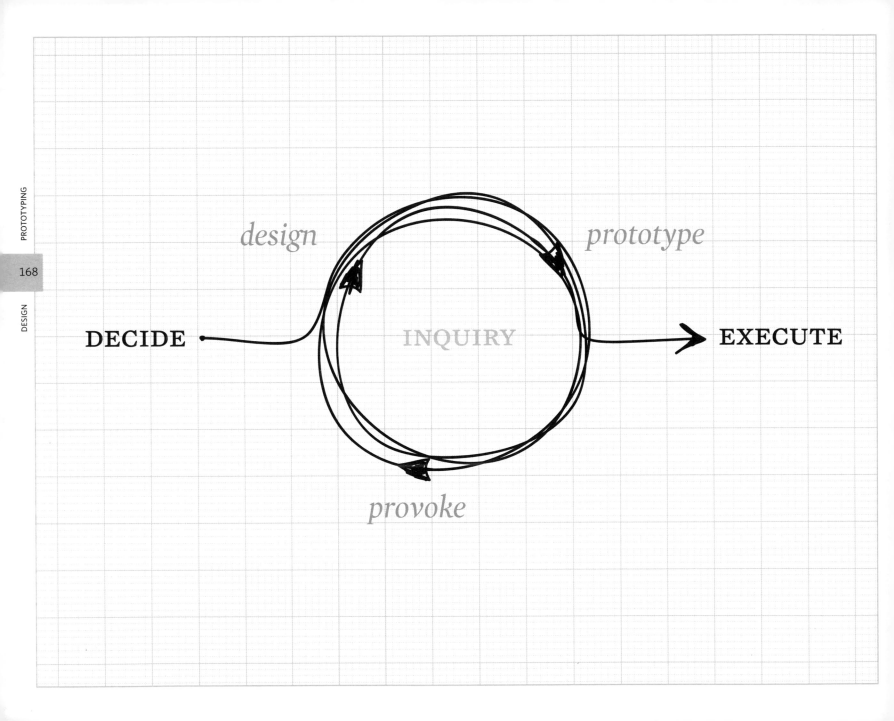

design

prototype

DECIDE

INQUIRY

EXECUTE

provoke

Wanted: A New Consulting Business Model

John Sutherland needs your help. John is the founder and CEO of a midsized global consulting firm that focuses on advising companies on strategy and organizational issues. He is looking for a fresh, outside perspective on his company because he believes that his business needs to be re-envisioned.

John built his company over two decades and now employs 210 people worldwide. The focus of his consultancy is helping executives develop effective strategies, improve their strategic management, and realign their organizations. He competes directly with McKinsey, Bain, and Roland Berger. One problem he faces is being smaller than his top-tier competitors, yet much larger than the typical niche-focused strategy consultancy. But John is not preoccupied with this issue, since his company is still doing reasonably well. What really troubles him is the strategic consulting profession's poor reputation in the marketplace, and growing client perception that the prevalent hourly and project-based billing model is outdated. Though his own firm's reputation remains good, he has heard from several clients that they think consultants overcharge, under-deliver, and show little genuine commitment to client projects.

Such comments alarm John, because he believes his industry employs some of the brightest minds in business. After much thought, he has concluded that this reputation results from an outdated business model, and he now wants to transform his own company's approach. John aims to make hourly and project billing a thing of the past, but isn't quite sure how to do so.

Help John by providing him with some fresh perspectives on innovative consulting business models.

John, 55
Founder & CEO
Strategy Consultancy
210 employees

1

OUTLINE BIG ISSUES

- *Think of a typical strategy-consulting client.*

- *Pick the Customer Segment and industry of your choice.*

- *Describe five of the biggest issues related to strategy consulting. Refer to the Empathy Map (see p. 131).*

2

GENERATE POSSIBILITIES

- *Take another close look at the five customer issues you selected.*

- *Generate as many consulting business model ideas as you can.*

- *Pick the five ideas you think are best (not necessarily the most realistic). Refer to the Ideation Process (see p. 134).*

3

PROTOTYPE THE BUSINESS MODEL

- *Choose the three most diverse ideas of the five generated.*

- *Develop three conceptual business model prototypes by sketching the elements of each idea on different Business Model Canvases.*

- *Annotate the pros and cons of each prototype.*

It is already far past midnight as Anab Jain watches the latest video footage she shot during the day …

… She's working on a series of small films for Colebrook Bosson Saunders, a designer and manufacturer of award-winning office furniture accessories. Anab is a storyteller and designer, and the films she is working on are part of a project to help Colebrook Bosson Saunders make sense of how the future of work and the workplace could look. To make this future tangible, she invented three protagonists and projected them into 2012. She gave them new jobs based on research into new and emerging technologies and the impact of demographics and environmental risks on our future lives. The films then show this near future. But rather than describing 2012, Anab takes the role of the storyteller, visiting this future environment and interviewing the three protagonists. They each explain their work and show objects they use. The films are real enough to cause viewers to suspend their disbelief and become intrigued by the different environment. That is exactly what companies that hire Anab Jain, like Microsoft and Nokia, are looking for: stories to make potential futures tangible.

Storytelling's Value

—

As parents, we read stories to our kids, sometimes the same ones we heard as children ourselves. As colleagues, we share the latest organizational gossip. And as friends, we tell one another stories of our personal lives. Somehow, it is only in our roles as business-people that we avoid using stories. This is unfortunate. When was the last time you heard a story used to introduce and discuss a business issue? Storytelling is an undervalued and underused art in the world of business. Let's examine how storytelling can serve as a powerful tool to make new business models more tangible.

By their very nature, new or innovative business models can be difficult to describe and understand. They challenge the status quo by arranging things in unfamiliar ways. They force listeners to open their minds to new possibilities. Resistance is one likely reaction to an unfamiliar model. Therefore, describing new business models in a way that overcomes resistance is crucial.

Just as the Business Model Canvas helps you sketch and analyze a new model, storytelling will help you effectively communicate what it is all about. Good stories engage listeners, so the story is the ideal tool to prepare for an in-depth discussion of a business model and its underlying logic. Storytelling takes advantage of the explanatory power of the Business Model Canvas by suspending disbelief in the unfamiliar.

Why Storytelling?

Introducing the New

New business model ideas can pop up anywhere in an organization. Some ideas may be good, some may be mediocre, and some may be, well, completely useless. But even outstanding business model ideas can have a tough time getting past layers of management and finding their way into an organization's strategy. So effectively pitching your business model ideas to management is crucial. This is where stories can help. Ultimately, managers are interested in numbers and facts, but having the right story can win their attention. A good story is a compelling way to quickly outline a broad idea before getting caught up in the details.

Pitching to Investors

If you are an entrepreneur, chances are you will pitch your idea or business model to investors or other potential shareholders (and you already know that investors stop listening the instant you tell them how you will become the next Google). What investors and other shareholders want to know is: How will you create value for customers? How will you make money doing so? That's the perfect setting for a story. It's the ideal way to introduce your venture and business model before getting into the full business plan.

Engaging Employees

When an organization transitions from an existing business model to a new business model, it must convince collaborators to follow. People need a crystal clear understanding of the new model and what it means for them. In short, the organization needs to powerfully engage its employees. That is where traditional text-based Power-Point presentations usually fail. Introducing a new business model through an engaging story-based presentation (delivered with PowerPoint, drawings, or other techniques) is far more likely to connect with listeners. Capturing people's attention and curiosity paves the way for in-depth presentations and discussions of the unfamiliar.

Make the New Tangible

Explaining a new, untested business model is like explaining a painting with words alone. But telling a story of how the model creates value is like applying bright colors to canvas. It makes things tangible.

Clarification

Telling a story that illustrates how your business model solves a customer problem is a clear way to introduce listeners to the idea. Stories give you the "buy-in" needed to subsequently explain your model in detail.

Engaging People

People are moved more by stories than by logic. Ease listeners into the new or unknown by building the logic of your model into a compelling narrative.

Making Business Models Tangible?

The goal of telling a story is to introduce a new business model in an engaging, tangible way. Keep the story simple and use only one protagonist. Depending on the audience, you can use a different protagonist with a different perspective. Here are two possible starting points.

COMPANY *perspective*

Employee Observer

Explain the business model in the form of a story told from an employee's perspective. Use the employee as the protagonist who demonstrates why the new model makes sense. This may be because the employee frequently observes customer problems that the new business model solves. Or it may be that the new model makes better or different use of resources, activities, or partnerships compared to the old model (e.g. cost reduction, productivity improvement, new revenue sources, etc.). In such a story, the employee embodies the inner workings of an organization and its business model and shows the reasons for transitioning to a new model.

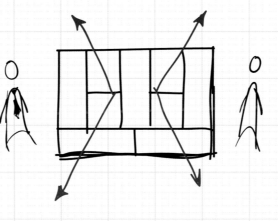

CUSTOMER *perspective*

Customer Jobs

The customer perspective provides a powerful starting point for a story. Cast a customer as the protagonist and tell the tale from her point of view. Show the challenges she faces and which jobs she must get done. Then outline how your organization creates value for her. The story can describe what she receives, how it fits into her life, and what she is willing to pay for. Add some drama and emotion to the story, and describe how your organization is making her life easier. Ideally, weave in how your organization gets these jobs done for the customer, with which resources and through which activities. The biggest challenge with stories told from a customer perspective is keeping them authentic and avoiding a facile or patronizing tone.

Making the Future Tangible

Stories offer a wonderful technique for blurring the lines separating reality and fiction. Thus stories provide a powerful tool for imparting tangibility to different versions of the future. This can help you challenge the status quo or justify adopting a new business model.

CURRENT BUSINESS MODEL

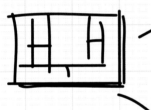

WHAT FUTURE BUSINESS MODEL?

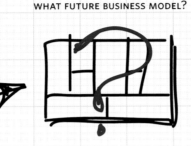

PLANNED FUTURE BUSINESS MODEL

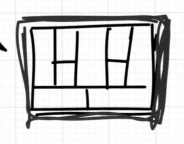

Provoke Ideas

Sometimes a story's sole purpose is to challenge the organizational status quo. Such a story must bring vividly to life a future competitive environment in which the current business model is severely challenged or even obsolete. Telling a story like this blurs the lines between reality and fiction and catapults listeners into the future. This suspends disbelief, instills a sense of urgency, and opens the audience's eyes to the need to generate new business models. Such a story can be told from either an organization or a customer perspective.

Justify Change

Sometimes an organization has strong ideas about how its competitive landscape will evolve. In this context, a story's purpose is to show how a new business model is ideally suited to help an organization compete in the new landscape. Stories temporarily suspend disbelief and help people imagine how the current business model should evolve to remain effective in the future. The story's protagonist could be a customer, an employee, or a top manager.

Developing the Story

The goal of telling a story is to introduce a new business model in an engaging, tangible way. Keep the story simple and use only one protagonist. Depending on the audience, you can use a different protagonist with a different perspective. Here are two possible starting points.

Company Perspective
Ajit, 32, Senior IT Manager, Amazon.com
Ajit has worked for Amazon.com as an IT manager for the past nine years. He and his colleagues have pulled countless all-nighters over the years to deliver the world-class IT infrastructure that serves and maintains the company's e-commerce business.

Ajit is proud of his work. Along with its fulfillment excellence (1, 6), Amazon.com's powerful IT infrastructure and software development capabilities (2, 3) form the heart of its success at selling everything from books to furniture online (7). Amazon.com (8) delivered over half a billion page impressions to online shoppers (9) in 2008, and spent over a billion dollars for technology and content (5), notably to run its e-commerce operations.

But now Ajit is even more excited, because Amazon.com is traveling far beyond its traditional retail offers. It's in the process of becoming one of the most important infrastructure providers in e-commerce.

With a service called Amazon Simple Storage Systems (Amazon S3) (11) the company is now using its own IT infrastructure to provide online storage to other companies at rock-bottom prices. This means that an online video hosting service can store all customer videos on Amazon's infrastructure rather than buying and maintaining its own servers. Similarly, Amazon Elastic Computing Cloud (Amazon EC2) (11) offers Amazon.com's own computing capability to outside clients.

Ajit knows that outsiders might view such services as distracting Amazon.com from its core retail operations. From the inside, though, the diversification makes perfect sense.

Ajit remembers that four years ago, his group spent much time coordinating the efforts of the network engineering groups, which managed IT infrastructure, and the applications programming groups, which managed Amazon.com's many Web sites. So they decided to build so-called application programming interfaces (APIs) (12) between these two layers, which would allow the latter to easily build on the former. Ajit also remembers exactly when they started to realize that this would be useful to external as well as internal customers. So under Jeff Bezos's leadership, Amazon.com decided to create a new business with the potential to generate a significant revenue source for the company. Amazon.com opened up its infrastructure APIs to provide what it calls Amazon Web Services to outside parties on a fee-for-service basis (14). Since Amazon.com had to design, create, implement, and maintain this infrastructure anyway, offering it to third parties was hardly a distraction.

1 FULFILLMENT
2 IT INFRASTRUCTURE & SOFTWARE DEVELOPMENT & MAINTENANCE
3 IT INFRASTRUCTURE & SOFTWARE
4 FULFILLMENT INFRASTRUCTURE
5 TECHNOLOGY & CONTENT
6 FULFILLMENT (MARKETING)

176 STORYTELLING DESIGN

E-commerce

9 CONSUMER MARKET

ONLINE RETAIL SHOP 7

AMAZON.COM 8

SALES MARGINS 10

AMAZON WEB SERVICES: S3, EC2, SQS, OTHER WEB SERVICES 11

COMPANIES AND DEVELOPERS 13

APIs 12

UTILITY COMPUTING FEES 14

Infrastructure NEW

Customer Perspective
Randy, 41, Web Entrepreneur

Randy is a passionate Web entrepreneur. After 18 years in the software industry he is now running his second startup, providing enterprise software through the Web. He spent 10 years of his career in large software companies and eight years in start-ups.

Throughout his career, one constant struggle has been getting infrastructure investments right. To him, running servers to provide services was basically a commodity business, but a tricky one due to the enormous costs involved. Tight management was crucial; when you're running a start-up you can't invest millions in a server farm.

But when serving the enterprise market, you'd better have a robust IT infrastructure in place. That's why Randy was intrigued when a friend at Amazon.com told him about the new IT infrastructure services his company was launching. That was the answer to one of Randy's most important in-house jobs: running his services on a world-class IT infrastructure, being able to scale quickly, and all the while paying only for what his company was actually using. That was exactly what Amazon's Web Services (11) promised. With Amazon Simple Storage Systems (Amazon S3), Randy could plug into Amazon's

infrastructure through a so-called application programming interface (API)(12) and store all the data and applications for his own services on Amazon.com's servers. The same went for Amazon's Elastic Computing Cloud (Amazon EC2). Randy didn't have to build and maintain his own infrastructure to crunch the numbers for his enterprise application service. He could simply plug into Amazon and use its computing power in return for hourly usage fees (14).

He immediately understood why the value was coming from the giant e-tailer rather than from IBM or Accenture. Amazon.com was providing and maintaining IT infrastructure (2, 3, 5) to serve its online retail business (7) every day on a global scale. This was its core competency. Taking the step to offer the same infrastructure services to other companies (9) was not much of a stretch. And since Amazon.com was in retail, a business with low margins (11), it had to be extremely cost-efficient (5), which explained the rock-bottom prices of its new Web Services.

Techniques

Telling an engaging story can be done in different ways. Each technique has advantages and disadvantages and is better suited for certain situations and audiences. Choose a suitable technique after you understand who your audience will be and the context in which you will present.

	Talk & Image	Video Clip	Role Play	Text & Image	Comic Strip
DESCRIPTION	Tell the story of a protagonist and his environment using one or several images	Tell the story of a protagonist and his environment using video to blur lines between reality and fiction	Have people play the roles of a story's protagonists to make the scenario real and tangible	Tell the story of a protagonist and his environment using text and one or several images	Use a series of cartoon images to tell the story of a protagonist in a tangible way
WHEN?	Group or conference presentation	Broadcast to large audiences or in-house use for decisions with important financial implications	Workshops where participants present newly developed business model ideas to each other	Reports or broadcasts to large audiences	Reports or broadcasts to large audiences
TIME & COST	Low	Medium to high	Low	Low	Low to medium

SuperToast, Inc.
Business Model

Start practicing your business model storytelling skills with this simple, slightly silly exercise: The business model of SuperToast, Inc. outlined in the Canvas below. You can start anywhere you like: with Customers, the Value Proposition, Key Resources, or elsewhere. Invent your own story. The only constraints are the nine images that outline SuperToast Inc.'s business model. Try telling the story several times, starting from different Building Blocks. Each starting point will give the story a slightly different twist and emphasize different aspects of the model.

By the way, this is a wonderful approach to introducing the Business Model Canvas to the "uninitiated" in a simple and engaging way—with a story.

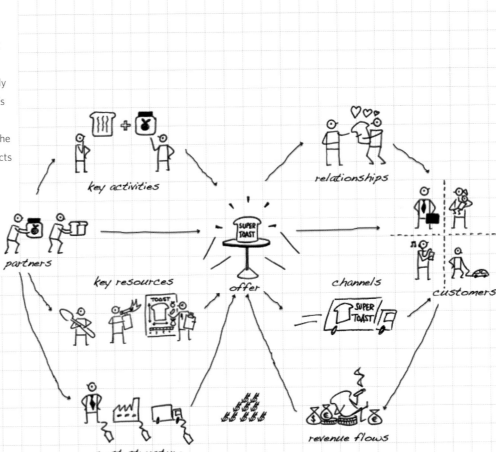

Technique_No. 6

Scenarios

Professor Jeffrey Huang and Muriel Waldvogel seem lost in thought as they ponder scale models of the Swisshouse, the new Swiss consulate facility to be built in Boston, Massachusetts …

… Huang and Waldvogel were brought in to conceive the architectural design of the building, which, rather than issuing visas, will serve as a networking and knowledge exchange hub. The two are studying several scenarios of how people will use the Swisshouse, and have constructed both physical models and screenplay-like texts designed to make tangible the purpose of this unprecedented government facility.

One scenario describes Nicolas, a brain surgeon who has just moved to Boston from Switzerland. He visits the Swisshouse to meet likeminded scientists and other members of the Swiss-American community. A second scenario tells the story of a Professor Smith, who uses the Swisshouse to present his MIT Media Lab research to Boston's Swiss community and to academics at two Swiss universities, using a high-speed Internet connection.

These scenarios, while simple, are the result of intensive research into roles the new type of consulate might play. The stories illustrate the Swiss government's intentions and serve as thinking tools to guide the building's design. Ultimately, the new facility effectively accommodated the applications imagined and fulfilled its objectives.

Today, almost a decade after its conception, the Swisshouse enjoys an outstanding reputation for helping build stronger international ties in greater Boston's science and technology communities. Under the banner of the Swiss Knowledge Network, or swissnex, the Swisshouse has inspired "colleague" facilities in Bangalore, San Francisco, Shanghai, and Singapore.

Scenario-Guided
Business Model Design

—

Scenarios can be useful in guiding the design of new business models or innovating around existing models. Like visual thinking (p. 146), prototyping (p. 160), and storytelling (p. 170), scenarios render the abstract tangible. For our purposes, their primary function is to inform the business model development process by making the design context specific and detailed.

Here we discuss two types of scenarios. The first describes different customer settings: how products or services are used, what kinds of customers use them, or customer concerns, desires, and objectives. Such scenarios build on customer insights (p. 126), but go a step further by incorporating knowledge about customers into a set of distinct, concrete images. By describing a specific situation, a customer scenario makes customer insights tangible.

A second type of scenario describes future environments in which a business model might compete. The goal here is not to predict the future, but rather to imagine possible futures in concrete detail. This exercise helps innovators reflect on the most appropriate business model for each of several future environ-

ments. The strategy literature discusses this practice in detail under the topic of "scenario planning." Applying scenario planning techniques to business model innovation forces reflection on how a model might have to evolve under certain conditions. This sharpens understanding of the model, and of potentially necessary adaptations. Most important, it helps us prepare for the future.

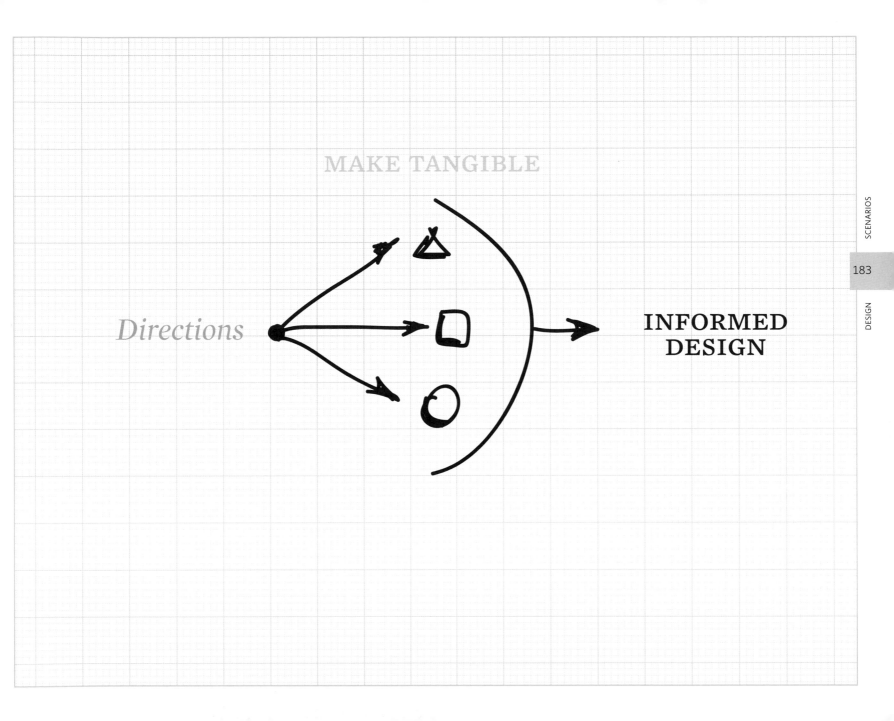

Explore Ideas

Customer scenarios guide us during business model design. They help us address issues such as which Channels are most appropriate, which relationships would be best to establish, and which problem solutions customers would be most willing to pay for. Once we've generated scenarios for different Customer Segments, we can ask ourselves whether a single business model is sufficient to serve them all—or if we need to adapt the model to each segment.

Here are three different scenarios describing location-based services that make use of Global Positioning Systems (GPS). They inform the business model design, but are deliberately left open to allow for specific questions around the Value Proposition, Distribution Channels, Customer Relationships, and Revenue Streams. The scenarios are written from the standpoint of a mobile telephone service operator working to develop innovative new business models.

THE HOME DELIVERY SERVICE

Tom has always dreamed of running his own small business. He knew it would be difficult, but earning a living by living his passion was definitely worth working more and earning less.

Tom is a film buff whose knowledge of movies is encyclopedic, and that's what customers of his home-delivery DVD movie service appreciate. They can query him about actors, production techniques, and just about anything else film-related before ordering movies for delivery to their doorsteps.

Given the formidable online competition, it's hardly an easy business. But Tom's been able to boost his productivity and improve customer service with a new GPS-based delivery planner acquired from his mobile phone operator. For a small fee he equipped his phone with software that easily integrated with his Customer Relationship management program. This software won back much of Tom's time by helping him better plan delivery routes and avoid traffic. It even integrated with the cell phones used by two aides who help out on weekends when demand for his service peaks. Tom knows his little business will never make him rich, but wouldn't trade his situation for any corporate job.

THE TOURISTS

Dale and Rose are traveling to Paris for an extended weekend. They are excited because they haven't visited Europe since their honeymoon 25 years ago. The couple organized this mini-escape from everyday work and family life just two weeks before departure, leaving their three kids with parents back in Portland. Lacking time and energy to plan the trip in detail, they decided to "wing it." As a consequence, they were intrigued to read an article in the inflight magazine about a new GPS-based tourist service that uses mobile phones. Dale and Rose, both technology fans, rented the recommended handset upon arrival at Charles de Gaulle airport. Now they're happily strolling around Paris on a customized tour proposed by the compact device—all without having consulted a single traditional tourist guide. They particularly appreciate the built-in audio guide that suggests various story and background information options as they approach particular sites. On the return flight, Dale and Rose muse about relocating to Paris after retiring. Laughing to themselves, they wonder whether the handy device would be enough to help them adapt to French culture.

THE WINE FARMER

Alexander inherited vineyards from his father, who in turn inherited them from Alexander's grandfather, who emigrated from Switzerland to California to grow wine. Carrying on this family history is hard work, but Alexander enjoys adding small innovations to his family's long wine-growing tradition.

His latest discovery is a simple land management application that now resides on his mobile phone. Though not aimed at vintners, it was designed in such a way that Alexander was easily able to customize it for his own particular needs. The application integrates with his task list, which means he now has a GPS-based to-do list that reminds him when and where to check soil or grape quality. Now he's pondering how to share the application with all of his managers. After all, the tool makes sense only if everyone on the management team updates the soil and grape quality database.

THE TOURISTS

- Should the service be based on a proprietary device or on an application that can be downloaded to customer handsets?
- Could airlines serve as Channel partners to distribute the service/device?
- Which prospective content partners would be interested in being part of the service?
- Which Value Propositions would customers be most willing to pay for?

THE HOME DELIVERY SERVICE

- Is the value added sufficient to motivate delivery services to pay monthly fees?
- Through which Channels could such Customer Segments most easily be reached?
- With what other devices and/or software would this service need to be integrated?

THE WINE FARMER

- Is the value added sufficient to motivate a landowner to pay a monthly service fee?
- Through which Channels could such Customer Segments most easily be reached?
- With what other devices and/or software would this service need to be integrated?

QUESTIONS REGARDING THE BUSINESS MODEL

Could one model serve all three Customer Segments?

Does each segment need a separate, specific Value Proposition?

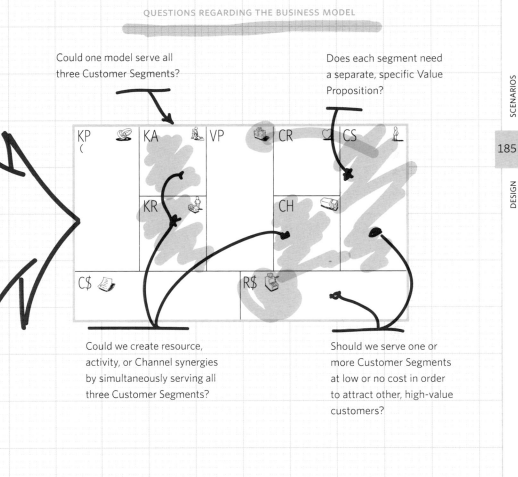

Could we create resource, activity, or Channel synergies by simultaneously serving all three Customer Segments?

Should we serve one or more Customer Segments at low or no cost in order to attract other, high-value customers?

Future Scenarios

The scenario is another thinking tool that helps us reflect on business models of the future. Scenarios kick-start our creativity by providing concrete future contexts for which we can invent appropriate business models. This is usually easier and more productive than free brainstorming about possible future business models. It does require, however, developing several scenarios, which can be costly depending on their depth and realism.

One sector under strong pressure to devise innovative new business models is the pharmaceutical industry. There are a number of reasons for this. Major player research productivity has declined in recent years, and these companies face enormous challenges discovering and marketing new blockbuster drugs—traditionally the core of their businesses. At the same time, patents on many of their cash cow drugs are expiring. This means revenues from those drugs are likely to be lost to generic drug manufacturers. This combination of empty product pipelines and evaporating revenue are just two headaches plaguing incumbent pharmaceutical makers.

In this turbulent context, combining business model brainstorming with the development of a set of future scenarios can be a powerful exercise. The scenarios help trigger out-of-the-box thinking, which is not always easy when trying to develop innovative business models. Here's an overview of how such an exercise might be conducted.

First, we must devise a set of scenarios that paint pictures of the future of the pharmaceutical industry. This is best left to scenario planning specialists equipped with the right tools and methodology. To illustrate, we developed four bare bones scenarios based on two criteria that may shape the evolution of the pharma industry over the next decade. There are, of course, several other drivers and many different scenarios that could be crafted based on deeper research into the industry.

The two drivers we've selected are (1) the emergence of personalized medicine and (2) the shift from treatment toward prevention. The former is based on advances in pharmacogenomics, the science of identifying underlying causes of diseases based on a person's DNA structure. Someday, this may result in completely personalized treatment, using customized drugs based on a person's genetic structure. The shift from treatment to prevention is driven in part by pharmacogenomics, in part by advances in diagnostics, and in part by renewed cost-consciousness amid growing awareness that prevention is less expensive than hospitalization and treatment. These two drivers suggest trends that may or may not materialize and thus provide four scenarios illustrated in the figure opposite. These are:

- BUSINESS AS USUAL: Personal medicine fails to materialize despite its technological feasibility (e.g. for privacy reasons, etc.) and treatment remains the core revenue generator.
- MY.MEDICINE: Personal medicine materializes, but treatment remains the core revenue generator.
- THE HEALTHY PATIENT: The shift toward preventive medicine continues, but personal medicine remains a fad despite technological feasibility.
- REINVENTING PHARMA: Personal and preventive medicine comprise the new growth areas of the drug industry.

Pharma Business Models
of the Future

C) The Healthy Patient:
- *What kind of Customer Relationship does effective preventive medicine require?*
- *Who are the main partners we should involve in developing our business model for preventive medicine?*
- *What does the shift toward preventive medicine imply about the relationship between doctors and our salespeople?*

D) Reinventing pharma:
- *What does our Value Proposition look like in this new landscape?*
- *What roles will Customer Segments play under our new business model?*
- *Should we develop relevant activities, such as bioinformatics and gene sequencing, in-house or through partnerships?*

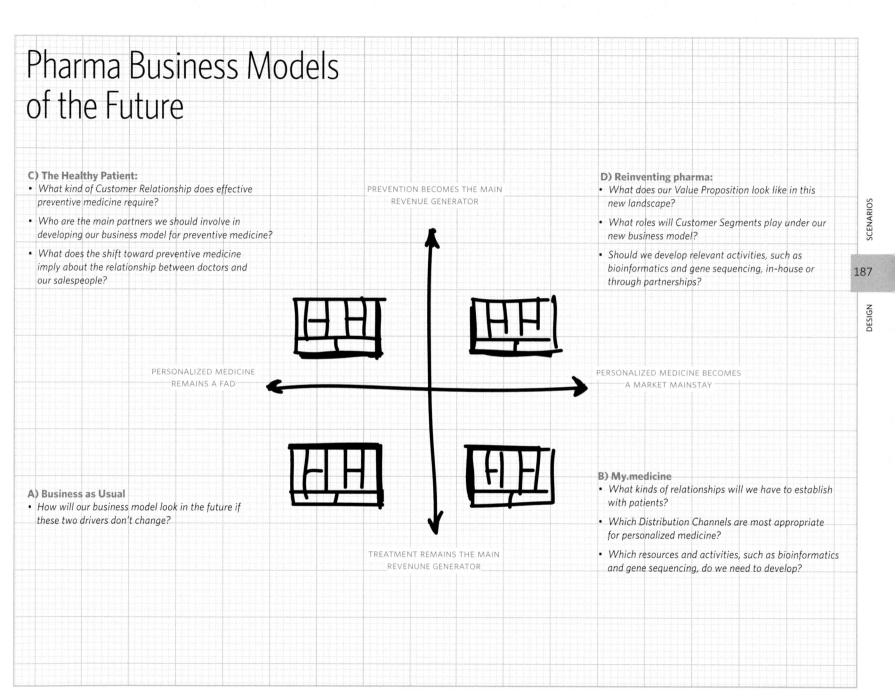

PREVENTION BECOMES THE MAIN
REVENUE GENERATOR

PERSONALIZED MEDICINE
REMAINS A FAD

PERSONALIZED MEDICINE BECOMES
A MARKET MAINSTAY

TREATMENT REMAINS THE MAIN
REVENUNE GENERATOR

A) Business as Usual
- *How will our business model look in the future if these two drivers don't change?*

B) My.medicine
- *What kinds of relationships will we have to establish with patients?*
- *Which Distribution Channels are most appropriate for personalized medicine?*
- *Which resources and activities, such as bioinformatics and gene sequencing, do we need to develop?*

Scenario D:
Reinventing Pharma

The landscape of the pharmaceutical industry has completely changed. Pharmacogenomic research has fulfilled its promise and is now a core part of the industry. Personalized drugs tailored to individual genetic profiles account for a large portion of industry revenues. All this has increased the importance of prevention—and is partially replacing treatment, thanks to substantially improved diagnostic tools and a better understanding of the links between diseases and individual genetic profiles.

These two trends—the rise of personalized drugs and the increasing importance of prevention—have completely transformed the traditional pharmaceutical manufacturing business model. The twin trends have had a dramatic impact on pharma's Key Resources and Activities. They've transformed the way drug makers approach customers and provoked substantial changes in how revenue is generated.

The new pharma landscape has taken a heavy toll on incumbents. A number were unable to adapt quickly enough and disappeared or were acquired by more agile players. At the same time, upstarts with innovative business models were able to acquire significant market share. Some were themselves acquired and integrated into the operations of larger but less nimble companies.

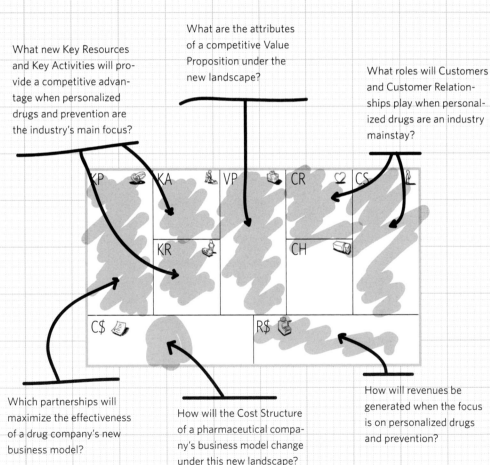

What new Key Resources and Key Activities will provide a competitive advantage when personalized drugs and prevention are the industry's main focus?

What are the attributes of a competitive Value Proposition under the new landscape?

What roles will Customers and Customer Relationships play when personalized drugs are an industry mainstay?

Which partnerships will maximize the effectiveness of a drug company's new business model?

How will the Cost Structure of a pharmaceutical company's business model change under this new landscape?

How will revenues be generated when the focus is on personalized drugs and prevention?

Future Scenarios and New Business Models

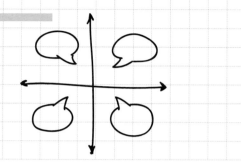

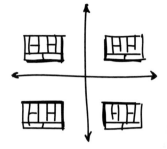

1 DEVELOP A SET OF FUTURE SCENARIOS BASED ON TWO OR MORE MAIN CRITERIA.

2 DESCRIBE EACH SCENARIO WITH A STORY THAT OUTLINES THE MAIN ELEMENTS OF THE SCENARIO

3 WORKSHOP DEVELOP ONE OR MORE APPROPRIATE BUSINESS MODELS FOR EACH SCENARIO

The goal of combining scenarios with business model innovation efforts is to help your organization prepare for the future. This process engenders meaningful discussion about a difficult topic, because it forces participants to project themselves into concrete "futures" underpinned by hard (though assumed) facts. When participants describe their business models they must be able to make a clear case for their choices within the context of the specific scenario.

Scenarios should be developed before the business model workshop begins. The sophistication of the "screenplays" will vary depending on your budget. Keep in mind that once you develop scenarios, they may be usable for other purposes as well. Even simple scenarios help jumpstart creativity and project participants into the future.

Ideally you should develop between two and four different scenarios based on two or more criteria in order to run a good business model scenario workshop. Each scenario should be titled and described with a short, specific narrative outlining the main elements.

Begin the workshop by asking participants to review the scenarios, then develop an appropriate business model for each. If your objective is to maximize a group's understanding of all the potential futures, you might want everyone to participate in a single group and let them collectively develop different business models for each scenario. If you are more interested in generating a set of very diverse future business models, you might decide to organize participants into different groups that work in parallel on separate solutions for the various scenarios.

Further Reading on Design and Business

Design Attitude

Managing as Designing
by Richard Boland Jr. and Fred Collopy
(Stanford Business Books, 2004)
A Whole New Mind: Why Right-Brainers Will Rule the Future
by Daniel H. Pink (Riverhead Trade, 2006)
The Ten Faces of Innovation: Strategies for Heightening Creativity
by Tom Kelley (Profile Business, 2008)

Customer Insights

Sketching User Experiences: Getting the Design Right and the Right Design
by Bill Buxton (Elsevier, 2007)
Designing for the Digital Age: How to Create Human-Centered Products and Services
by Kim Goodwin (John Wiley & Sons, Inc. 2009)

Ideation

The Art of Innovation: Lessons in Creativity from IDEO, America's Leading Design Firm
by Tom Kelley, Jonathan Littman, and Tom Peters (Broadway Business, 2001)
IdeaSpotting: How to Find Your Next Great Idea
by Sam Harrison (How Books, 2006)

Visual Thinking

The Back of the Napkin: Solving Problems and Selling Ideas with Pictures
by Dan Roam (Portfolio Hardcover, 2008)
Brain Rules: 12 Principles for Surviving and Thriving at Work, Home, and School
by John Medina (Pear Press, 2009)
(pp. 221-240)

Prototyping

Serious Play: How the World's Best Companies Simulate to Innovate
by Michael Schrage (Harvard Business Press, 1999)
Designing Interactions
by Bill Moggridge (MIT Press, 2007) (ch. 10)

Storytelling

The Leader's Guide to Storytelling: Mastering the Art and Discipline of Business Narrative
by Stephen Denning (Jossey-Bass, 2005)
Made to Stick: Why Some Ideas Survive and Others Die
by Chip Heath and Dan Heath (Random House, 2007)

Scenarios

The Art of the Long View: Planning for the Future in an Uncertain World
by Peter Schwartz (Currency Doubleday, 1996)
Using Trends and Scenarios as Tools for Strategy Development
by Ulf Pillkahn (Publicis Corporate Publishing, 2008)

Do you have the guts to start from scratch?

WHAT STANDS IN YOUR WAY?

194

In my work with non-profit organizations, the biggest obstacles to business model innovation are **1.** inability to understand the existing business model, **2.** lack of a language to talk about business model innovation, and **3.** counterproductive constraints on imagining the design of new business models.
Jeff De Cagna, United States

The management of an SME (wood manufacturing industry-WMI) did not begin changing its business model until the bank no longer wanted to give them credit. The biggest obstacle to business model innovation (in the WMI case and likely every case) is the people who resist any changes until problems appear and need corrective actions.
Danilo Tic, Slovenia

EVERYONE LOVES INNOVATION UNTIL IT AFFECTS THEM.

The biggest obstacle to business model innovation is not technology: it is we humans and the institutions we live in. Both are stubbornly resistant to experimentation and change.
Saul Kaplan, United States

I have found that the management and key employees in many SME companies lack a common framework and language for discussing business model innovation. They do not have the theoretical background, but they are essential to the process because they are the ones who know the business.
Michael N. Wilkens, Denmark

METRICS OF SUCCESS:

They can direct the scope and ambition of behavior. At best they can allow for the agility that brings truly disruptive innovation; at worst they reduce vision to near term iterative cycles of evolution that fail to take opportunity from changing environments.
Nicky Smyth, U.K.

Fear to take risks. As a CEO you need courage to take a business model innovation decision. In 2005, Dutch telecom provider KPN decided to migrate proactively to IP and thus to cannibalize its traditional business. KPN is now internationally recognized as an outperformer in the telco industry.
Kees Groeneveld, Netherlands

In my experience with a large archive, the biggest hurdle was to make them understand that even an archive has a business model. We overcame this by starting a small project and showed them this would affect their current model.
Harry Verwayen, Netherlands

GET EVERYBODY INVOLVED

and keep up the speed of change. For our disruptive meeting concept Seats-2meet.com we trained the staff almost daily for a period of four months just on communicating this new business model to all stakeholders.
Ronald van Den Hoff, Netherlands

1. Organizational antibodies that attack a project as resources drawn from their area conflict with their business objectives. **2.** Project management processes that can't deal with risks/uncertainties associated with bold ideas so leaders decline or claw ideas back to existing comfort zones.
John Sutherland, Canada

The biggest obstacle is a belief that models must contain every detail—experience shows that clients ask for a lot but settle for simplicity once they have insight into their business.
David Edwards, Canada

1. Not knowing: What is a business model? What is business model innovation? **2.** Not able: How to innovate a business model? **3.** Not willing: Why should I innovate my business model? Is there a sense of urgency? **4.** Combinations of the above.

Ray Lai, Malaysia

In my experience, the biggest obstacle is failure to change the thinking process from the traditional linear way to holistic and systemic.

Entrepreneurs need to make a concerted effort to develop the capability to envision the model as a system whose parts interact with each other and affect each other in a holistic and non-linear manner.

Jeaninne Horowitz Gassol, Spain

As an Internet marketer for 15 years I've seen new business models live and die.

The key for the winners was that the major stakeholders completely understood and advanced the model.

Stephanie Diamond, United States

THE MENTAL MODELS
of executives and the board.

The lack of candor and fear of deviating from the status quo sets in groupthink. Executives are comfortable with exploit phase and not 'explore' phase, which is unknown and hence risky.

Cheenu Srinivasan, Australia

In my experience as an Internet entrepreneur and investor, the biggest obstacles are lack of vision and bad governance. Without good vision and governance a company will miss the emerging industry paradigm and avoid reinventing the business model in time.

Nicolas De Santis, U.K.

Within large multinationals it is key to create cross-functional understanding and synergies. Business model innovation does not hold itself to the organizational constraints that the people in it experience. For successful execution it is key to have all disciplines on board and interconnected!

Bas van Oosterhout, Netherlands

FUG: FEAR, UNCERTAINTY & GREED

of the people vested in the current business model…

Frontier Service Design, LLC, United States

A lack of entrepreneurship in the organization.

Innovation is about taking risks, wisely. If there is no room for creative insights or if people can't think and act outside the boundaries of the existing model, don't even try to innovate: you will fail.

Ralf de Graaf, Netherlands

On an organizational level, the biggest obstacle for a large, successful company is a reluctance to risk doing anything that may jeopardize their current model. On a leader/personal level, **their very success was likely a product of the current business model…**

Jeffrey Murphy, United States

"If it ain't broke, don't fix it"

thinking. Established companies stick to current ways of doing business until it is obvious that the customers want something else.

Ola Dagberg, Sweden

STRENGTH OF LEADERSHIP

can be an obstacle. Risk management and due diligence color the perceived purpose of many boards. Where innovation is assessed as a risk issue it's easy to relegate it to tokenism, especially within cultural institutions that tend not to have championing cultures. Here innovation often dies the death of a thousand cuts inflicted by entrenched critical business processes, instead of being placed front and center as the fuel for future strategy.

Anne McCrossan, U.K.

Oftentimes, companies design an innovative business model, but do a poor job of constructing a compensation structure that is properly aligned with the model and its objectives.

Andrew Jenkins, Canada

CURRENT SUCCESS

prevents companies from asking themselves how their business model could be innovated. Organizational structures are not typically designed for new business models to emerge.

Howard Brown, United States

The companies that are the most successful in continuously improving the efficiency of their current business model often get blinded by

"this is the way things are done in our business"

and fail to see the emergence of innovative business models.

Wouter van der Burg, Netherlands

"There's not a single business model . . . There are really a lot of opportunities and a lot of options and we just have to discover all of them."

Tim O'Reilly, CEO, O'Reilly

In previous sections we taught you a language for describing, discussing, and designing business models, described business model patterns, and explained techniques that facilitate the design and invention of new business models. This next section is about re-interpreting strategy through the lens of the Business Model Canvas. This will help you constructively question established business models and strategically examine the environment in which your own business model functions.

The following pages explore four strategic areas: the Business Model Environment, Evaluating Business Models, a Business Model Perspective on Blue Ocean Strategies, and how to Manage Multiple Business Models within an enterprise.

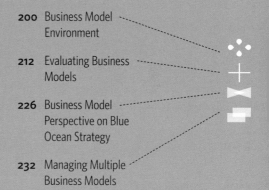

BUSINESS MODEL ENVIRONMENT: CONTEXT, DESIGN DRIVERS, AND CONSTRAINTS

BUSINESS MODELS ARE DESIGNED AND EXECUTED IN SPECIFIC ENVIRONMENTS. Developing a good understanding of your organization's environment helps you conceive stronger, more competitive business models.

Continuous environmental scanning is more important than ever because of the growing complexity of the economic landscape (e.g. networked business models), greater uncertainty (e.g. technology innovations) and severe market disruptions (e.g. economic turmoil, disruptive new Value Propositions). Understanding changes in the environment helps you adapt your model more effectively to shifting external forces.

You may find it helpful to conceive of the external environment as a sort of "design space." By this we mean thinking of it as a context in which to conceive or adapt your business model, taking into account a number of design drivers (e.g. new customer needs, new technologies, etc.) and design constraints (e.g. regulatory trends, dominant competitors, etc.). This environment should in no way limit your creativity or predefine your business model. It should, however, influence your design choices and help you make more informed decisions. With a breakthrough business model, you may even become a shaper and transformer of this environment, and set new standards for your industry.

To get a better grasp on your business model "design space," we suggest roughly mapping four main areas of your environment. These are (1) market forces, (2) industry forces, (3) key trends, and (4) macroeconomic forces. If you'd like to deepen your analysis of the landscape beyond the simple mapping we propose, each of these four areas is backed by a large body of literature and specific analytical tools.

In the following pages, we describe the key external forces that influence business models and categorize them using the four areas just mentioned. The pharmaceutical industry, introduced in the previous chapter, is used to illustrate each external force. The pharma sector is likely to undergo substantial transformation in coming years, though it is unclear how the changes will play out. Will biotechnology companies, which are currently copying the pharmaceutical sector's blockbuster drug model, come up with new, disruptive business models? Will technological change lead to transformation? Will consumers and market demand force changes?

We strongly advocate mapping your own business model environment and reflecting on what trends mean for the future of your enterprise. A good understanding of the environment will allow you to better evaluate the different directions in which your business model might evolve. You may also want to consider creating scenarios of future business model environments (see p. 186). This can be a valuable tool for jumpstarting business model innovation work or simply preparing your organization for the future.

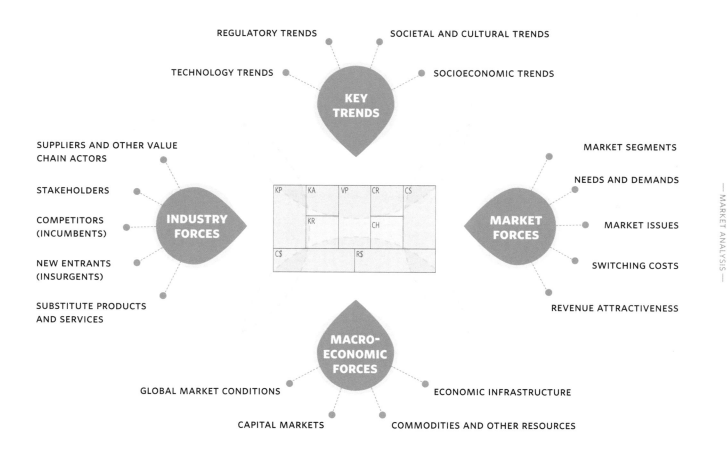

KEY
TRENDS

REGULATORY TRENDS

SOCIETAL AND CULTURAL TRENDS

TECHNOLOGY TRENDS

SOCIOECONOMIC TRENDS

INDUSTRY
FORCES

SUPPLIERS AND OTHER VALUE
CHAIN ACTORS

STAKEHOLDERS

COMPETITORS
(INCUMBENTS)

NEW ENTRANTS
(INSURGENTS)

SUBSTITUTE PRODUCTS
AND SERVICES

KP   KA   VP   CR   CS
KR   CH
C$ R$

MARKET
FORCES

MARKET SEGMENTS

NEEDS AND DEMANDS

MARKET ISSUES

SWITCHING COSTS

REVENUE ATTRACTIVENESS

201

MACRO-
ECONOMIC
FORCES

GLOBAL MARKET CONDITIONS

ECONOMIC INFRASTRUCTURE

CAPITAL MARKETS

COMMODITIES AND OTHER RESOURCES

MARKET FORCES

— MARKET ANALYSIS —

MARKET ISSUES	Identifies key issues driving and transforming your market from Customer and Offer perspectives	What are the crucial issues affecting the customer landscape? Which shifts are underway? Where is the market heading?
MARKET SEGMENTS	Identifies the major market segments, describes their attractiveness, and seeks to spot new segments	What are the most important Customer Segments? Where is the biggest growth potential? Which segments are declining? Which peripheral segments deserve attention?
NEEDS AND DEMANDS	Outlines market needs and analyzes how well they are served	What do customers need? Where are the biggest unsatisfied customer needs? What do customers really want to get done? Where is demand increasing? Declining?
SWITCHING COSTS	Describes elements related to customers switching business to competitors	What binds customers to a company and its offer? What switching costs prevent customers from defecting to competitors? Is it easy for customers to find and purchase similar offers? How important is brand?
REVENUE ATTRACTIVENESS	Identifies elements related to revenue attractiveness and pricing power	What are customers really willing to pay for? Where can the largest margins be achieved? Can customers easily find and purchase cheaper products and services?

Pharmaceutical Industry Landscape

- Skyrocketing healthcare costs
- Emphasis shifting from treatment to prevention
- Treatments, diagnostics, devices, and support services are converging
- Emerging markets becoming more important

- Doctors and healthcare providers
- Governments/regulators
- Distributors
- Patients
- Strong potential in emerging markets
- U.S. remains the predominant global market

- Strong, with dispersed need for niche treatments
- Need to manage exploding cost of health care
- Large, unsatisfied health care needs in emerging markets and developing countries
- Consumers are better informed

- Monopoly on patent-protected drugs
- Low switching costs for patent-expired drugs replaceable by generic versions
- Growing amount of quality information available online
- Deals with governments, large-scale healthcare providers increase switching costs

---

- High margins on patent-protected drugs
- Low margins on generic drugs
- Healthcare providers, governments enjoy growing influence over prices
- Patients continue to have little influence over prices

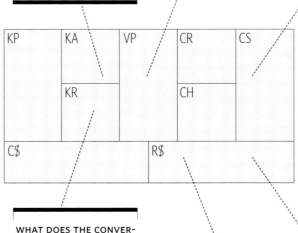

WHAT NEW KEY RESOURCES DO WE NEED TO DEVELOP OR ACQUIRE IN LIGHT OF THE ONGOING SHIFT FROM TREATMENT TO PREVENTION?

HOW CAN OUR VALUE PROPOSITION ADDRESS THE ISSUE OF EXPLODING HEALTH COSTS?

WHAT WOULD A GREATER FOCUS ON EMERGING MARKETS MEAN FOR THE OTHER BUILDING BLOCKS IN OUR MODEL?

WHAT DOES THE CONVERGENCE OF TREATMENT, DIAGNOSTICS, DEVICES, AND SUPPORT SERVICES MEAN FOR OUR KEY RESOURCES AND ACTIVITIES?

HOW CAN WE MAINTAIN EARNINGS WHILE ADDRESSING THE PUBLIC STRUGGLE TO COPE WITH SKYROCKETING HEALTHCARE COSTS?

WHAT KIND OF NEW REVENUE OPPORTUNITIES MIGHT BE CREATED BY THE SHIFT IN EMPHASIS FROM TREATMENT TO PREVENTION?

INDUSTRY FORCES

— COMPETITIVE ANALYSIS —

Main Qs

COMPETITORS (INCUMBENTS)	Identifies incumbent competitors and their relative strengths		Who are our competitors? Who are the dominant players in our particular sector? What are their competitive advantages or disadvantages? Describe their main offers. Which Customer Segments are they focusing on? What is their Cost Structure? How much influence do they exert on our Customer Segments, Revenue Streams, and margins?
NEW ENTRANTS (INSURGENTS)	Identifies new, insurgent players and determines whether they compete with a business model different from yours		Who are the new entrants in your market? How are they different? What competitive advantages or disadvantages do they have? Which barriers must they overcome? What are their Value Propositions? Which Customer Segments are they focused on? What is their Cost Structure? To what extent do they influence your Customer Segments, Revenue Streams, and margins?
SUBSTITUTE PRODUCTS AND SERVICES	Describes potential substitutes for your offers—including those from other markets and industries		Which products or services could replace ours? How much do they cost compared to ours? How easy it is for customers to switch to these substitutes? What business model traditions do these substitute products stem from (e.g. high-speed trains versus airplanes, mobile phones versus cameras, Skype versus long-distance telephone companies)?
SUPPLIERS AND OTHER VALUE CHAIN ACTORS	Describes the key value chain incumbents in your market and spots new, emerging players		Who are the key players in your industry value chain? To what extent does your business model depend on other players? Are peripheral players emerging? Which are most profitable?
STAKEHOLDERS	Specifies which actors may influence your organization and business model		Which stakeholders might influence your business model? How influential are shareholders? Workers? The government? Lobbyists?

Pharmaceutical Industry Landscape

- Several large and medium size players compete in pharma
- Most players are struggling with empty product pipelines and low R&D productivity
- Growing trend toward consolidation through mergers and acquisitions
- Major players acquire biotech, specialty drug developers to fill product pipeline
- Several players starting to build on open innovation processes

- Little disruption of the pharmaceutical industry over the last decade
- Main new entrants are generic drug companies, particularly from India

- To a certain extent, prevention represents a substitution for treatment
- Patent-expired drugs replaced by low-cost generics

- Increasing use of research contractors
- Biotech firms and specialty drug developers as important new product generators
- Doctors and healthcare providers
- Insurance companies
- Bioinformatics providers growing in importance
- Laboratories

- Shareholder pressure forces drug companies to focus on short term (quarterly) financial results
- Governments/regulators have a strong stake in the actions of pharmaceutical companies because of their pivotal role in healthcare services
- Lobbyists, social enterprise groups and/or foundations, particularly those pursuing agendas such as low-cost treatments for developing countries
- Scientists, who represent the core talent of the drug manufacturing industry

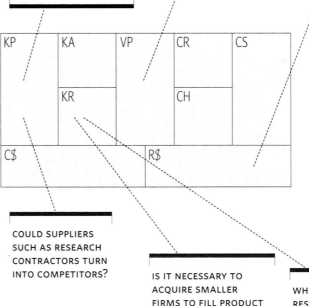

FOR WHICH PARTS OF THE INDUSTRY VALUE CHAIN SHOULD KEY PARTNERSHIPS BE BUILT AS OPPOSED TO DEVELOPING KEY RESOURCES AND ACTIVITIES IN-HOUSE?

MUST THE VALUE PROPOSITION CHANGE TO ACCOMMODATE SHIFTS IN THE INDUSTRY (E.G. THE GROWING IMPORTANCE OF BIOTECH FIRMS)?

WHICH PART OF THE PHARMA INDUSTRY OFFERS THE GREATEST EARNINGS POTENTIAL?

COULD SUPPLIERS SUCH AS RESEARCH CONTRACTORS TURN INTO COMPETITORS?

IS IT NECESSARY TO ACQUIRE SMALLER FIRMS TO FILL PRODUCT PIPELINES?

WHICH OF THE KEY RESOURCES EMERGING AMONG NEW ACTORS IN THE VALUE CHAIN NEED TO BE DEVELOPED IN-HOUSE (E.G. BIOINFORMATICS)?

KEY TRENDS

— FORESIGHT —

TECHNOLOGY TRENDS

Identifies technology trends that could threaten your business model—or enable it to evolve or improve

What are the major technology trends both inside and outside your market? Which technologies represent important opportunities or disruptive threats? Which emerging technologies are peripheral customers adopting?

REGULATORY TRENDS

Describes regulations and regulatory trends that influence your business model

Which regulatory trends influence your market? What rules may affect your business model? Which regulations and taxes affect customer demand?

SOCIETAL AND CULTURAL TRENDS

Identifies major societal trends that may influence your business model

Describe key societal trends. Which shifts in cultural or societal values affect your business model? Which trends might influence buyer behavior?

SOCIOECONOMIC TRENDS

Outlines major socioeconomic trends relevant to your business model

What are the key demographic trends? How would you characterize income and wealth distribution in your market? How high are disposable incomes? Describe spending patterns in your market (e.g. housing, health-care, entertainment, etc.). What portion of the population lives in urban areas as opposed to rural settings?

Pharmaceutical Industry Landscape

- Emergence of pharmacogenomics, declining cost of gene sequencing, and the immenent rise of personalized medicine
- Major advances in diagnostics
- Use of pervasive computing and nanotechnology for the injection/delivery of drugs

- Heterogeneous global regulatory landscape in the pharmaceutical industry
- Many countries prohibit drug companies from marketing directly to consumers
- Regulatory agency pressure to publish data on unsuccessful clinical trials

- Generally unfavorable image of big drug makers
- Growing social consciousness among consumers
- Customers increasingly conscious of global warming, sustainability issues, prefer "green" purchases
- Customers are better informed about drug maker activity in developing countries (e.g. HIV/AIDS drugs)

- Aging society in many mature markets
- Good but costly healthcare infrastructure in mature markets
- Growing middle class in emerging markets
- Large, unsatisfied healthcare needs in developing countries

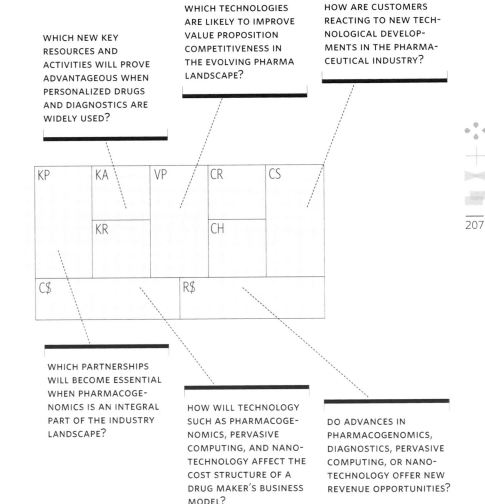

WHICH NEW KEY RESOURCES AND ACTIVITIES WILL PROVE ADVANTAGEOUS WHEN PERSONALIZED DRUGS AND DIAGNOSTICS ARE WIDELY USED?

WHICH TECHNOLOGIES ARE LIKELY TO IMPROVE VALUE PROPOSITION COMPETITIVENESS IN THE EVOLVING PHARMA LANDSCAPE?

HOW ARE CUSTOMERS REACTING TO NEW TECHNOLOGICAL DEVELOPMENTS IN THE PHARMACEUTICAL INDUSTRY?

WHICH PARTNERSHIPS WILL BECOME ESSENTIAL WHEN PHARMACOGENOMICS IS AN INTEGRAL PART OF THE INDUSTRY LANDSCAPE?

HOW WILL TECHNOLOGY SUCH AS PHARMACOGENOMICS, PERVASIVE COMPUTING, AND NANOTECHNOLOGY AFFECT THE COST STRUCTURE OF A DRUG MAKER'S BUSINESS MODEL?

DO ADVANCES IN PHARMACOGENOMICS, DIAGNOSTICS, PERVASIVE COMPUTING, OR NANOTECHNOLOGY OFFER NEW REVENUE OPPORTUNITIES?

MACRO-ECONOMIC FORCES

— MACROECONOMICS —

● **GLOBAL MARKET CONDITIONS**	Outlines current overall conditions from a macroeconomic perspective		Is the economy in a boom or bust phase? Describe general market sentiment. What is the GDP growth rate? How high is the unemployment rate?
● **CAPITAL MARKETS**	Describes current capital market conditions as they relate to your capital needs		What is the state of the capital markets? How easy is it to obtain funding in your particular market? Is seed capital, venture capital, public funding, market capital, or credit readily available? How costly is it to procure funds?
● **COMMODITIES AND OTHER RESOURCES**	Highlights current prices and price trends for resources required for your business model		Describe the current status of markets for commodities and other resources essential to your business (e.g. oil prices and labor costs). How easy is it to obtain the resources needed to execute your business model (e.g. attract prime talent)? How costly are they? Where are prices headed?
● **ECONOMIC INFRASTRUCTURE**	Describes the economic infrastructure of the market in which your business operates		How good is the (public) infrastructure in your market? How would you characterize transportation, trade, school quality, and access to suppliers and customers? How high are individual and corporate taxes? How good are public services for organizations? How would you rate the quality of life?

Pharmaceutical Industry Landscape

- Global recession
- Negative GDP growth in Europe, Japan, and the United States
- Slower growth rates in China and India
- Uncertainty as to when recovery will occur

- Tight capital markets
- Credit availability restricted due to banking crisis
- Little venture capital available
- Risk capital availability extremely limited

- Fierce "battles" for prime talent
- Employees seek to join pharmaceutical companies with positive public image
- Commodity prices rising from recent lows
- Demand for natural resources likely to pick up with economic recovery
- Oil prices continue to fluctuate

- Specific to the region in which a company operates

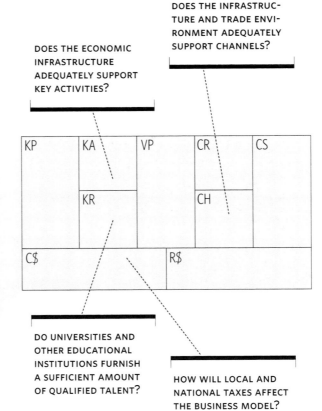

DOES THE ECONOMIC INFRASTRUCTURE ADEQUATELY SUPPORT KEY ACTIVITIES?

DOES THE INFRASTRUCTURE AND TRADE ENVIRONMENT ADEQUATELY SUPPORT CHANNELS?

DO UNIVERSITIES AND OTHER EDUCATIONAL INSTITUTIONS FURNISH A SUFFICIENT AMOUNT OF QUALIFIED TALENT?

HOW WILL LOCAL AND NATIONAL TAXES AFFECT THE BUSINESS MODEL?

HOW SHOULD YOUR BUSINESS MODEL EVOLVE IN LIGHT OF A CHANGING ENVIRONMENT?

A competitive business model that makes sense in today's environment might be outdated or even obsolete tomorrow. We all have to improve our understanding of a model's environment and how it might evolve. Of course we can't be certain about the future, because of the complexities, uncertainties, and potential disruptions inherent in the evolving business environment. We can, however, develop a number of hypotheses about the future to serve as guidelines for designing tomorrow's business models. Assumptions about how market forces, industry forces, key trends, and macroeconomic forces unfold give us the "design space" to develop potential business model options or prototypes (see p. 160) for the future. The role of business model scenarios (see p. 186) in forecasting should also be evident by now. Painting pictures of the future makes it much easier to generate potential business models. Depending on your own criteria (e.g. acceptable level of risk, growth potential sought, etc.) you may then select one option over another.

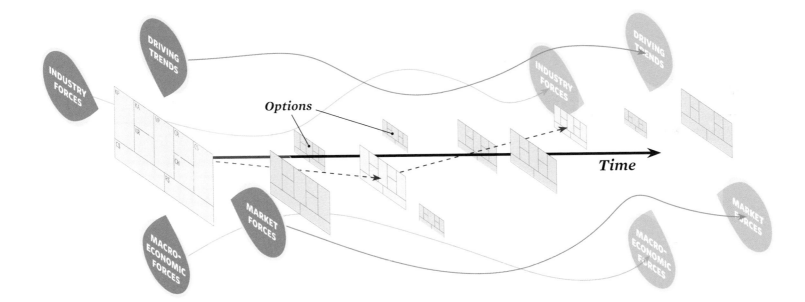

Options

Time

EVALUATING BUSINESS MODELS

LIKE SEEING THE DOCTOR FOR AN ANNUAL EXAM, REGULARLY ASSESSING a business model is an important management activity that allows an organization to evaluate the health of its market position and adapt accordingly. This checkup may become the basis for incremental business model improvements, or it might trigger a serious intervention in the form of a business model innovation initiative. As the automobile, newspaper, and music industries have shown, failing to conduct regular checkups may prevent early detection of business model problems, and may even lead to a company's demise.

In the previous chapter on the business models environment (see p. 200), we evaluated the influence of external forces. In this chapter, we adopt the point of view of an existing business model and analyze external forces from the inside out.

The following pages outline two types of assessment. First, we provide a big picture assessment of Amazon.com's online retailing model circa 2005 and describe how the company has built strategically on that model since. Second, we provide a set of checklists for assessing your business model's strengths, weaknesses, opportunities, and threats (SWOT) and to help you evaluate each Building Block. Keep in mind that assessing a business model from a big picture perspective and assessing it from a Building Block perspective are complementary activities. A weakness in one Building Block, for example, may have consequences for one or several other Building Blocks—or for the entire model. Business model assessment, therefore, alternates between individual elements and overall integrity.

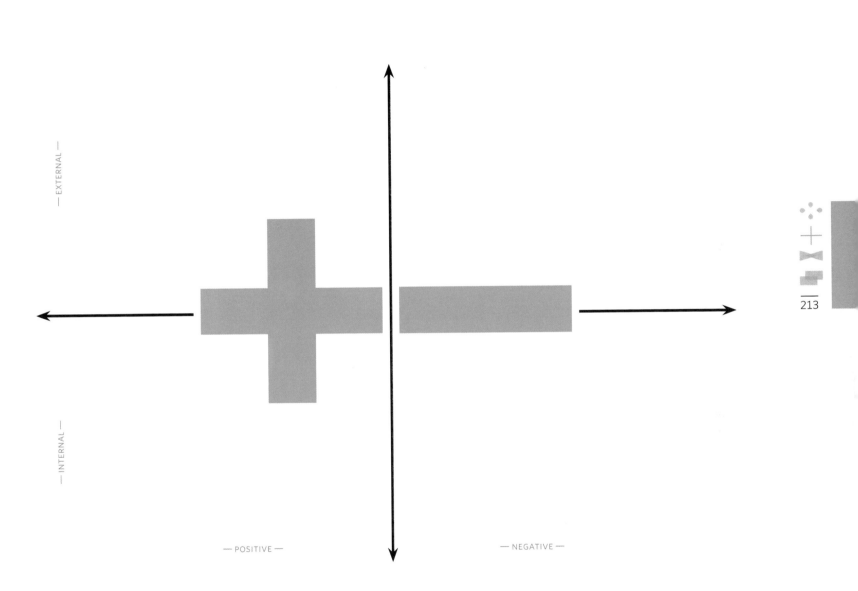

POSITIVE

NEGATIVE

BIG PICTURE ASSESSMENT: AMAZON.COM

Amazon.com's main strengths and weaknesses in 2005:

Amazon.com provides a powerful illustration of implementing business model innovation based on an analysis of strengths and weaknesses. We've already described why it made sense for Amazon.com to launch a series of new service offers under the moniker Amazon Web Services (see p. 176). Now let's examine how those new offers launched in 2006 related to Amazon.com's strengths and weaknesses the previous year.

Assessing the strengths and weaknesses of Amazon.com's business model circa 2005 reveals an enormous strength and a dangerous weakness. Amazon.com's strength was its extraordinary customer reach and huge selection of products for sale. The company's main costs lay in the activities in which it excelled, namely fulfillment ($745 million, or 46.3 percent of operating expenses) and technology and content ($451 million, or 28.1 percent of operating expenses). The key weakness of Amazon.com's business model was weak margins, the result of selling primarily low-value, low-margin products such as books, music CDs, and DVDs. As an online retailer, Amazon.com recorded sales of $8.5 billion in 2005 with a net margin of only 4.2 percent. At the time, Google enjoyed a net margin of 23.9 percent on sales of $6.1 billion while eBay achieved a net margin of 23.7 percent on sales of $4.6 billion.

Looking to the future, founder Jeff Bezos and his management team took a two-pronged approach to building on Amazon.com's business model. First, they aimed to grow the online retail business through a continuing focus on customer satisfaction and efficient fulfillment. Second, they began growth initiatives in new areas. Management was clear on the requirements for these new initiatives. They had to (1) target underserved markets, (2) be scalable with potential for significant growth, and (3) leverage existing Amazon.com capabilities to bring strong customer-facing differentiation to that marketplace.

Opportunities Amazon.com explored in 2006:

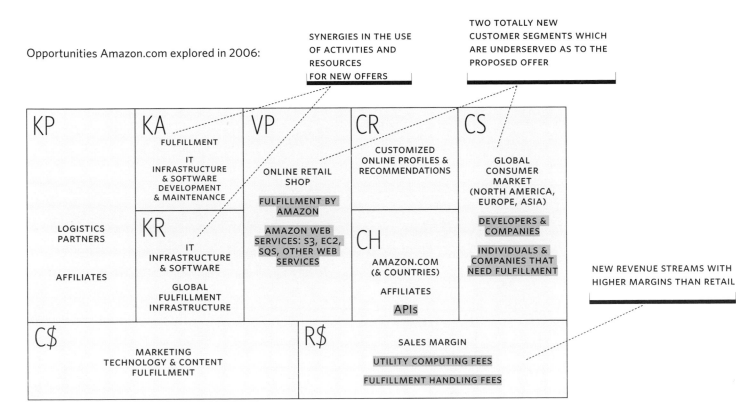

The diagram contains the following labels:

SYNERGIES IN THE USE OF ACTIVITIES AND RESOURCES FOR NEW OFFERS

TWO TOTALLY NEW CUSTOMER SEGMENTS WHICH ARE UNDERSERVED AS TO THE PROPOSED OFFER

KP
LOGISTICS PARTNERS

AFFILIATES

KA
FULFILLMENT

IT INFRASTRUCTURE & SOFTWARE DEVELOPMENT & MAINTENANCE

KR
IT INFRASTRUCTURE & SOFTWARE

GLOBAL FULFILLMENT INFRASTRUCTURE

VP
ONLINE RETAIL SHOP

FULFILLMENT BY AMAZON

AMAZON WEB SERVICES: S3, EC2, SQS, OTHER WEB SERVICES

CR
CUSTOMIZED ONLINE PROFILES & RECOMMENDATIONS

CH
AMAZON.COM (& COUNTRIES)

AFFILIATES

APIs

CS
GLOBAL CONSUMER MARKET (NORTH AMERICA, EUROPE, ASIA)

DEVELOPERS & COMPANIES

INDIVIDUALS & COMPANIES THAT NEED FULFILLMENT

NEW REVENUE STREAMS WITH HIGHER MARGINS THAN RETAIL

C$
MARKETING
TECHNOLOGY & CONTENT
FULFILLMENT

R$
SALES MARGIN

UTILITY COMPUTING FEES

FULFILLMENT HANDLING FEES

In 2006 Amazon.com focused on two new initiatives that satisfied the above requirements and which promised to powerfully extend the existing business model. The first was a service called Fulfillment by Amazon, and the second was a series of new Amazon Web Services. Both initiatives built on the company's core strengths—order fulfillment and Web IT expertise—and both addressed underserved markets. What's more, both initiatives promised higher margins than the company's core online retailing business.

Fulfillment by Amazon allows individuals and companies to use Amazon.com's fulfillment infrastructure for their own businesses in exchange for a fee. Amazon.com stores a seller's inventory in its warehouses, then picks, packs, and ships on the seller's behalf when an order is received. Sellers can sell through Amazon.com, their own Channels, or a combination of both.

Amazon Web Services targets software developers and any party requiring high-performance server capability by offering on-demand storage and computing capacity. Amazon Simple Storage Systems (Amazon S3) allows developers to use Amazon.com's massive data center infrastructure for their own data storage needs. Similarly, Amazon Elastic Compute Cloud (EC2), allows developers to "rent" servers on which to run their own applications. Thanks to its deep expertise and unprecedented experience scaling an online shopping site, the company can offer both at cutthroat prices, yet still earn higher margins compared to its online retail operations.

Investors and investment analysts were initially skeptical about these new long-term growth strategies. Unconvinced that the diversification made sense, they contested Amazon.com's investments in even more IT infrastructure. Eventually, Amazon.com overcame their skepticism. Nonetheless, the true returns from this long-term strategy may not be known for several more years—and after even more investment in the new business model.

DETAILED SWOT
ASSESSMENT OF EACH
BUILDING BLOCK

Assessing your business model's overall integrity is crucial, but looking at its components in detail can also reveal interesting paths to innovation and renewal. An effective way to do this is to combine classic strengths, weaknesses, opportunities, and threats (SWOT) analysis with the Business Model Canvas. SWOT analysis provides four perspectives from which to assess the elements of a business model, while the Business Model Canvas provides the focus necessary for a structured discussion.

SWOT analysis is familiar to many businesspeople. It is used to analyze an organization's strengths and weaknesses and identify potential opportunities and threats. It is an attractive tool because of its simplicity, yet its use can lead to vague discussions because its very openness offers little direction concerning which aspects of an organization to analyze. A lack of useful outcomes may result, which has lead to a certain SWOT-fatigue among managers. When combined with the Business Model Canvas, though, SWOT enables a focused assessment and evaluation of an organization's business model and its Building Blocks.

SWOT asks four big, simple questions. The first two—what are your organization's strength and weaknesses?—assess your organization internally. The second two—what opportunities does your organization have and what potential threats does it face?—assess your organization's position within its environment. Of these four questions, two look at helpful areas (strengths and opportunities) and two address harmful areas. It is useful to ask these four questions with respect to both the overall business model and each of its nine Building Blocks. This type of SWOT analysis provides a good basis for further discussions, decision-making, and ultimately innovation around business models.

The following pages contain non-exhaustive sets of questions to help you assess the strengths and weaknesses of each of your business model Building Blocks. Each set can help jumpstart your own assessments. Results from this exercise can become the foundation for business model change and innovation in your organization.

What are your business model's ...

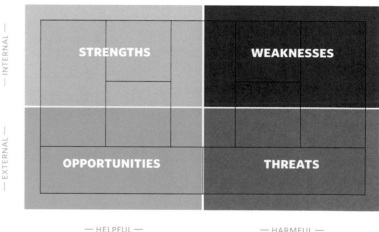

Value Proposition Assessment

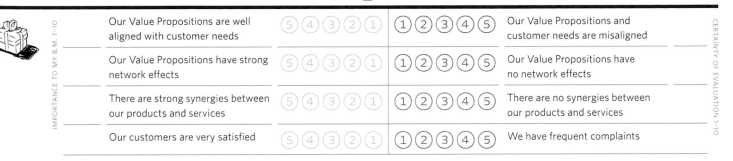

				IMPORTANCE TO MY B.M. 1-10											CERTAINTY OF EVALUATION 1-10

Our Value Propositions are well aligned with customer needs — (5)(4)(3)(2)(1) | (1)(2)(3)(4)(5) — Our Value Propositions and customer needs are misaligned

Our Value Propositions have strong network effects — (5)(4)(3)(2)(1) | (1)(2)(3)(4)(5) — Our Value Propositions have no network effects

There are strong synergies between our products and services — (5)(4)(3)(2)(1) | (1)(2)(3)(4)(5) — There are no synergies between our products and services

Our customers are very satisfied — (5)(4)(3)(2)(1) | (1)(2)(3)(4)(5) — We have frequent complaints

Cost/Revenue Assessment

We benefit from strong margins — (5)(4)(3)(2)(1) | (1)(2)(3)(4)(5) — Our margins are poor

Our revenues are predictable — (5)(4)(3)(2)(1) | (1)(2)(3)(4)(5) — Our revenues are unpredictable

We have recurring Revenue Streams and frequent repeat purchases — (5)(4)(3)(2)(1) | (1)(2)(3)(4)(5) — Our revenues are transactional with few repeat purchases

Our Revenue Streams are diversified — (5)(4)(3)(2)(1) | (1)(2)(3)(4)(5) — We depend on a single Revenue Stream

Our Revenue Streams are sustainable — (5)(4)(3)(2)(1) | (1)(2)(3)(4)(5) — Our revenue sustainability is questionable

We collect revenues before we incur expenses — (5)(4)(3)(2)(1) | (1)(2)(3)(4)(5) — We incur high costs before we collect revenues

We charge for what customers are really willing to pay for — (5)(4)(3)(2)(1) | (1)(2)(3)(4)(5) — We fail to charge for things customers are willing to pay for

Our pricing mechanisms capture full willingness to pay — (5)(4)(3)(2)(1) | (1)(2)(3)(4)(5) — Our pricing mechanisms leave money on the table

Our costs are predictable — (5)(4)(3)(2)(1) | (1)(2)(3)(4)(5) — Our costs are unpredictable

Our Cost Structure is correctly matched to our business model — (5)(4)(3)(2)(1) | (1)(2)(3)(4)(5) — Our Cost Structure and business model are poorly matched

Our operations are cost-efficient — (5)(4)(3)(2)(1) | (1)(2)(3)(4)(5) — Our operations are cost-inefficient

We benefit from economies of scale — (5)(4)(3)(2)(1) | (1)(2)(3)(4)(5) — We enjoy no economies of scale

IMPORTANCE TO MY B.M. 1–10				CERTAINTY OF EVALUATION 1–10
	Our Key Resources are difficult for competitors to replicate	⑤ ④ ③ ② ①	① ② ③ ④ ⑤	Our Key Resources are easily replicated
	Resource needs are predictable	⑤ ④ ③ ② ①	① ② ③ ④ ⑤	Resource needs are unpredictable
	We deploy Key Resources in the right amount at the right time	⑤ ④ ③ ② ①	① ② ③ ④ ⑤	We have trouble deploying the right resources at the right time
	We efficiently execute Key Activities	⑤ ④ ③ ② ①	① ② ③ ④ ⑤	Key Activity execution is inefficient
	Our Key Activities are difficult to copy	⑤ ④ ③ ② ①	① ② ③ ④ ⑤	Our Key Activities are easily copied
	Execution quality is high	⑤ ④ ③ ② ①	① ② ③ ④ ⑤	Execution quality is low
	Balance of in-house versus outsourced execution is ideal	⑤ ④ ③ ② ①	① ② ③ ④ ⑤	We execute too many or too few activities ourselves
	We are focused and work with partners when necessary	⑤ ④ ③ ② ①	① ② ③ ④ ⑤	We are unfocused and fail to work sufficiently with partners
	We enjoy good working relationships with Key Partners	⑤ ④ ③ ② ①	① ② ③ ④ ⑤	Working relationships with Key Partners are conflict-ridden

Customer Interface Assessment

IMPORTANCE TO MY B.M. 1–10		+	—		CERTAINTY OF EVALUATION 1–10
	Customer churn rates are low	⑤④③②①	①②③④⑤	Customer churn rates are high	
	Customer base is well segmented	⑤④③②①	①②③④⑤	Customer base is unsegmented	
	We are continuously acquiring new customers	⑤④③②①	①②③④⑤	We are failing to acquire new customers	
	Our Channels are very efficient	⑤④③②①	①②③④⑤	Our Channels are inefficient	
	Our Channels are very effective	⑤④③②①	①②③④⑤	Our Channels are ineffective	
	Channel reach is strong among customers	⑤④③②①	①②③④⑤	Channel reach among prospects is weak	
	Customers can easily see our Channels	⑤④③②①	①②③④⑤	Prospects fail to notice our Channels	
	Channels are strongly integrated	⑤④③②①	①②③④⑤	Channels are poorly integrated	
	Channels provide economies of scope	⑤④③②①	①②③④⑤	Channels provide no economies of scope	
	Channels are well matched to Customer Segments	⑤④③②①	①②③④⑤	Channels are poorly matched to Customer Segments	
	Strong Customer Relationships	⑤④③②①	①②③④⑤	Weak Customer Relationships	
	Relationship quality correctly matches Customer Segments	⑤④③②①	①②③④⑤	Relationship quality is poorly matched to Customer Segments	
	Relationships bind customers through high switching costs	⑤④③②①	①②③④⑤	Customers switching costs are low	
	Our brand is strong	⑤④③②①	①②③④⑤	Our brand is weak	

ASSESSING THREATS

We've described how business models are situated within specific environments, and shown how external forces such as competition, the legal environment, or technology innovation can influence or threaten a business model (see p. 200). In this section we look at threats specific to each business model Building Block, and provide a non-exhaustive set of questions to help you think about ways to address each threat.

220

Value Proposition Threats

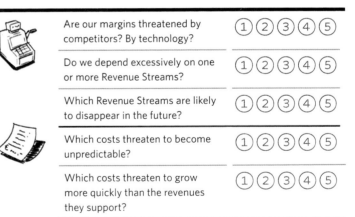

Are substitute products and services available?		① ② ③ ④ ⑤
Are competitors threatening to offer better price or value?		① ② ③ ④ ⑤

Cost/Revenue Threats

Are our margins threatened by competitors? By technology?	① ② ③ ④ ⑤
Do we depend excessively on one or more Revenue Streams?	① ② ③ ④ ⑤
Which Revenue Streams are likely to disappear in the future?	① ② ③ ④ ⑤
Which costs threaten to become unpredictable?	① ② ③ ④ ⑤
Which costs threaten to grow more quickly than the revenues they support?	① ② ③ ④ ⑤

Infrastructure Threats

	Could we face a disruption in the supply of certain resources?	① ② ③ ④ ⑤
	Is the quality of our resources threatened in any way?	① ② ③ ④ ⑤
	What Key Activities might be disrupted?	① ② ③ ④ ⑤
	Is the quality of our activities threatened in any way?	① ② ③ ④ ⑤
	Are we in danger of losing any partners?	① ② ③ ④ ⑤
	Might our partners collaborate with competitors?	① ② ③ ④ ⑤
	Are we too dependent on certain partners?	① ② ③ ④ ⑤

Customer Interface Threats

	Could our market be saturated soon?	① ② ③ ④ ⑤
	Are competitors threatening our market share?	① ② ③ ④ ⑤
	How likely are customers to defect?	① ② ③ ④ ⑤
	How quickly will competition in our market intensify?	① ② ③ ④ ⑤
	Do competitors threaten our Channels?	① ② ③ ④ ⑤
	Are our Channels in danger of becoming irrelevant to customers?	① ② ③ ④ ⑤
	Are any of our Customer Relationships in danger of deteriorating?	① ② ③ ④ ⑤

ASSESSING OPPORTUNITIES

As with threats, we can assess the opportunities that may lie within each business model Building Block. Here's a non-exhaustive set of questions to help you think about opportunities that could emerge from each of the Building Blocks in your business model.

Value Proposition Opportunities

Could we generate recurring revenues by converting products into services?	① ② ③ ④ ⑤	
Could we better integrate our products or services?	① ② ③ ④ ⑤	
Which additional customer needs could we satisfy?	① ② ③ ④ ⑤	
What complements to or extensions of our Value Proposition are possible?	① ② ③ ④ ⑤	
What other jobs could we do on behalf of customers?	① ② ③ ④ ⑤	

Cost/Revenue Opportunities

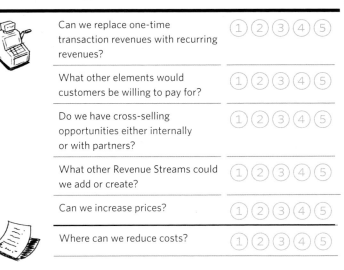

Can we replace one-time transaction revenues with recurring revenues?	① ② ③ ④ ⑤
What other elements would customers be willing to pay for?	① ② ③ ④ ⑤
Do we have cross-selling opportunities either internally or with partners?	① ② ③ ④ ⑤
What other Revenue Streams could we add or create?	① ② ③ ④ ⑤
Can we increase prices?	① ② ③ ④ ⑤
Where can we reduce costs?	① ② ③ ④ ⑤

Infrastructure Opportunities

Question	Rating
Could we use less costly resources to achieve the same result?	① ② ③ ④ ⑤
Which Key Resources could be better sourced from partners?	① ② ③ ④ ⑤
Which Key Resources are under-exploited?	① ② ③ ④ ⑤
Do we have unused intellectual property of value to others?	① ② ③ ④ ⑤
Could we standardize some Key Activities?	① ② ③ ④ ⑤
How could we improve efficiency in general?	① ② ③ ④ ⑤
Would IT support boost efficiency?	① ② ③ ④ ⑤
Are there outsourcing opportunities?	① ② ③ ④ ⑤
Could greater collaboration with partners help us focus on our core business?	① ② ③ ④ ⑤
Are there cross-selling opportunities with partners?	① ② ③ ④ ⑤
Could partner Channels help us better reach customers?	① ② ③ ④ ⑤
Could partners complement our Value Proposition?	① ② ③ ④ ⑤

Customer Interface Opportunities

Question	Rating
How can we benefit from a growing market?	① ② ③ ④ ⑤
Could we serve new Customer Segments?	① ② ③ ④ ⑤
Could we better serve our customers through finer segmentation?	① ② ③ ④ ⑤
How could we improve channel efficiency or effectiveness?	① ② ③ ④ ⑤
Could we integrate our Channels better?	① ② ③ ④ ⑤
Could we find new complementary partner Channels?	① ② ③ ④ ⑤
Could we increase margins by directly serving customers?	① ② ③ ④ ⑤
Could we better align Channels with Customer Segments?	① ② ③ ④ ⑤
Is there potential to improve customer follow-up?	① ② ③ ④ ⑤
How could we tighten our relationships with customers?	① ② ③ ④ ⑤
Could we improve personalization?	① ② ③ ④ ⑤
How could we increase switching costs?	① ② ③ ④ ⑤
Have we identified and "fired" unprofitable customers? If not, why not?	① ② ③ ④ ⑤
Do we need to automate some relationships?	① ② ③ ④ ⑤

USING SWOT ASSESSMENT ANALYSIS RESULTS TO DESIGN NEW BUSINESS MODEL OPTIONS

A structured SWOT assessment of your business model yields two results.
It provides a snapshot of where you are now (strengths and weaknesses)
and it suggests some future trajectories (opportunities and threats). This is
valuable input that can help you design new business model options toward
which your enterprise can evolve. SWOT analysis is thus a significant part
of the process of designing both business model prototypes (see p. 160) and,
with luck, a new business model that you will eventually implement.

Future Model(s)

Current Model

— SWOT PROCESS —

BUSINESS MODEL PERSPECTIVE ON BLUE OCEAN STRATEGY

IN THIS SECTION WE BLEND OUR BUSINESS MODEL TOOLS WITH THE Blue Ocean Strategy concept coined by Kim and Mauborgne in their million-selling book of the same name. The Business Model Canvas is a perfect extension of the analytical tools presented by Kim and Mauborgne. Together they provide a powerful framework for questioning incumbent business models and creating new, more competitive models.

Blue Ocean Strategy is a potent method for questioning Value Propositions and business models and exploring new Customer Segments. The Business Model Canvas complements Blue Ocean by providing a visual "big picture" that helps us understand how changing one part of a business model impacts other components.

In a nutshell, Blue Ocean Strategy is about creating completely new industries through fundamental differentiation as opposed to competing in existing industries by tweaking established models. Rather than outdoing competitors in terms of traditional performance metrics, Kim and Mauborgne advocate creating new, uncontested market space through what the authors call value innovation. This means increasing value for customers by creating new benefits and services, while simultaneously reducing costs by eliminating less valuable features or services. Notice how this approach rejects the traditionally accepted trade-off between differentiation and lower cost.

To achieve value innovation, Kim and Mauborgne propose an analytical tool they call the Four Actions Framework. These four key questions challenge an industry's strategic logic and established business model:

1. Which of the factors that the industry takes for granted should be eliminated?
2. Which factors should be reduced well below the industry standard?
3. Which factors should be raised well above the industry standard?
4. Which factors should be created that the industry has never offered?

In addition to value innovation, Kim and Mauborgne propose exploring non-customer groups to create Blue Oceans and tap untouched markets.

Blending Kim and Mauborgne's value innovation concept and Four Actions Framework with the Business Model Canvas creates a powerful new tool. In the Business Model Canvas the right-hand side represents value creation and the left-hand side represents costs. This fits well with Kim and Mauborgne's value innovation logic of increasing value and reducing costs.

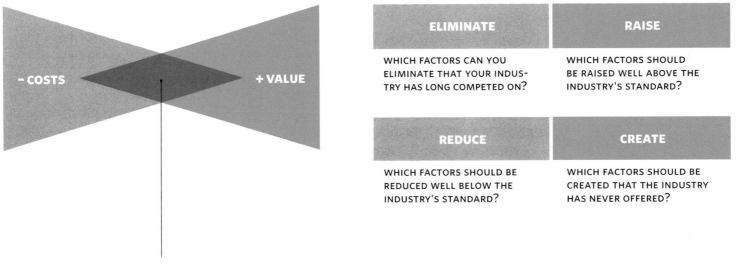

− COSTS **+ VALUE**

— VALUE INNOVATION —

ELIMINATE	RAISE
WHICH FACTORS CAN YOU ELIMINATE THAT YOUR INDUSTRY HAS LONG COMPETED ON?	WHICH FACTORS SHOULD BE RAISED WELL ABOVE THE INDUSTRY'S STANDARD?

REDUCE	CREATE
WHICH FACTORS SHOULD BE REDUCED WELL BELOW THE INDUSTRY'S STANDARD?	WHICH FACTORS SHOULD BE CREATED THAT THE INDUSTRY HAS NEVER OFFERED?

— FOUR ACTIONS FRAMEWORK —

Source: Adapted from Blue Ocean Strategy.

BLENDING THE BLUE OCEAN STRATEGY FRAMEWORK WITH THE BUSINESS MODEL CANVAS

Business Model Canvas

Value innovation

Blending approaches

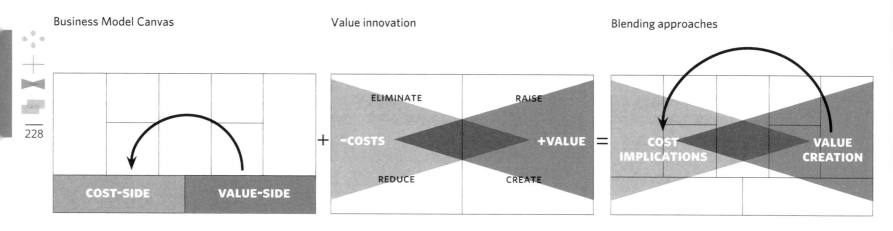

The Business Model Canvas consists of a right-hand value and customer-focused side, and a left-hand cost and infrastructure side, as described earlier (see p. 49). Changing elements on the right-hand side has implications for the left-hand side. For example, if we add to or eliminate parts of the Value Proposition, Channels, or Customer Relationship Building Blocks, this will have immediate implications for Resources, Activities, Partnerships, and Costs.

Blue Ocean Strategy is about simultaneously increasing value while reducing costs. This is achieved by identifying which elements of the Value Proposition can be eliminated, reduced, raised, or newly created. The first goal is to lower costs by reducing or eliminating less valuable features or services. The second goal is to enhance or create high-value features or services that do not significantly increase the cost base.

Blending Blue Ocean Strategy and the Business Model Canvas lets you systematically analyze a business model innovation in its entirety. You can ask the Four Actions Framework questions (eliminate, create, reduce, raise) about each business model Building Block and immediately recognize implications for the other parts of the business model, (e.g. what are the implications for the cost side when we make changes on the value side? and vice versa).

CIRQUE DU SOLEIL

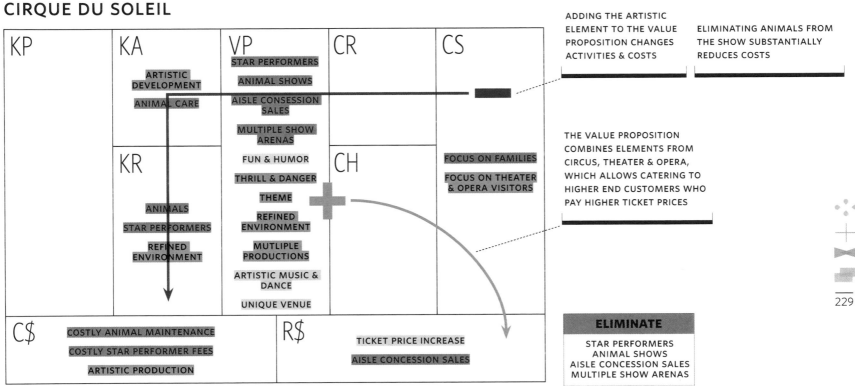

KP	KA	VP	CR	CS
	ARTISTIC DEVELOPMENT ANIMAL CARE	STAR PERFORMERS ANIMAL SHOWS AISLE CONSESSION SALES MULTIPLE SHOW ARENAS		

ADDING THE ARTISTIC ELEMENT TO THE VALUE PROPOSITION CHANGES ACTIVITIES & COSTS

ELIMINATING ANIMALS FROM THE SHOW SUBSTANTIALLY REDUCES COSTS

KR		VP (cont.)	CH	CS (cont.)
ANIMALS STAR PERFORMERS REFINED ENVIRONMENT		FUN & HUMOR THRILL & DANGER THEME REFINED ENVIRONMENT MUTLIPLE PRODUCTIONS ARTISTIC MUSIC & DANCE UNIQUE VENUE		FOCUS ON FAMILIES FOCUS ON THEATER & OPERA VISITORS

THE VALUE PROPOSITION COMBINES ELEMENTS FROM CIRCUS, THEATER & OPERA, WHICH ALLOWS CATERING TO HIGHER END CUSTOMERS WHO PAY HIGHER TICKET PRICES

C$	R$
COSTLY ANIMAL MAINTENANCE COSTLY STAR PERFORMER FEES ARTISTIC PRODUCTION	TICKET PRICE INCREASE AISLE CONCESSION SALES

229

ELIMINATE
STAR PERFORMERS ANIMAL SHOWS AISLE CONCESSION SALES MULTIPLE SHOW ARENAS
REDUCE
FUN & HUMOR THRILL & DANGER
RAISE
UNIQUE VENUE
CREATE
THEME REFINED ENVIRONMENT MULTIPLE PRODUCTIONS ARTISTIC MUSIC & DANCE

Cirque du Soleil features prominently among Blue Ocean Strategy examples. Next we apply the blended Blue Ocean and Business Model Canvas approach to this intriguing and highly successful Canadian business.

First, the Four Actions Framework shows how Cirque du Soleil "played" with the traditional elements of the circus business Value Proposition. It eliminated costly elements, such as animals and star performers, while adding other elements, such as theme, artistic atmosphere, and refined music. This revamped Value Proposition allowed Cirque du Soleil to broaden its appeal to theatergoers and other adults seeking sophisticated entertainment, rather than the traditional circus audience of families.

As a consequence, it was able to substantially raise ticket prices. The Four Actions Framework, outlined in blue and gray in the business model canvas above, illustrates the effects of changes in the Value Proposition.

Source: Adapted from Blue Ocean Strategy.

NINTENDO'S Wii

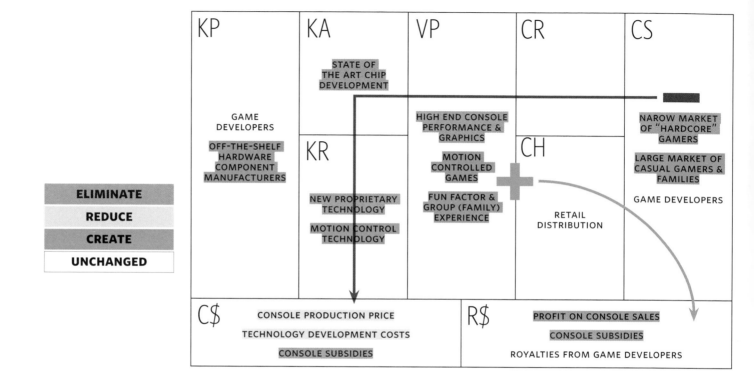

KP	KA	VP	CR	CS
	STATE OF THE ART CHIP DEVELOPMENT			
GAME DEVELOPERS		HIGH END CONSOLE PERFORMANCE & GRAPHICS		NAROW MARKET OF "HARDCORE" GAMERS
OFF-THE-SHELF HARDWARE COMPONENT MANUFACTURERS	KR	MOTION CONTROLLED GAMES	CH	LARGE MARKET OF CASUAL GAMERS & FAMILIES
	NEW PROPRIETARY TECHNOLOGY	FUN FACTOR & GROUP (FAMILY) EXPERIENCE	RETAIL DISTRIBUTION	GAME DEVELOPERS
	MOTION CONTROL TECHNOLOGY			

C$		R$	
CONSOLE PRODUCTION PRICE		PROFIT ON CONSOLE SALES	
TECHNOLOGY DEVELOPMENT COSTS		CONSOLE SUBSIDIES	
CONSOLE SUBSIDIES		ROYALTIES FROM GAME DEVELOPERS	

ELIMINATE
REDUCE
CREATE
UNCHANGED

We've discussed Nintendo's successful Wii game console as an example of a multi-sided platform business model pattern (see p. 76). Now we look at how Nintendo differentiated itself from competitors Sony and Microsoft from the standpoint of Blue Ocean Strategy. Compared to Sony's PlayStation 3 and Microsoft's Xbox 360, Nintendo pursued a fundamentally different strategy and business model with Wii.

The heart of Nintendo's strategy was the assumption that consoles do not necessarily require leading-edge power and performance. This was a radical stance in an industry that traditionally competed on technological performance, graphic quality, and game realism: factors valued primarily by diehard gaming fans. Nintendo shifted its focus to providing a new form of player interaction targeted at a wider demographic than the traditional avid gamer audience. With the Wii, Nintendo brought to market a console that technologically underperformed rival machines, but boosted the fun factor with new motion control technology. Players could control games through a sort of "magic wand," the Wii Remote, simply through physical movement. The console was an instant success with casual gamers, and outsold rival consoles focused on the traditional market of "hardcore" gamers.

Nintendo's new business model has the following characteristics: A shift in focus from "hardcore" to casual gamers, which allowed the company to reduce console performance and add a new element of motion control that created more fun; elimination of state-of-the-art chip development and increased use of off-the-shelf components, reducing costs and allowing lower console prices; elimination of console subsidies resulting in profits on each console sold.

QUESTIONING YOUR CANVAS WITH THE FOUR ACTIONS FRAMEWORK

The combination of Blue Ocean Strategy tools and the Business Model Canvas provide a solid foundation upon which to question your business model from value creation, customer, and Cost Structure perspectives. We propose that three different perspectives—the Customer Segment perspective, the Value Proposition perspective, and the cost perspective—provide ideal starting points from which to start questioning your business model using the Four Actions Framework. Changes to each starting point then allow you to analyze impacts on other areas of the Business Model Canvas (see also innovation epicenters on p. 138).

(see also innovation epicenters on p. 138).

Cost Impact Exploration

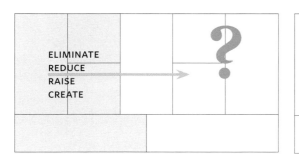

Identify the highest cost infrastructure elements and evaluate what happens if you eliminate or reduce them. What value elements disappear, and what would you have to create to compensate for their absence? Then, identify infrastructure investments you may want to make and analyze how much value they create.

- Which activities, resources, and partnerships have the highest costs?
- What happens if you reduce or eliminate some of these cost factors?
- How could you replace, using less costly elements, the value lost by reducing or eliminating expensive resources, activities, or partnerships?
- What value would be created by planned new investments?

Exploring Value Proposition Impact

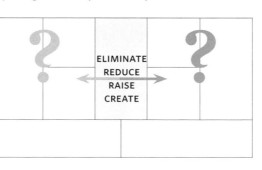

Begin the process of transforming your Value Proposition by asking the Four Actions Framework questions. Simultaneously, consider the impact on the cost side and evaluate what elements you need to (or could) change on the value side, such as Channels, Relationships, Revenue Streams, and Customer Segments.

- What less-valued features or services could be eliminated or reduced?
- What features or services could be enhanced or newly created to produce a valuable new customer experience?
- What are the cost implications of your changes to the Value Proposition?
- How will changes to the Value Proposition affect the customer side of the model?

Exploring Customer Impact

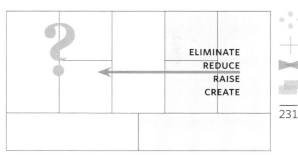

Ask yourself the Four Actions Framework questions about each business model Building Block on the customer side of the Canvas: Channels, Relationships, and Revenue Streams. Analyze what happens to the cost side if you eliminate, reduce, raise, or create value side elements.

- Which new Customer Segments could you focus on, and which segments could you possibly reduce or eliminate?
- What jobs do new Customer Segments really want to have done?
- How do these customers prefer to be reached and what kind of relationship do they expect?
- What are the cost implications of serving new Customer Segments?

231

MANAGING MULTIPLE BUSINESS MODELS

VISIONARIES, GAME CHANGERS, AND CHALLENGERS ARE GENERATING innovative business models around the world—as entrepreneurs and as workers within established organizations. An entrepreneur's challenge is to design and successfully implement a new business model. Established organizations, though, face an equally daunting task: how to implement and manage new models while maintaining existing ones.

Business thinkers such as Constantinos Markides, Charles O'Reilly III, and Michael Tushman have a word for groups that successfully meet this challenge: ambidextrous organizations. Implementing a new business model in a longstanding enterprise can be extraordinarily difficult because the new model may challenge or even compete with established models. The new model might require a different organizational culture, or it might target prospective customers formerly ignored by the enterprise. This begs a question: How do we implement innovative business models within long-established organizations?

Scholars are divided on the issue. Many suggest spinning off new business model initiatives into separate entities. Others propose a less drastic approach and argue that innovative new business models can thrive within established organizations, either as-is or in separate business units. Constantinos Markides, for example, proposes a two-variable framework for deciding on how to manage new and traditional business models simultaneously. The first variable expresses the severity of conflict between the models, while the second expresses strategic similarity. Yet, he also shows that success depends not only on the correct choice—integrated versus standalone implementation—but also on *how* the choice is implemented.

Synergies, Markides claims, should be carefully exploited even when the new model is implemented in a standalone unit.

Risk is a third variable to consider when deciding whether to integrate or separate an emerging model. How big is the risk that the new model will negatively affect the established one in terms of brand image, earnings, legal liability, and so forth?

During the financial crisis of 2008, ING, the Dutch financial group, was nearly toppled by its ING Direct unit, which provides online and telephone retail banking services in overseas markets. In effect, ING treated ING Direct more as a marketing initiative than as a new, separate business model that would have been better housed in a separate entity.

Finally, choices evolve over time. Markides emphasizes that companies may want to consider a phased integration or a phased separation of business models. e.Schwab, the Internet arm of Charles Schwab, the U.S. retail securities broker, was initially set up as a separate unit, but later was integrated back into the main business with great success. Tesco.com, the Internet branch of Tesco, the giant U.K. retailer, made a successful transition from integrated business line into standalone unit.

In the following pages we examine the issue of integration versus separation with three examples described using the Business Model Canvas. The first, Swiss watch manufacturer SMH, chose the integration route for its new Swatch business model in the 1980s. The second, Swiss foodmaker Nestlé, chose the separation route for bringing Nespresso to the marketplace. As of this writing, the third, German vehicle manufacturer Daimler, has yet to choose an approach for its car2go vehicle rental concept.

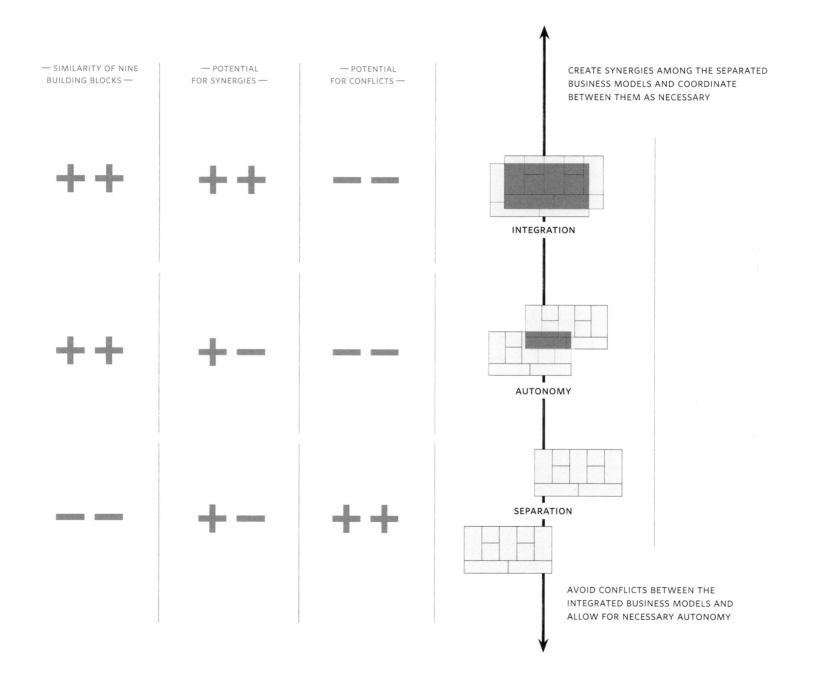

SMH'S AUTONOMOUS MODEL FOR SWATCH

In the mid-seventies the Swiss watch industry, which had historically dominated the timepiece sector, found itself in deep crisis. Japanese and Hong Kong watch manufacturers had dislodged the Swiss from their leadership position with cheap quartz watches designed for the low-end market. The Swiss continued to focus on traditional mechanical watches for the mid- and high-end markets, but all the while Asian competitors threatened to intrude on these segments as well.

In the early 1980s competitive pressure intensified to the point that most Swiss manufacturers, with the exception of a handful of luxury brands, were teetering on collapse. Then Nicolas G. Hayek took over the reigns of SMH (later renamed Swatch Group). He completely restructured a newly formed group cobbled together from companies with roots in the two biggest ailing Swiss watchmakers.

Hayek envisioned a strategy whereby SMH would offer healthy, growing brands in all three market segments: low, mid, and luxury. At the time, Swiss firms dominated the luxury watch market with a 97 percent share. But the Swiss owned only 3 percent of the middle market and were non-players in the low end, leaving the entire segment of inexpensive timepieces to Asian rivals.

Launching a new brand at the bottom end was provocative and risky, and triggered fears among investors that the move would cannibalize Tissot, SMH's middle-market brand. From a strategic point of view, Hayek's vision meant nothing less than combining a high-end luxury business model with a low-cost business model under the same roof, with all the attending conflicts and trade-offs. Nevertheless, Hayek insisted on this three-tiered strategy, which triggered development of the Swatch, a new type of affordable Swiss watch priced starting at around U.S. $40.

The specifications for the new watch were demanding: inexpensive enough to compete with Japanese offers yet providing Swiss quality, plus sufficient margins and the potential to anchor a larger product line. This forced engineers to entirely rethink the very idea of a timepiece and its manufacture; they were essentially deprived of the ability to apply their traditional watchmaking knowledge.

The result was a watch made with far fewer components. Manufacturing was highly automated: molding replaced screws, direct labor costs were driven down to less than 10 percent, and the watches were produced in large quantities. Innovative guerrilla marketing concepts were used to bring the watch to market under several different designs. Hayek saw the new product communicating a lifestyle message, rather than just telling time on the cheap.

Thus the Swatch was born: high quality at a low price, for a functional, fashionable product. The rest is history. Fifty-five million Swatches were sold in five years, and in 2006 the company celebrated aggregate sales of over 333 million Swatches.

SMH's choice to implement the low end Swatch business model is particularly interesting in light of its potential impact on SMH's higher end brands. Despite a completely different organizational and brand culture, Swatch was launched under SMH and not as a standalone entity.

SMH, though, was careful to give Swatch and all its other brands near-complete autonomy regarding product and marketing decisions, while centralizing everything else. Manufacturing, purchasing, and R&D were each regrouped under a single entity serving all of SMH's brands. Today, SMH maintains a strong vertical integration policy in order to achieve scale and defend itself against Asian competitors.

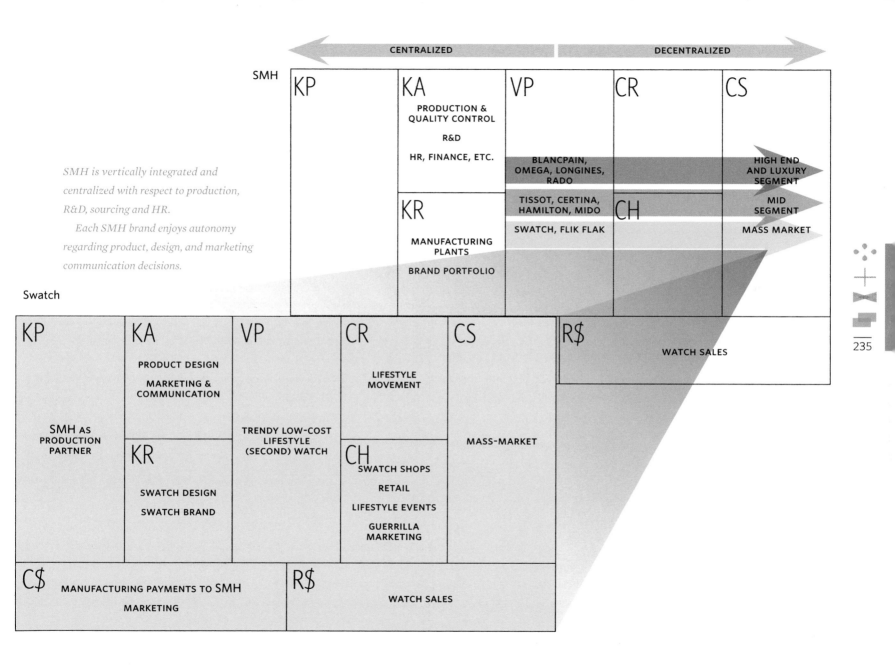

SMH

SMH is vertically integrated and centralized with respect to production, R&D, sourcing and HR.

Each SMH brand enjoys autonomy regarding product, design, and marketing communication decisions.

KP	KA	VP	CR	CS
	PRODUCTION & QUALITY CONTROL / R&D / HR, FINANCE, ETC.			
		BLANCPAIN, OMEGA, LONGINES, RADO		HIGH END AND LUXURY SEGMENT
	KR	TISSOT, CERTINA, HAMILTON, MIDO	CH	MID SEGMENT
		SWATCH, FLIK FLAK		MASS MARKET
	MANUFACTURING PLANTS			
	BRAND PORTFOLIO			

CENTRALIZED — DECENTRALIZED

Swatch

KP	KA	VP	CR	CS	R$
SMH AS PRODUCTION PARTNER	PRODUCT DESIGN / MARKETING & COMMUNICATION	TRENDY LOW-COST LIFESTYLE (SECOND) WATCH	LIFESTYLE MOVEMENT	MASS-MARKET	WATCH SALES
	KR / SWATCH DESIGN / SWATCH BRAND		CH / SWATCH SHOPS / RETAIL / LIFESTYLE EVENTS / GUERRILLA MARKETING		

C$	R$
MANUFACTURING PAYMENTS TO SMH / MARKETING	WATCH SALES

THE NESPRESSO SUCCESS MODEL

1976
FIRST PATENT FILED FOR NESPRESSO SYSTEM

1982
FOCUS ON THE OFFICE MARKET

1986
SEPARATE COMPANY CREATED

1988
NEW CEO OVERHAULS STRATEGY

1991
NESPRESSO IS LAUNCHED INTERNATIONALLY

1997
FIRST AD CAMPAIGNS LAUNCHED

1998
FOCUS ON INTERNET WITH WEB SITE REDESIGN

2006
GEORGE CLOONEY RETAINED AS SPOKESMAN FOR NESPRESSO

2000–2008
AVERAGE ANNUAL GROWTH OF OVER 35%

Another ambidextrous organization is Nespresso, part of Nestlé, the world's largest food company with 2008 sales of approximately U.S. $101 billion.

Nespresso, which each year sells over U.S.$1.9 billion worth of single-serve premium coffee for home consumption, offers a potent example of an ambidextrous business model. In 1976, Eric Favre, a young researcher at a Nestlé research lab, filed his first patent for the Nespresso system. At the time Nestlé dominated the huge instant coffee market with its Nescafé brand, but was weak in the roast and ground coffee segments. The Nespresso system was designed to bridge that gap with a dedicated espresso machine and pod system that could conveniently produce restaurant-quality espresso.

An internal unit headed by Favre was set up to eliminate technical problems and bring the system to market. After a short, unsuccessful attempt to enter the restaurant market, in 1986 Nestlé created Nespresso SA, a wholly-owned subsidiary that would start marketing the system to offices in support of another Nestlé joint venture with a coffee machine manufacturer already active in the office segment. Nespresso SA was completely independent of Nescafé, Nestlé's established coffee business. But by 1987 Nespresso's sales had sagged far below expectations and it was kept alive only because of its large remaining inventory of high-value coffee machines.

In 1988 Nestlé installed Jean-Paul Gaillard as the new CEO of Nespresso. Gaillard completely overhauled the company's business model with two drastic changes. First, Nespresso shifted its focus from offices to high-income households and started selling coffee capsules directly by mail. Such a strategy was unheard of at Nestlé, which traditionally focused on targeting mass markets through retail Channels (later on Nespresso would start selling online and build high-end retail stores at premium locations such as the Champs-Élysées, as well as launch its own in-store boutiques in high-end

department stores). The model proved successful, and over the past decade Nespresso has posted average annual growth rates exceeding of 35 percent.

Of particular interest is how Nespresso compares to Nescafé, Nestlé's traditional coffee business. Nescafé focuses on instant coffee sold to consumers indirectly through mass-market retailers, while Nespresso concentrates on direct sales to affluent consumers. Each approach requires completely different logistics, resources, and activities. Thanks to the different focus there was no risk of direct cannibalization. Yet, this also meant little potential for synergy between the two businesses. The main conflict between Nescafé and Nespresso arose from the considerable time and resource drain imposed on Nestlé's coffee business until Nespresso finally became successful. The organizational separation likely kept the Nespresso project from being cancelled during hard times.

The story does not end there. In 2004 Nestlé aimed to introduce a new system, complementary to the espresso-only Nespresso devices, that could also serve cappuccino and lattes. The question, of course, was with which business model and under which brand should the system be launched? Or should a new company be created, as with Nespresso? The technology was originally developed at Nespresso, but cappuccinos and lattes seemed more appropriate for the mid-tier mass market. Nestlé finally decided to launch under a new brand, Nescafé Dolce Gusto, but with the product completely integrated into Nescafé's mass-market business model and organizational structure. Dolce Gusto pods sell on retail shelves alongside Nescafé's soluble coffee, but also via the Internet—a tribute to Nespresso's online success.

NESTLÉ'S PORTFOLIO OF COFFEE BUSINESS MODELS

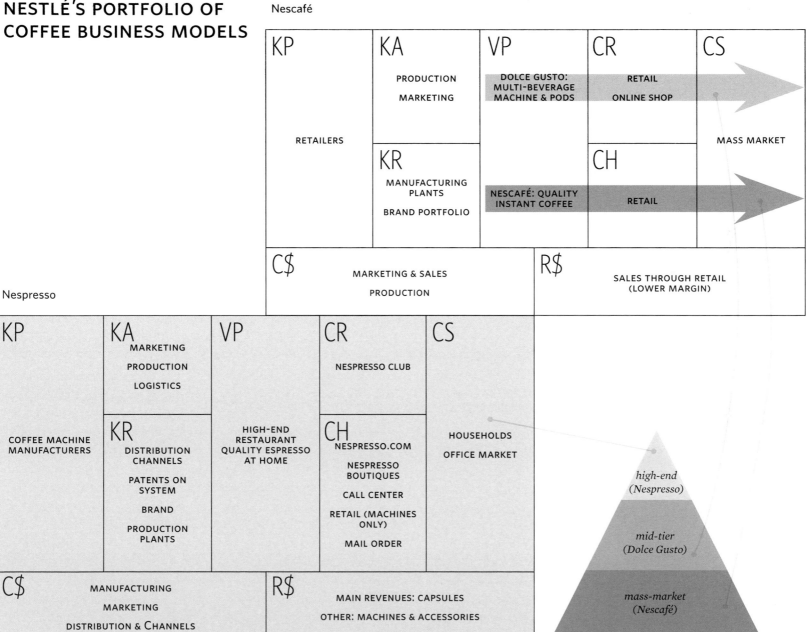

Nescafé

KP
RETAILERS

KA
PRODUCTION
MARKETING

KR
MANUFACTURING PLANTS
BRAND PORTFOLIO

VP
DOLCE GUSTO: MULTI-BEVERAGE MACHINE & PODS

NESCAFÉ: QUALITY INSTANT COFFEE

CR
RETAIL
ONLINE SHOP

CH
RETAIL

CS
MASS MARKET

C$
MARKETING & SALES
PRODUCTION

R$
SALES THROUGH RETAIL (LOWER MARGIN)

237

Nespresso

KP
COFFEE MACHINE MANUFACTURERS

KA
MARKETING
PRODUCTION
LOGISTICS

KR
DISTRIBUTION CHANNELS
PATENTS ON SYSTEM
BRAND
PRODUCTION PLANTS

VP
HIGH-END RESTAURANT QUALITY ESPRESSO AT HOME

CR
NESPRESSO CLUB

CH
NESPRESSO.COM
NESPRESSO BOUTIQUES
CALL CENTER
RETAIL (MACHINES ONLY)
MAIL ORDER

CS
HOUSEHOLDS
OFFICE MARKET

C$
MANUFACTURING
MARKETING
DISTRIBUTION & CHANNELS

R$
MAIN REVENUES: CAPSULES
OTHER: MACHINES & ACCESSORIES

high-end (Nespresso)

mid-tier (Dolce Gusto)

mass-market (Nescafé)

DAIMLER'S CAR2GO BUSINESS MODEL

Market introduction of car2go

CONCEPT DEVELOPMENT	INTERNAL PILOT	EXTENDED INTERNAL PILOT	ULM PUBLIC PILOT	AUSTIN INTERNAL PILOT	AUSTIN PUBLIC PILOT	WHICH ORGANIZATIONAL FORM?

Our final example is still emerging as of this writing. Car2go is a new concept in mobility created by German vehicle manufacturer Daimler. Car2go provides an example of a business model innovation that complements the parent company's core model of manufacturing, selling, and financing vehicles ranging from luxury cars to trucks and buses.

Daimler's core business generates annual revenue exceeding U.S. $136 billion through sales of more than two million vehicles. Car2go, on the other hand, is a startup business offering city dwellers mobility on demand using a citywide fleet of *smart* cars (*smart* is Daimler's smallest and lowest-priced vehicle brand). The service is currently being tested in the German city of Ulm, one of Daimler's key operational bases. The business model was developed by Daimler's Business Innovation Department, which is tasked with developing new business ideas and supporting their implementation.

Here's how car2go works: a fleet of *smart* "fortwo" two-person vehicles is made available throughout the city, serving as a vehicle pool accessible by customers at any time. Following a one-time registration process, customers can rent fortwo cars on the spot (or reserve them in advance) then use them for as long as they like. Once a trip is completed, the driver simply parks the car somewhere within the city limits.

Rentals cost the equivalent $0.27 per minute, all-inclusive, or $14.15 per hour with a maximum of $70 per day. Customers pay monthly. The concept resembles popular car-sharing companies such as Zipcar in North America and the U.K. Distinctive characteristics of car2go include freedom from the obligation to use an assigned parking place, on-the-spot rental for as long as one likes, and a simple pricing structure.

Daimler launched car2go in response to the accelerating global trend toward urbanization, and saw the service as an intriguing complement to its core business. As a pure service model, car2go naturally has completely different dynamics compared to Daimler's traditional business, and revenues will likely remain comparatively small for some years. But Daimler clearly has high hopes for car2go over the long term.

In the pilot phase, launched in October of 2008, 50 fortwo cars were made available to some 500 employees of the Daimler Research Center in Ulm. These 500, plus 200 family members, participated as initial customers. The aim was to test the technical systems, gather data on user acceptance and behavior, and give the service an overall "road test." In February 2009, the pilot was extended to include employees of Mercedes-Benz sales and service outlets and other Daimler subsidiaries, with the number of vehicles increased to 100. At the end of March, a public test was initiated with 200 vehicles and car2go was made available to all 120,000 of Ulm's residents and visitors.

At the same time, Daimler announced a U.S. pilot in Austin, Texas, a city with 750,000 residents. As in the first phase of the German test, car2go will begin with a limited user group, such as city employees, then be opened to the public. These pilots can be seen as prototypes of a business model (see p. 160). Now, car2go's business model prototype is being fixed into organizational form.

As of this writing, Daimler had not yet decided whether to internalize car2go or spin it off as a separate company. Daimler chose to start with business model design, then test the concept in the field, and defer decisions regarding organizational structure until it could assess car2go's relationship to its long-established core business.

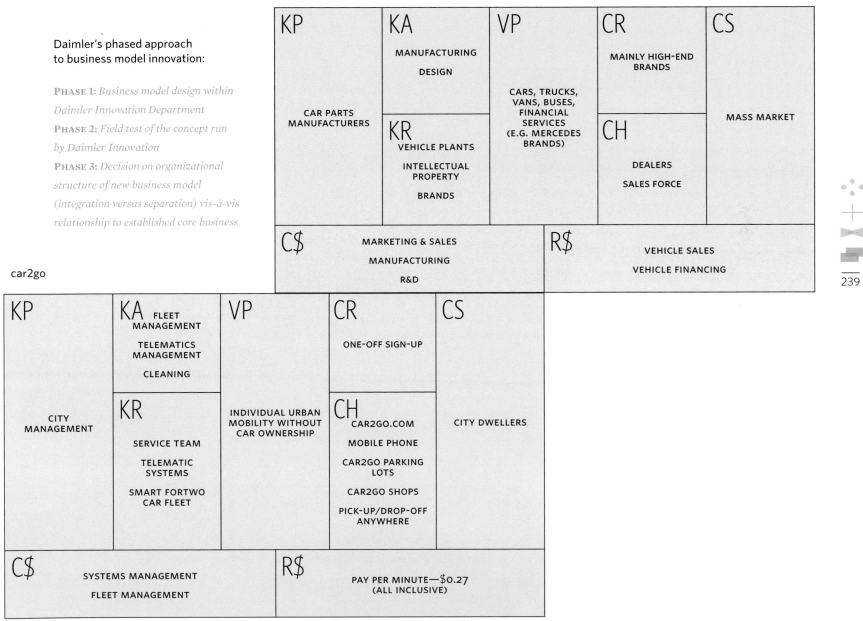

Daimler

Daimler's phased approach to business model innovation:

PHASE 1: *Business model design within Daimler Innovation Department*
PHASE 2: *Field test of the concept run by Daimler Innovation*
PHASE 3: *Decision on organizational structure of new business model (integration versus separation) vis-à-vis relationship to established core business*

KP
CAR PARTS MANUFACTURERS

KA
MANUFACTURING
DESIGN

KR
VEHICLE PLANTS
INTELLECTUAL PROPERTY
BRANDS

VP
CARS, TRUCKS, VANS, BUSES, FINANCIAL SERVICES (E.G. MERCEDES BRANDS)

CR
MAINLY HIGH-END BRANDS

CH
DEALERS
SALES FORCE

CS
MASS MARKET

C$
MARKETING & SALES
MANUFACTURING
R&D

R$
VEHICLE SALES
VEHICLE FINANCING

239

car2go

KP
CITY MANAGEMENT

KA
FLEET MANAGEMENT
TELEMATICS MANAGEMENT
CLEANING

KR
SERVICE TEAM
TELEMATIC SYSTEMS
SMART FORTWO CAR FLEET

VP
INDIVIDUAL URBAN MOBILITY WITHOUT CAR OWNERSHIP

CR
ONE-OFF SIGN-UP

CH
CAR2GO.COM
MOBILE PHONE
CAR2GO PARKING LOTS
CAR2GO SHOPS
PICK-UP/DROP-OFF ANYWHERE

CS
CITY DWELLERS

C$
SYSTEMS MANAGEMENT
FLEET MANAGEMENT

R$
PAY PER MINUTE—$0.27
(ALL INCLUSIVE)

improve

invent

Business Model Design Process

In this chapter we tie together the concepts and tools from the book to simplify the task of setting up and executing a business model design initiative. We propose a generic business model design process adaptable to your organization's specific needs.

Every business model design project is unique, and presents its own challenges, obstacles, and critical success factors. Every organization starts from a different point and has its own context and objectives when it begins addressing an issue as fundamental as its business model. Some may be reacting to a crisis situation, some may be seeking new growth potential, some may be in startup mode, and still others may be planning to bring a new product or technology to market.

The process we describe provides a starting point upon which just about any organization can customize its own approach. Our process has five phases: Mobilize, Understand, Design, Implement, and Manage. We describe each of these phases in a general way, then revisit them from the perspective of the established organization, as business model innovation in enterprises already executing on one or more existing business models requires taking additional factors into account.

Business model innovation results from one of four objectives: (1) to satisfy existing but unanswered market needs, (2) to bring new technologies, products, or services to market, (3) to improve, disrupt, or transform an existing market with a better business model, or (4) to create an entirely new market.

In longstanding enterprises, business model innovation efforts typically reflect the existing model and organizational structure. The effort usually has one of four motivations: (1) a crisis with the existing business model (in some cases a "near death" experience), (2) adjusting, improving, or defending the existing model to adapt to a changing environment, (3) bringing new technologies, products, or services to market, or (4) preparing for the future by exploring and testing completely new business models that might eventually replace existing ones.

Business Model Design and Innovation

Satisfy market: Fulfill an unanswered market need
(e.g. Tata car, NetJets, GrameenBank, Lulu.com)

Bring to market: Bring a new technology, product, or service to market or exploit existing intellectual property (IP) *(e.g. Xerox 914, Swatch, Nespresso, Red Hat)*

Improve market: Improve or disrupt an existing market *(e.g. Dell, EFG Bank, Nintendo Wii, IKEA, Bharti Airtel, Skype, Ryanair, Amazon.com retail, better place)*

Create market: Create an entirely new type of business *(Diners Club, Google)*

CHALLENGES

• Finding the right model

• Testing the model before a full-scale launch

• Inducing the market to adopt the new model

• Continuously adapting the model in response to market feedback

• Managing uncertainty

Factors Specific to Established Organizations

Reactive: Arising out of a crisis with the existing business model *(e.g. IBM in the 1990s, Nintendo Wii, Rolls Royce jet engines)*

Adaptive: Adjusting, improving, or defending the existing business model *(Nokia "comes with music," P&G open innovation, Hilti)*

Expansive: Launching a new technology, product, or service *(e.g. Nespresso, Xerox 914 in the 1960s, iPod/iTunes)*

Pro-active/explorative: Preparing for the future *(e.g. car2go by Daimler, Amazon Web Services)*

CHALLENGES

• Developing an appetite for new models

• Aligning old and new models

• Managing vested interests

• Focusing on the long term

245

Design Attitude

Business model innovation rarely happens by coincidence. But neither is it the exclusive domain of the creative business genius. It is something that can be managed, structured into processes, and used to leverage the creative potential of an entire organization.

The challenge, though, is that business model innovation remains messy and unpredictable, despite attempts to implement a process. It requires the ability to deal with ambiguity and uncertainty until a good solution emerges. This takes time. Participants must be willing to invest significant time and energy exploring many possibilities without jumping too quickly to adopt one solution. The reward for time invested will likely be a powerful new business model that assures future growth.

We call this approach design attitude, which differs sharply from the decision attitude that dominates traditional business management. Fred Collopy and Richard Boland of the Weatherhead School of Management eloquently explain this point in their article "Design Matters" in the book *Managing as Designing*. The decision attitude, they write, assumes that it is easy to come up with alternatives but difficult to choose between them. The design attitude, in contrast, assumes that it is difficult to design an outstanding alternative, but once you have, the decision about which alternative to select becomes trivial (see p. 164).

This distinction is particularly applicable to business model innovation. You can do as much analysis as you want yet still fail to develop a satisfactory new business model. The world is so full of ambiguity and uncertainty that the design attitude of exploring and prototyping multiple possibilities is most likely to lead to a powerful new business model. Such exploration involves messy, opportunistic bouncing back and forth between market research, analysis, business model prototyping, and idea generation. Design attitude is far less linear and uncertain than decision attitude, which focuses on analysis, decision, and optimization. Yet a purposeful quest for new and competitive growth models demands the design approach.

Damien Newman of the design firm Central eloquently expressed the design attitude in an image he calls the "Design Squiggle." The Design Squiggle embodies the characteristics of the design process: Uncertain at the outset, it is messy and opportunistic, until it focuses on a single point of clarity once the design has matured.

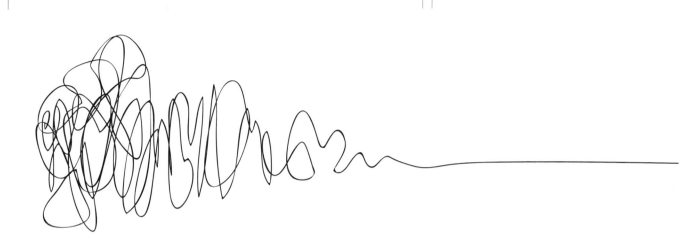

*research
& understand*   *design business
model prototypes*   *implement business
model design*

247

Source: Adapted from Damien Newman, Central

5 Phases

The business model design process we propose has five phases: Mobilize, Understand, Design, Implement, and Manage. As previously mentioned, the progression through these phases is rarely as linear as depicted in the table on the right. In particular, the Understanding and Design phases tend to proceed in parallel. Business model prototyping can start early in the Understanding phase, in the form of sketching preliminary business model ideas. Similarly, prototyping during the design phase may lead to new ideas requiring additional research—and a revisiting of the Understand phase.

Finally, the last phase, Manage, is about continuously managing your business model(s). In today's climate, it's best to assume that most business models, even successful ones, will have a short lifespan. Considering the substantial investment an enterprise makes in producing a business model, it makes sense to extend its life through continuous management and evolution until it needs complete rethinking. Management of the model's evolution will determine which components are still relevant and which are obsolete.

For each process phase we outline the objective, the focus, and which content in *Business Model Generation* supports that phase. Then we outline the five phases in more detail, and explain how the circumstances and focus can change when you are working with an existing business model in an established organization.

OBJECTIVE

FOCUS

DESCRIPTION

BOOK SECTIONS

			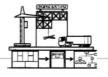	
## Mobilize	## Understand	## Design	## Implement	## Manage
Prepare for a successful business model design project	Research and analyze elements needed for the business model design effort	Generate and test viable business model options, and select the best	Implement the business model prototype in the field	Adapt and modify the business model in response to market reaction
Setting the stage	**Immersion**	**Inquiry**	**Execution**	**Evolution**
Assemble all the elements for successful business model design. Create awareness of the need for a new business model, describe the motivation behind the project, and establish a common language to describe, design, and analyze and discuss business models.	You and the business model design team immerse yourselves in relevant knowledge: customers, technology, and environment. You collect information, interview experts, study potential customers, and identify needs and problems.	Transform the information and ideas from the previous phase into business model prototypes that can be explored and tested. After an intensive business model inquiry, select the most satisfactory business model design.	Implement the selected business model design.	Set up the management structures to continuously monitor, evaluate, and adapt or transform your business model.
• Business Model Canvas (p. 44) • Storytelling (p. 170)	• Business Model Canvas (p. 44) • Business Model Patterns (p. 52) • Customer Insights (p. 126) • Visual Thinking (p. 146) • Scenarios (p. 180) • Business Model Environment (p. 200) • Evaluating Business Models (p. 212)	• Business Model Canvas (p. 44) • Business Model Patterns (p. 52) • Ideation (p. 134) • Visual Thinking (p. 146) • Prototyping (p. 160) • Scenarios (p. 180) • Evaluating Business Models (p. 212) • Business Model Perspective on Blue Ocean Strategy (p. 226) • Managing Multiple Business Models (p. 232)	• Business Model Canvas (p. 44) • Visual Thinking (p. 146) • Storytelling (p. 170) • Managing Multiple Business Models (p. 232)	• Business Model Canvas (p. 44) • Visual Thinking (p. 146) • Scenarios (p. 180) • Business Model Environment (p. 200) • Evaluating Business Models (p. 212)

Canvas

Mobilize

Prepare for a successful business
model design project

ACTIVITIES	CRITICAL SUCCESS FACTORS	KEY DANGERS
• Frame project objectives	• Appropriate people, experience, and knowledge	• Overestimating value of initial idea(s)
• Test preliminary business ideas		
• Plan		
• Assemble team		

The main activities of this first phase are framing the project objectives, testing preliminary ideas, planning the project, and assembling the team.

How objectives are framed will vary depending on the project, but this usually covers establishing the rationale, project scope, and main objectives. Initial planning should cover the first phases of a business model design project: Mobilize, Understand, and Design. The Implementation and Management phases depend heavily on the outcome of these first three phases—namely the business model direction—and therefore can only be planned later.

Crucial activities in this first phase include assembling the project team and gaining access to the right people and information. While there are no rules about training the perfect team—again, each project is unique—it makes sense to seek a mix of people with broad management and industry experience, fresh ideas, the right personal networks, and a deep commitment to business model innovation. You may want to start doing some preliminary testing of the basic business idea during the mobilization phase. But since the potential of a business idea depends heavily on the choice of the right business model, this is easier said than done. When Skype launched its business, who would have imagined it would become the world's largest long-distance call carrier?

In any case, establish the Business Model Canvas as the shared language of the design effort. This will help you structure and present preliminary ideas more effectively and improve communications. You may also want to try weaving your business model ideas into some stories to test them.

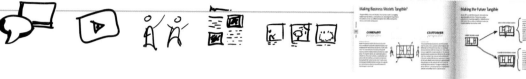

One clear danger in the Mobilization phase is that people tend to overestimate the potential of initial business model ideas. This can lead to a closed mindset and limited exploration of other possibilities. Try to mitigate this risk by continuously testing the new ideas with people from varied backgrounds. You may also want to consider organizing a so-called kill/thrill session in which all participants are tasked first with brainstorming for 20 minutes on reasons why the idea won't work (the "kill" portion), then spend 20 minutes brainstorming exclusively on why the idea will fly (the "thrill" portion). It's a powerful way to challenge an idea's fundamental worth.

Working from the Established Company Perspective

● *Project legitimacy* Building project legitimacy is a critical success factor when working within established organizations. Since business model design projects affect people across organizational boundaries, a strong and visible commitment by the board and/or top management is indispensable to obtaining cooperation. A straightforward way to create legitimacy and visible sponsorship is to directly involve a respected member of top management from the very beginning.

● *Manage vested interests* Take care to identify and manage vested interests throughout the organization. Not everybody in an organization is interested in reinventing the current business model. In fact, the design effort may threaten some people.

● *Cross-functional team* As described previously (see p. 143), the ideal business model task force is composed of people from across the organization, including different business units, business functions (e.g. marketing, finance, IT), levels of seniority and expertise, and so forth. Different organizational perspectives help generate better ideas, and increase the likelihood that the project will succeed. A cross-functional team helps identify and overcome potential obstacles to reinvention early in the game and encourages buy-in.

● *Orienting decision makers* You should plan on spending a considerable amount of time orienting and educating decision makers on business models, their importance, and the design and innovation process. This is critical to gaining buy-in and overcoming resistance to the unknown or not-yet-understood. Depending on your organization's management style you may want to avoid overemphasizing the conceptual aspects of business models. Stay practical and deliver your message with stories and images rather than concepts and theory.

Understanding

Research and analyze the elements needed
for the business model design effort

ACTIVITIES

- Scan environment
- Study potential customers
- Interview experts
- Research what has already been tried (e.g. examples of failures and their causes)
- Collect ideas and opinions

CRITICAL SUCCESS FACTORS

- Deep understanding of potential target markets
- Looking beyond the traditional boundaries defining target markets

KEY DANGERS

- Over-researching: disconnect between research and objectives
- Biased research because of precommitment to a certain business idea

This second phase consists of developing a good understanding of the context in which the business model will evolve.

Scanning the business model environment is a mix of activities, including market research, studying and involving customers, interviewing domain experts, and sketching out competitor business models. The project team should immerse itself in the necessary materials and activities to develop a deep understanding of the business model "design space."

Scanning, though, is inevitably accompanied by the risk of over-researching. Make your team aware of this risk at the outset and ensure that everyone agrees to avoid excessive researching. "Analysis paralysis" can also be avoided by prototyping business models early on (see Prototyping, p. 160). This has the added benefit of allowing you to quickly collect feedback. As mentioned earlier, research, understanding, and designing go hand in hand, and the boundaries separating them are often unclear.

During research, one area that deserves careful attention is developing deep knowledge of the customer. This sounds obvious, but it is often neglected, particularly in technology-focused projects. The Customer Empathy Map (see p. 131) can serve as a powerful tool to help you structure customer research. One common challenge is that the Customer Segment is not necessarily clear from the outset. A technology "still in search of a problem to solve" may be applicable in several different markets.

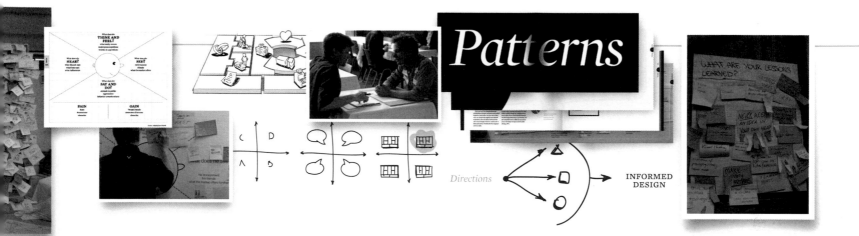

A critical success factor in this phase is questioning industry assumptions and established business model patterns. The game console industry was building and selling cutting edge subsidized consoles until the Nintendo Wii overturned commonly accepted assumptions (see p. 82). Questioning assumptions includes exploring the potential of "the low end" of established markets, as Scott Anthony points out in *The Silver Lining*. As you scan the environment and assess trends, markets, and competitors, remember that the seeds of business model innovation can be found just about anywhere.

During the Understanding phase you should also actively seek input from varied sources, including customers. Start testing preliminary business model directions early by soliciting feedback on Business Model Canvas sketches. Bear in mind, though, that breakthrough ideas may encounter strong resistance.

Working from the Established Company Perspective

● *Mapping/assessing existing business models* Established organizations start with existing business models. Ideally, mapping and assessing your current business model should be done in separate workshops involving people throughout the organization, at the same time ideas and opinions for new business models are being collected. This will provide multiple perspectives on the strengths and weaknesses of your business model, and provide the first ideas for new models.

● *Looking beyond the status-quo* It is particularly challenging to see beyond the current business model and business model patterns. Because the status quo is usually the result of a successful past, it is deeply embedded in organizational culture.

● *Searching beyond the existing client base* Searching beyond your existing client base is critical when seeking lucrative new business models. Tomorrow's profit potential may well lie elsewhere.

● *Demonstrate progress* Excessive analysis risks losing senior management support due to a perceived lack of productivity. Demonstrate your progress by describing customer insights or showing a series of business model sketches based on what you've learned from research.

Design

Adapt and modify the business model
in response to market response

ACTIVITIES

- Brainstorm
- Prototype
- Test
- Select

CRITICAL SUCCESS FACTORS

- Co-create with people from across
  the organization
- Ability to see beyond status quo
- Taking time to explore multiple
  business model ideas

KEY DANGERS

- Watering down or suppressing
  bold ideas
- Falling in love with ideas too quickly

The key challenge during the Design phase is to generate and stick with bold new models. Expansive thinking is the critical success factor here. In order to generate breakthrough ideas, team members must develop the ability to abandon the status quo (current business models and patterns) during ideation. An inquiry-focused design attitude is also crucial. Teams must take the time to explore multiple ideas, because the process of exploring different paths is most likely to yield the best alternatives.

Avoid "falling in love" with ideas too early. Take the time to think through multiple business model options before selecting the one you want to implement. Experiment with different partnership models, seek alternative revenue streams, and explore the value of multiple distribution channels. Try out different business model patterns (see p. 52) to explore and test new possibilities.

To test potential business models with outside experts or prospective clients, develop a narrative for each and seek feedback on your telling of each model's "story." This is not to imply that you need to modify your model based on each and every comment. You will hear feedback such as "this won't work, customers don't need it," "that's not doable, it goes against industry logic," or "the marketplace just isn't ready." Such comments indicate potential roadblocks ahead but should not be considered showstoppers. Further inquiry may well enable you to successfully refine your model.

Iqbal Quadir's quest to bring mobile telephony to poor rural villagers in Bangladesh in the late 1990s provides a powerful example. Most industry experts rejected his idea, saying poor villagers were pressed by more basic needs and wouldn't pay for mobile telephones. But seeking feedback and developing contacts outside the telecommunications

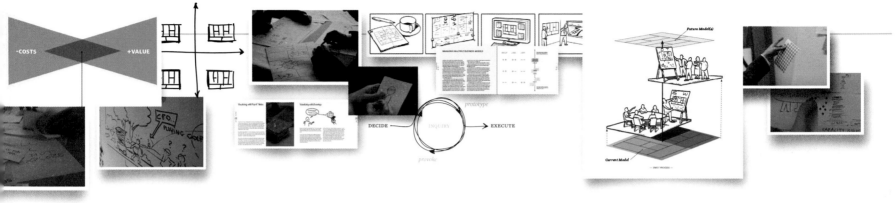

industry led to a partnership with microfinance institution Grameen Bank, which became the cornerstone of Grameenphone's business model. Contrary to expert opinion, poor villagers were indeed willing to pay for mobile connectivity, and Grameenphone became Bangladesh's leading telecommunications provider.

Working from the Established Company Perspective

● *Prevent taming of bold ideas* Established organizations tend to water down bold business model ideas. Your challenge is to defend their boldness—while assuring that they won't face overwhelming obstacles if implemented.

To achieve this tricky balance it can be helpful to draw a risk/reward profile of each model. The profile could include questions such as, What is the profit/loss potential? Describe potential conflicts with existing business units. How might this affect our brand? How will existing customers react? This approach can help you clarify and address the uncertainties in each model. The bolder the model, the higher the level of uncertainty. If you clearly define the uncertainties involved (e.g. new pricing mechanisms, new Distribution Channels), you can prototype and test them in the market to better predict how the model will perform when launched full-scale.

● *Participatory design* Another way to improve the likelihood of having bold ideas adopted and subsequently implemented is to be especially inclusive when assembling the design team. Co-create with people from different business units, different levels of the organizational hierarchy, and different areas of expertise. By integrating comments and concerns from across the organization, your design can anticipate and possibly circumvent implementation roadblocks.

● *Old versus new* One big design question is whether the old and new business models should be separated or integrated into one. The right design choice will greatly affect chances of success (see Managing Multiple Business Models, p. 232).

● *Avoid short-term focus* One limitation to avoid is a short-term focus on ideas with large first-year revenue potential. Big corporations, in particular, can experience huge absolute growth. A company with annual sales of U.S. $5 billion, for example, generates $200 million in new revenues by growing at the modest rate of four percent. Few breakthrough business models can achieve such revenues during their first year (doing so would require acquiring 1.6 million new customers, each paying an annual fee of $125). Therefore, a longer-term perspective is required when exploring new business models. Otherwise, your organization is likely to miss out on many future growth opportunities. How much do you imagine Google earned in its first year?

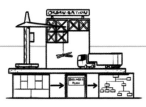

Implement

Implement the business model
prototype in the field

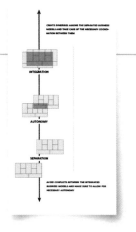

ACTIVITIES

- Communicate and involve
- Execute

CRITICAL SUCCESS FACTORS

- Best practice project management
- Ability and willingness to rapidly adapt the business model
- Align "old" and "new" business models

KEY DANGERS

- Weak or fading momentum

Business Model Generation focuses on understanding and developing innovative business models, but we'd also like to offer some suggestions on implementing new business models, particularly within established organizations.

Once you've arrived at a final business model design, you will start translating this into an implementation design. This includes defining all related projects, specifying milestones, organizing any legal structures, preparing a detailed budget and project roadmap, and so forth. The implementation phase is often outlined in a business plan and itemized in a project management document.

Particular attention needs to be paid to managing uncertainties. This implies closely monitoring how risk/reward expectations play out against actual results. It also means developing mechanisms to quickly adapt your business model to market feedback.

For example, when Skype started becoming successful and was signing up tens of thousands of new users each day, it had to immediately develop mechanisms to cost-effectively handle user feedback and complaints. Otherwise, skyrocketing expenses and user dissatisfaction would have brought the company to its knees.

Working from the Established Company Perspective

● *Proactively managing "roadblocks"* The single element that most increases the likelihood of a new business model's success is in place long before actual implementation. By this we are referring to the participation of people from throughout the organization during the Mobilization, Understanding, and Design phases. Such a participatory approach will have already established buy-in and uncovered obstacles before the imple-

mentation of the new model is even planned. Deep, cross-functional participation allows you to directly address any concerns regarding the new business model before drawing the roadmap for its implementation.

● *Project sponsorship* A second success element is the sustained and visible support of your project sponsor, something that signals the importance and legitimacy of the business model design effort. Both elements are crucial to keeping vested interests from undermining the successful implementation of a new business model.

● *Old versus new business model* A third element is creating the right organizational structure for your new business model (see Managing Multiple Business Models, p. 232). Should it be a standalone entity or a business unit within the parent organization? Will it draw on resources shared with an existing business model? Will it inherit the parent's organizational culture?

● *Communication campaign* Finally, conduct a highly visible, multi-channel internal communication campaign announcing the new business model. This will help you counter "fear of the new" in your organization. As outlined earlier, stories and visualizations are powerful, engaging tools that help people understand the logic of and rationale for the new business model.

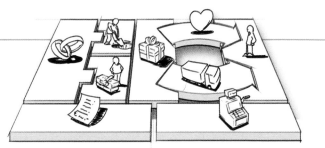

Manage

Adapt and modify the business model
in response to market reaction

ACTIVITIES

- Scan the environment

- Continuously assess your
  business model

- Rejuvenate or rethink your model

- Align business models throughout
  the enterprise

- Manage synergies or conflicts
  between models

CRITICAL SUCCESS FACTORS

- Long-term perspective

- Proactiveness

- Governance of business models

KEY DANGERS

- Becoming a victim of your own
  success, failing to adapt

For successful organizations, creating a new business model or
rethinking an existing one is not a one-time exercise. It's an activity
that continues beyond implementation. The Manage phase includes
continuously assessing the model and scanning the environment
to understand how it might be affected by external factors over the
long term.

At least one person on the organizational strategy team—if not a new
team—should be assigned responsibility for business models and
their long-term evolution. Consider organizing regular workshops with
cross-functional teams to evaluate your business model. This will help
you judge whether a model needs minor adjustments or a complete
overhaul.

Ideally, improving and rethinking the organization's business model
should be every employee's obsession rather than something that
preoccupies only top management. With the Business Model Canvas
you now have a formidable tool with which to make business models
clear to everybody throughout the enterprise. New business model
ideas often emerge from unlikely places within an organization.

Proactive response to market evolutions is also increasingly important
Consider managing a "portfolio" of business models. We live in the
business model generation, a time when the shelf life of successful
business models is shrinking quickly. As with traditional product life-

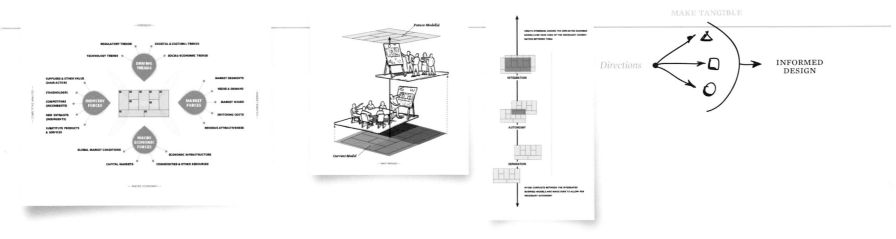

cycle management, we all need to start thinking about replacing our current cash-generating business models with growth models for tomorrow's marketplace.

Dell disrupted the PC industry when it introduced the build-to-order format and direct online sales. Over the years, Dell grew so successfully that it established itself as the industry leader. But the company failed to fully rethink its once disruptive business model. Now that the industry landscape has changed, Dell risks remaining stuck in a commoditized PC market, while growth and profits, generated elsewhere, lie outside its reach.

Working from the Established Company Perspective

● *Business Model Governance* Consider establishing a "business model governance" authority to help better manage business models across the enterprise. This group's role would be to orchestrate business models, engage stakeholders, launch inno-

vation or redesign projects, and track the overall evolution of the organization's business models. It should also manage the "master" business model that describes the entire organization. This master template could serve as the starting point for each business model project within the organization. The master business model would also help different functional groups, such as operations, manufacturing, or sales align with the organization's overarching goals.

● *Manage synergies and conflicts* One of the business model governance authority's main tasks would be to align business models with each other to exploit synergies and avoid or manage conflicts. A Canvas document describing each business model in the organization would help illuminate the big picture and achieve better alignment.

● *Business model portfolio* Successful, established companies should proactively manage a "portfolio" of business models. Many formerly successful companies in the music, newspaper, and automotive industries failed to proactively examine their business models and slid into crisis as a result. A promising approach to avoiding this fate is to develop a portfolio of business models whereby cash-generating businesses finance business model experiments for the future.

● *A beginner's mindset* Maintaining a beginner's mindset helps keep us from becoming victims of our own successes. We all need to constantly scan the landscape and continuously assess our own business models. Take a fresh look at your model regularly. You may need to overhaul a successful model sooner than you thought.

WHAT ELSE?

Prototyping is potentially the most important part of the book and tools provided.

My reasoning is based upon the stress and resistance that established organizations are facing in the process of innovating their own business models. Therefore a very potent strategy is prototyping—in order to create buy-in processes needed.
Terje Sand, Norway

Typically when an organization looks at improving their business model, it is as a result of gaps. Visualizing your current business model can demonstrate the logical gaps that exist and make them tangible as action items.
Ravila White, United States

In established companies, there are often ample physical "product ideas" that never get serious consideration because they don't immediately fit the prevailing business model.
Gert Steens, Netherlands

Do not get too attached to the first idea or implementation.
Build in feedback loops and monitor early warning signals to explicitly challenge your original concept and be willing and able to completely change it if required.
Erwin Fielt, Australia

The freemium business model as the reverse of insurance—insightful! Makes me want to turn other models upside down!
Victor Lombardi, United States

A business model is the **"CORE CONTENT"** *or the* **"SHORT STORY"** of the company (actual or prospective). A business plan is the "guideline for the action" or the "full story."
Fernando Saenz-Marrero, Spain

When I work with non-profits the first thing I tell them is that they in fact have a "business" (model) in that they must create and capture value, whether that value comes from donations, subscriptions, and so on.
Kim Korn, United States

Begin with the end in mind while taking the end client perspective.
Karl Burrow, Japan

It's one thing to map out a Business Model Canvas. But for creating a business model that in itself is a breakthrough innovation, it is helpful to use tools used to create breakthrough innovation in other industries, such as in design.

Ellen Di Resta, United States

Aravind uses the Freemium Business Model to enable FREE eye surgery for the poor in India. Business model innovation can really make a difference!

Anders Sundelin, Sweden

I find that although most managers understand strategy concepts, they have a tough time applying these concepts at their level of the organization.

However, discussions about business models connect the high-level concepts to day-to-day decision-making. It's a great middle ground.

Bill Welter, United States

Personas, Scenarios, Visualization, Empathy maps, and so on are techniques that I have used since the late 1990s in user experience type projects. In the last few years I have seen that they are incredibly effective at a strategy/business level.

Eirik V Johnsen, Norway

If solving humanity's current problems requires rethinking how value is generated and for whom, then business model innovation is the premier tool to organize, communicate, and implement that new thinking.

Nabil Harfoush, Canada

I'm interested in hearing how people are integrating technology ideas into their models using the Canvas. We've explored adding it as a separate layer (above or below financial) but have now settled on integrating it as notes on each of the 9 key areas. From this we then step back and develop a separate integrated technology plan.

Rob Manson, Australia

YOUR BUSINESS MODEL IS **NOT** YOUR BUSINESS

It's a method of inquiry to help you understand what to do next. Testing and iteration is key.

Matthew Milan, Canada

Multi-sided platforms are actually rather easy at the business model level; the difficulty comes in execution: attracting the "subsidized side," pricing on both sides, vertical or horizontal integration, how to change the business model in step with the size of the market on each side.

Hampus Jakobsson, Sweden

BUSINESS MODEL INNOVATION COMBINES *creativity* WITH A *structured approach*—THE BEST OF BOTH WORLDS.

Ziv Baida, Netherlands

Many of my clients do not have a holistic view of their business model and tend to focus on trying to address the immediate problem. The Business Model Canvas provides a framework that helps clarify the why, who, what, when, where, and how.

Patrick van Abbema, Canada

I love the idea of using these tools to design businesses and to tinker under the hood of the engine of an organization.

Michael Anton Dila, Canada

There are **thousands of business models to be investigated** and many **thousands of people who are interested** in them.

Steven Devijver, Belgium

Simplicity is very important to explain the patterns and to trigger the non-professional's involvement in business innovation.

Gertjan Verstoep, Netherlands

We have been working too long and too hard for companies with bad or improper business models.

Lytton He, China

The term business model is thrown around a lot and more frequently than not to mean an incomplete understanding of what makes a business a business (mostly just the financial/revenue aspect).

Livia Labate, United States

Business model innovation is one of the

LEAST USED **& MOST POWERFUL**

ways to create sustainable profit growth, economic development and create new 'markets' and 'industries'.

Deborah Mills-Scofield, United States

Outlook

We hope we've shown you how visionaries, game changers, and challengers can tackle the vital issue of business models. We hope we've provided you with the language, the tools and techniques, and the dynamic approach needed to design innovative and competitive new models. But much remains to be said. So here we touch on five topics, each of which might well merit its own book.

The first examines business models beyond profit: how the Canvas can drive business model innovation in the public and non-profit sectors. The second suggests how computer-aided business model design might leverage the paper-based approach and allow for complex manipulation of business model elements. The third discusses the relationship between business models and business plans. The fourth addresses issues that arise when implementing business models in either new or existing organizations. The final topic examines how to better achieve business model and IT alignment.

Beyond-Profit Business Models

The application of the Canvas is in no way limited to for-profit corporations. You can easily apply the technique to non-profit organizations, charities, public sector entities, and for-profit social ventures.

Every organization has a business model, even if the word "business" is not used as a descriptor. To survive, every organization that creates and delivers value must generate enough revenue to cover its expenses. Hence it has a business model. The difference is merely a matter of focus: the for-profit business's goal is to maximize earnings, while the organizations discussed in the following pages have strong non-financial missions focused on ecology, social causes, and public service mandates. We find useful entrepreneur Tim Clark's suggestion that the term "enterprise model" be applied to such organizations.

We distinguish between two categories of beyond-profit models: third-party funded enterprise models (e.g. philanthropy, charities, government) and so-called triple bottom line business models with a strong ecological and/or social mission ("triple bottom line" refers to the practice of accounting for environmental and social, as well as financial, costs). It is mainly the source of revenue that distinguishes these two, but as a direct consequence they have two very different business model patterns and drivers. Many organizations are experimenting with blending the two models in order to exploit the best of both.

Third-Party Funded Models
In this type of enterprise model, the product or service recipient is not the payer. Products and services are paid for by a third party, which might be a donor or the public sector. The third party pays the organization to fulfill a mission, which may be of a social, ecological, or public service nature. For example, government (and indirectly, taxpayers) pays schools to deliver education services. Likewise, donors to Oxfam, a large U.K. non-profit organization, help finance its efforts to end poverty and social injustice. Third parties rarely expect to receive direct economic benefits from the exchange, unlike advertisers—who are players in for-profit business models which also feature third party financing.

One risk of the third-party enterprise model is that value creation incentives can become misaligned. The third-party financer becomes the main "customer," so to speak, while the recipient becomes a mere receiver. Since the very existence of the enterprise depends on contributions, the incentive to create value for donors may be stronger than the incentive to create value for recipients.

All this is not to say that third-party funded enterprise models are bad and recipient-funded business models are good. Conventional businesslike selling of products and services doesn't always work: education, healthcare, and utility services are clear examples. There are no simple answers to the questions raised by third-party financed enterprise models and the resulting risks of misaligned incentives. We must explore which models make sense, then strive to design optimal solutions.

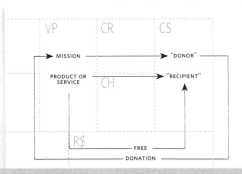

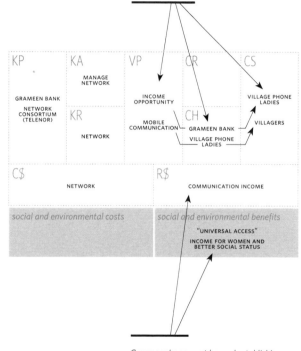

Villagers in Bangladesh were too poor to afford phones, so Grameenphone partnered with Grameen Bank, the microfinance institution, to provide local women with microloans to purchase mobile phones. The women sold calling services in their villages, repaid the loans, earned income, and thereby improved their social status.

Grameenphone went beyond establishing near universal access to telephone service and earning a profit. It also had substantial social impact by providing "village phone ladies" with earning opportunities and improved social status.

Solving the big issues of our generation requires bold new business models

Triple Bottom Line Business Models

Earlier we shared the story of how Iqbal Quadir, an investment banker in New York, set out to build Grameenphone. His goal was to provide universal access to telecommunications services in remote, rural areas of his home country of Bangladesh. He achieved his aim with a for-profit model that had a profound, positive impact on rural Bangladesh. Grameenphone eventually provided over 200,000 women in rural areas with income-earning opportunities, raised their social status, connected 60,000 villages to a mobile phone network, reached 100 million people, turned a profit, and became the Bangladeshi government's biggest taxpayer.

To accommodate triple bottom line business models, we can extend the Canvas with Blocks illustrating two outcomes: (1) the social and environmental costs of a business model (i.e. its negative impact), and (2) the social and environmental benefits of a business model (i.e. its positive impact). Just as earnings are increased by minimizing financial costs and maximizing income, the triple bottom line model seeks to minimize negative social and environmental impacts and maximize the positive.

Computer-Aided Business Model Design

Improving the process

Mike, a senior business analyst with a large financial group, wraps up the first of a two-day workshop he is facilitating with a group of 24 executives. He collects the business model prototypes and ideas that participants sketched on large Canvas posters and hurries to his office.

There, Mike and his team enter the ideas into a collaborative computer-aided business model design program to further develop the prototypes. Other business analysts working overseas add resource and activity cost estimates, as well as calculations of potential Revenue Streams. The software then spits out four different financial scenarios, with business model data and prototype diagrams for each plotted on large posters. The following morning Mike presents the results to the executives, who have gathered for the second day of their workshop to discuss the potential risks and rewards of each prototype.

This scenario doesn't yet describe reality, but that is changing rapidly. A Business Model Canvas printed on a large poster and a big box of Post-it notes will always be a very powerful tool for triggering creativity and generating innovative business model ideas. However, we extended this paper-based approach with the help of the computer, the Internet, and the iPad. Turning a prototype business model into a spreadsheet is time-consuming, and each change to the prototype usually requires a manual modification of the spreadsheet. Therefore we developed the Business Model Toolbox, Web and iPad-based platform that combines the speed of a napkin sketch with the smarts of a spreadsheet.

Scratching the Surface: a Prototype

The Business Model Toolbox makes the creation, storage, manipulation, tracking, and communication of business models far easier. The toolbox also supports collaborative work on business models for geographically disparate teams. With this software our aim is to bring the same computer support to business models than what we take for granted when we design, simulate, and build airplanes or develop software across continents. Inventing innovative business models certainly requires human creativity, but computer-aided systems can help us manipulate business models in more sophisticated and complex ways.

Try our prototype of computer aided business model editor free
at www.businessmodeltoolbox.com

CAD's Influence Past, Present and Future

An example from the field of architecture is helpful in illustrating the power of computer-aided design. In the 1980s so-called Computer-Aided Design (CAD) systems started becoming more affordable and slowly were adopted by architectural firms. CAD made it much easier and cheaper for architects to create threedimensionalmodels and prototypes. They brought speed, integration, improved collaboration, simulation, and better planning to architecture practices, Cumbersome manual tasks, such as constant redrawing and blueprint sharing, were eliminated, and a whole new world of opportunity, such as rapid visual 3-D exploration and prototyping, opened up. Today paper-based sketching and CAD happily co-exist, each method retaining its own strengths and weaknesses.

In the realm of business models, too, computer-aided systems could make many tasks easier and quicker, while revealing as-yet unseen opportunity. At the least, CAD systems could help visualize, store, manipulate, track, annotate, and communicate business models just as the Business Model Toolbox does.

More complex functions could involve manipulating layers or business model versions, or moving business model elements dynamically and evaluating the impact in real-time. Systems might facilitate business model critiquing, provide a repository of business model patterns and off-the-shelf building blocks,simulate models, or integrate with other enterprise systems (e.g. ERP or business process management).

Computer-aided business model design systems like the Business Model Toolbox will likely evolve in step with interface improvements. Manipulating business models on wall-sized touch screens would bring computer-aided design closer to the intuitive paper-based approach and improve usability.

	Paper-based	Computer-aided
Advantages	• Paper or poster-based Canvases can be easily created and used just about anywhere • Paper and poster-based Canvases impose few barriers: no need to learn a specific computer application • Very intuitive and engaging in group settings • Fosters creativity, spurs ideation when used on large surfaces	Easy to create, store, manipulate, and track business models • Enable remote collaboration • Quick, comprehensive financial, other simulations • Provide business model design guidance (critiquing systems, business model database, pattern ideas, control mechanisms)
Applications	• Napkin sketches to draw, understand, or explain business models • Collaborative brainstorming sessions to develop business model ideas • Collaborative assessment of business models	• Collaborative business model design with remote teams • Complex manipulations of business models (navigation, business model layers, merging models) • Deep, comprehensive analysis

Business Models and Business Plans

The purpose of a business plan is to describe and communicate a for-profit or non-profit project and how it can be implemented, either inside or outside an organization. The motivation behind the business plan may be to "sell" a project, either to potential investors or internal organizational stakeholders. A business plan may also serve as an implementation guide.

In fact, the work you may have done designing and thinking through your own business model is the perfect basis for writing a strong business plan. We suggest giving business plans a five-section structure: The Team, The Business Model, Financial Analysis, External Environment, Implementation Roadmap, and Risk Analysis.

The Team

One business plan element that venture capitalists particularly emphasize is the management team. Is the team experienced, knowledgeable, and connected enough to accomplish what they propose? Do the members have successful track records? Highlight why your team is the right one to successfully build and execute the business model you propose.

The Business Model

This section showcases the attractiveness of the business model. Use the Canvas to provide readers with an immediate visual portrait of your model. Ideally, illustrate the elements with drawings. Then, describe the Value Proposition, show evidence of customer need, and explain how you will reach the market. Use stories. Highlight the attractiveness of your target segments to pique the reader's interest. Finally, describe the Key Resources and Activities needed to build and execute the business model.

Financial Analysis

This is traditionally an important business plan component that attracts much attention. You can make pro forma calculations based on your Canvas Building Blocks and estimate how many customers can be acquired. Include elements such as breakeven analysis, sales scenarios, and operating costs. The Canvas can also help with capital spending calculations and other implementation cost estimates. Total cost, revenue, and cash flow projections determine your funding requirements.

External Environment

This section of the business plan describes how your business model is positioned with respect to the external environment. The four external forces covered earlier (see p. 201) provide the basis for this description. Summarize your business model's competitive advantages.

Implementation Roadmap

This section shows the reader what it will take to implement your business model and how you will do it. Include a summary of all projects and the overarching milestones. Outline the implementation agenda with a project roadmap that includes Gantt charts. Projects can be derived directly from your Canvas.

Risk Analysis

In closing, describe limiting factors and obstacles, as well as critical success factors. These can be derived from a SWOT analysis of your business model (see p. 216).

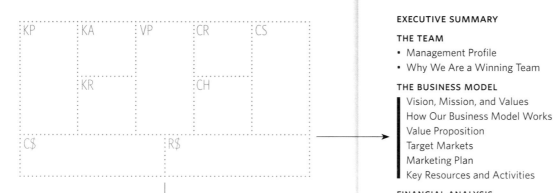

BUSINESS PLAN

EXECUTIVE SUMMARY

THE TEAM
- Management Profile
- Why We Are a Winning Team

THE BUSINESS MODEL
Vision, Mission, and Values
How Our Business Model Works
Value Proposition
Target Markets
Marketing Plan
Key Resources and Activities

FINANCIAL ANALYSIS
Breakeven Analysis
Sales Scenarios and Projections
Capital Spending
Operating Costs
Funding Requirements

EXTERNAL ENVIRONMENT
The Economy
Market Analysis and Key Trends
Competitor Analysis
Competitive Advantages of Our Business Model

IMPLEMENTATION ROADMAP
Projects
Milestones
Roadmap

RISK ANALYSIS
Limiting Factors and Obstacles
Critical Success Factors
Specific Risks and Countermeasures

CONCLUSION

ANNEXES

financial spreadsheets

environmental analysis

implementation roadmap

SWOT and uncertainty analysis

KP KA VP CR CS
KR CH
C$ R$

Implementing Business Models in Organizations

We've laid out the fundamentals of business model innovation, explained the dynamics of different patterns, and outlined techniques for inventing and designing models. Naturally there is much more to say about the implementation that is critical to a business model's success.

We've already addressed the question of how to manage multiple business models (see p. 232). Now let's turn to another aspect of implementation: turning your business model into a sustainable enterprise, or implementing it in an existing organization. To illustrate, we've combined the Canvas with Jay Galbraith's Star Model to suggest aspects of organizational design you may want to consider when executing a business model.

Galbraith specifies five areas that should be aligned in an organization: Strategy, Structure, Processes, Rewards, and People. We place the business model in the middle of the star as a "center of gravity" that holds the five areas together.

Strategy

Strategy drives the business model. Do you want to grow 20 percent in new market segments? Then that should be reflected in your business model in terms of new Customer Segments, Channels, or Key Activities.

Structure

The characteristics of a business model determine the optimal organizational structure for its execution. Does your business model call for a highly centralized or decentralized organizational structure? If you will implement the model in an established business, should the new operation be integrated or spun off (see p. 233)?

Processes

Each business model demands different processes. Operations run under a low-cost business model should be lean and highly automated. If the model calls for selling high-value machines, quality processes must be exceptionally rigorous.

Rewards

Different business models require different reward systems. A reward system must use appropriate incentives to motivate workers to do the right things. Does your model require a direct sales force to acquire new customers? Then your reward system should be highly performance oriented. Does your model depend heavily on customer satisfaction? Then your reward system must reflect that commitment.

People

Certain business models call for people with particular mindsets. For example, some business models call for particularly entrepreneurial mechanisms to bring products and services to market. Such models must give employees significant leeway, which means hiring proactive, but dependable, free-thinkers.

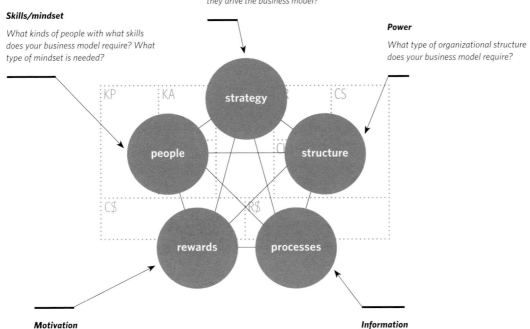

Direction

What are your strategic goals? How do they drive the business model?

Skills/mindset

What kinds of people with what skills does your business model require? What type of mindset is needed?

Power

What type of organizational structure does your business model require?

Motivation

What reward system does your business model require? How can you motivate your people?

Information

What information flows, processes, and workflows does your business model require?

Aligning IT with Business

Aligning information systems and business goals is fundamental to the success of an enterprise. Chief executives officers ask their chief information officers (CIOs), Do we have the right IT? How do we know? How can we best align our business with our technology systems?

Information technology research and advisory firm Gartner highlights this issue in a report called "Getting the Right IT: Using Business Models." Gartner asserts that the Business Model Canvas is a powerful tool that helps CIOs quickly grasp how a business works without getting bogged down in operational details. Gartner recommends that CIOs use the Business Model Canvas to align IT and key business processes. This helps them align business and IT decisions without diving too deeply into tactical issues.

We find it useful to pair the Canvas with an Enterprise Architecture approach. Many of the various Enterprise Architecture concepts describe the enterprise from three perspectives: the business perspective, the applications perspective, and the technology perspective. We recommend using the Canvas to guide the business perspective, then align the business with the applications and technology perspectives.

In the application perspective, you describe the portfolio of applications that leverage aspects of your business model (e.g. recommendation systems, supply chain management applications, etc.) and you describe all the business model's information requirements (e.g. customer profiles, warehousing, etc.). In the technology perspective you describe the technology infrastructure that drives your business model (e.g. server farms, data storage systems, etc.).

Authors Weill and Vitale propose another interesting way to explore IT alignment. They pair categories of IT infrastructure service with business models. Weill and Vitale propose aligning business models with application infrastructure, communications management, data management, IT management, security, IT architecture, channel management, IT research and development, and IT training and education.

On the opposite page we've brought these elements together in a graphic to help you pose some fundamental questions regarding business and IT alignment.

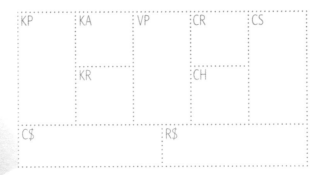

strategy
business model
operational models

Business

Applications

Technology

How can IT support the processes and workflows required by my business models?

What information do I need to capture, store, share, and manage to improve my business model?

How does my application portfolio leverage the specific dynamics of my business model?

How will IT architecture, standards, and interface choices limit or leverage my business model?

Which technology infrastructure is required and crucial to the success of my business model (e.g. server farms, communications, and so on)?

Where in my business model does security play an important role and how does that influence my IT?

Do I need to invest in IT training and education to leverage my business model?

Could investments in IT research and development improve my business model in the future?

WHERE DID THIS BOOK COME FROM?

CONTEXT

2004: Alexander Osterwalder completes a Ph.D. dissertation on the topic of business model innovation with Professor Yves Pigneur at HEC Lausanne, Switzerland. Fast forward. **2006:** The approach outlined in the dissertation starts being applied around the world based on Alexander's business model blog, notably in companies such as 3M, Ericsson, Deloitte, and Telenor. During a workshop in the Netherlands Patrick van der Pijl asks **"why is there no book accompanying the method?"** Alexander and Yves take up the challenge. **But how does one stand out in a market where countless strategy and management books are published every year?**

INNOVATING THE MODEL

Alexander and Yves decide **they can't credibly write a book about business model innovation without an innovative business model.** They ditch publishers and launch the Hub, an online platform to share their writings from day one. Anybody with an interest in the topic can join the platform for a fee (initially U.S. $24, which is gradually raised to U.S. $243 to keep the platform exclusive). That this and other innovative Revenue Streams finance the book production in advance itself is an innovation as well. It breaks the format of conventional strategy and management books in order to create more value for readers: it is co-created highly visual, and complemented by exercises and workshop tips.

KEY AUDIENCE
visionary and game changing …
entrepreneurs / consultants / executives

MADE IN…

Written: **Lausanne, CH**
Designed: **London, UK**
Edited: **Portland, USA**
Photographed: **Toronto, CA**
Produced: **Amsterdam, NL**
Events: **Amsterdam & Toronto**

PROCESS

The core team, consisting of Alexander, Yves, and Patrick start the project with a number of meetings to sketch out the business model of the book. The Hub is launched to co-create the book with business model innovation practitioners throughout the world. Creative Director Alan Smith of The Movement hears about the project and puts his company behind it. Finally, Hub member Tim Clark joins the core team after recognizing the need for an editor. The group is completed by JAM, a company that uses visual thinking to solve business problems. An engagement cycle is started to pump fresh "chunks" of content out to the Hub community for feedback and contributions. The writing of the book becomes completely transparent. Content, design, illustrations, and structure are constantly shared and thoroughly commented upon by Hub members worldwide. The core team responds to every comment and integrates the feedback back into the book and design. A "soft launch" of the book is organized in Amsterdam, Netherlands, so members of the Hub can meet in person and share their experiences with business model innovation. Sketching out participant business models with JAM becomes the core exercise of the day. Two hundred special limited edition prototypes of the (unfinished) book go to print and a video of the writing process is produced by Fisheye Media. After several more iterations the first print run is produced.

TOOLS USED

STRATEGY:
- Environmental Scanning
- Business Model Canvas
- Customer Empathy Map

CONTENT AND R&D:
- Customer Insights
- Case Studies

OPEN PROCESS:
- Online Platform
- Co-Creation
- Access to Unfinished Work
- Commenting & Feedback

DESIGN:
- Open Design Process
- Moodboards
- Paper Mockups
- Visualization
- Illustration
- Photography

THE NUMBERS

9
years of research and practice

470
co-authors

19
book chunks

8
prototypes

200
copies of a messed up test print

77
forum discussions

287
Skype calls

1,360
comments

45
countries

137,757
views of method online before book publishing

13.18
GB of content

28,456
Post-it™ notes used

4,000+
hours of work

521
photos

REFERENCES

Boland, Richard Jr., and Collopy, Fred. *Managing as Designing*. Stanford: Stanford Business Books. 2004.

Buxton, Bill. *Sketching User Experience, Getting the Design Right and the Right Design*. New York: Elsevier. 2007.

Denning, Stephen.*The Leader's Guide to Storytelling: Mastering the Art and Discipline of Business Narrative*. San Francisco: Jossey-Bass. 2005.

Galbraith, Jay R. *Designing Complex Organizations*. Reading: Addison Wesley. 1973.

Goodwin, Kim. *Designing for the Digital Age: How to Create Human-Centered Products and Services*. New York: John Wiley & Sons, Inc. 2009.

Harrison, Sam. *Ideaspotting: How to Find Your Next Great Idea*. Cincinnati: How Books. 2006.

Heath, Chip, and Heath, Dan. *Made to Stick: Why Some Ideas Survive and Others Die*. New York: Random House. 2007.

Hunter, Richard, and McDonald, Mark, "Getting the Right IT: Using Business Models." *Gartner EXP CIO Signature report*, October 2007.

Kelley, Tom, et. al. *The Art of Innovation: Lessons in Creativity from IDEO, America's Leading Design Firm*. New York: Broadway Business. 2001.

Kelley, Tom. *The Ten Faces of Innovation: Strategies for Heightening Creativity*. New York: Profile Business. 2008.

Kim, W. Chan, and Mauborgne, Renée. *Blue Ocean Strategy: How to Create Uncontested Market Space and Make Competition Irrelevant*. Boston: Harvard Business School Press. 2005.

Markides, Constantinos C. *Game-Changing Strategies: How to Create New Market Space in Established Industries by Breaking the Rules*. San Francisco: Jossey-Bass. 2008.

Medina, John. *Brain Rules: 12 Principles for Surviving and Thriving at Work, Home, and School*. Seattle: Pear Press. 2009.

Moggridge, Bill. *Designing interactions*. Cambridge: MIT Press. 2007.

O'Reilly, Charles A., III, and Michael L. Tushman. "The Ambidextrous Organization." *Harvard Business Review* 82, no. 4 (April 2004): 74–81.

Pillkahn, Ulf. *Using Trends and Scenarios as Tools for Strategy Development*. New York: John Wiley & Sons, Inc. 2008.

Pink, Daniel H. *A Whole New Mind: Why Right-Brainers Will Rule the Future*. New York: Riverhead Trade. 2006.

Porter, Michael. *Competitive Strategy: Techniques for Analyzing Industries and Competitors*. New York: Free Press. 1980.

Roam, Dan. *The Back of the Napkin: Solving Problems and Selling Ideas with Pictures*. New York: Portfolio Hardcover. 2008.

Schrage, Michael. *Serious Play: How the World's Best Companies Simulate to Innovate*. Boston: Harvard Business School Press. 1999.

Schwartz, Peter. *The Art of the Long View: Planning for the Future in an Uncertain World*. New York: Currency Doubleday. 1996.

Stabell, Charles and Fjeldstad, Øystein, "Configuring Value for Competitive Advantage: on Chain, Shops, and Networks," *Strategic Management Journal*, no.19, 1998: 413–437.

Weill, Peter, and Vitale, Michael. *Place to Space: Migrating to Ebusiness Models*. Boston: Harvard Business School Press. 2001.

NO JUNK MAIL

MARKET RESPONSE

The market response to *Business Model Generation* has been extremely gratifying. The first print run of 5,000 books sold out in two months, with no marketing budget and without the support of a traditional publisher. News about the book spread exclusively by word-of-mouth, blogs, Web sites, e-mail, and Twitter. Most gratifying of all, local meetups, where readers and Hub followers got together to discuss *Business Model Generation's* content, formed spontaneously worldwide.

#BMGEN

@business_design Three steps to effective use of "Business Model Generation": 1) Buy book 2) Test live 3) Be amazed ;-) http://bit.ly/OzZh0
@Acluytens

Excitement! Business Model Generation book arrived! It's going to be an "I'm reading weekend," sorry darling! :-) #bmgen
@tkeppins

Still quiet in the house this sunday morning. Enjoying a cappuccino and reading Business Model Generation.
@hvandenbergh

I have a dilemma now: to catch up on class reading or have fun with Business Model Generation by @business_design...
@vshamanov

Just got my copy of Business Model Generation by @business_design designed by @thinksmith Even more beautiful than I imagined #bmgen
@remarkk

Heading over to #ftjco to visit @ryan-taylor and borrow his copy of #bmgen tonight. Exciting evening all-around!
@bgilham

I'm SO tempted to write all over my copy of #bmgen, but it's too beautiful to destroy. Think I need 2 copies. #bmgento
@skanwar

Just got my copy of Business Model Generation - looks to be as beautifully made as it is useful. Congrats!
@francoisnel

@business_design I am BLOWN AWAY by the stuff I've learned from #bmgen!! I can't thank you guys enough for writing it!
@will_lam

Is reading Business Model Generation... This is perhaps the neatest and most innovative book I have ever read!
@jhemlig

I am so in love with my copy! Thanks @business_design #bmgen
@evelynso

Business Model Generation

Just got my copy of Business Model Generation.. Too good!! The new age of innovation in book-writing
@Neerumarya

Just received my copy of the book 'Business Model Generation'. It's a musthave for entrepreneurs who think out of the box
@Peter_Engel

Business model generatiom really is a stunning book. Feeling like a kid at Christmas with it in my hands. #bmgen
@mrchrisadams

my edition of http://www.businessmodelgeneration.com has arrived! This is the coolest business book ever! WOW! #bmgen
@snuikas

The Business Model Generation book will bring a lot more depth to current, often superficial BM discussions #bmgen http://pic.gd/6671ef
@provice

Reading Business Model Generation over a lonely dinner in London. The book is exquisitely designed. Once you see it, there's no going back.
@roryoconnor

Excited to have participated in the Business Model Generation book. Now published!!
@pvanabbema

giddy as a little kid. just received my copy of Business Model Generation http://tinyurl.com/l847fj awesome book design.
@santiago_rdm

Reading Business Model Generation by Alex Osterwalder and Yves Pigneur: best mngt book in a long time
@JoostC

your big experiment just arrived in Japan. First printing of "Business Model Generation." Electrifying hands-on book.
@CoCreatr

My Business Model Generation by @business_design & Yves Pigneur arrived! So awesome to have been a TINY part.
@jaygoldman

@thinksmith @business_design @patrickpijl Guys, I am happy! Insane. What a wonderful result.
@dulk

Got my hands on the #bmgen book a few days ago, very nice! Great job, @business_design, @thinksmith et al!
@evangineer

It was so amazing to experience 40+ people all embracing business model gen thinking in Toronto #bmgento - this city is exploding!
@davidfeldt

278

Is it me or is everybody in Toronto picking up a copy of Business Model Generation? #bmgen
@will_iam

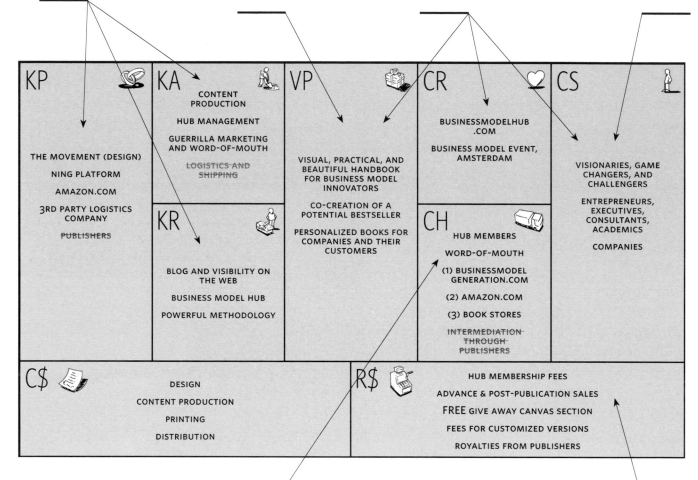

THE CANVAS OF BUSINESS MODEL GENERATION

Production and Logistics

Anything beyond content creation is outsourced to readily available service providers.

Differentiation

An entirely different format, business model, and story for the book makes it stand out in a crowded market.

Community

The book is co-created with practitioners from around the world who feel owner-ship thanks to attribution as contributing co-authors.

Buyers

Paying customers are not only readers, but co-creators and companies that want customized books for their employees and clients.

Reach

A mix of direct and indirect Channels and a phased approach optimizes reach and margins. The story of the book lends itself well to viral marketing and word-of-mouth promotion.

Revenues

The book was financed through advance sales and fees paid by co-creators. Additional revenues come from custom-ized versions for companies and their clients.

KP
THE MOVEMENT (DESIGN)
NING PLATFORM
AMAZON.COM
3RD PARTY LOGISTICS COMPANY
PUBLISHERS

KA
CONTENT PRODUCTION
HUB MANAGEMENT
GUERRILLA MARKETING AND WORD-OF-MOUTH
LOGISTICS AND SHIPPING

KR
BLOG AND VISIBILITY ON THE WEB
BUSINESS MODEL HUB
POWERFUL METHODOLOGY

VP
VISUAL, PRACTICAL, AND BEAUTIFUL HANDBOOK FOR BUSINESS MODEL INNOVATORS
CO-CREATION OF A POTENTIAL BESTSELLER
PERSONALIZED BOOKS FOR COMPANIES AND THEIR CUSTOMERS

CR
BUSINESSMODELHUB.COM
BUSINESS MODEL EVENT, AMSTERDAM

CH
HUB MEMBERS
WORD-OF-MOUTH
(1) BUSINESSMODEL GENERATION.COM
(2) AMAZON.COM
(3) BOOK STORES
INTERMEDIATION THROUGH PUBLISHERS

CS
VISIONARIES, GAME CHANGERS, AND CHALLENGERS
ENTREPRENEURS, EXECUTIVES, CONSULTANTS, ACADEMICS
COMPANIES

C$
DESIGN
CONTENT PRODUCTION
PRINTING
DISTRIBUTION

R$
HUB MEMBERSHIP FEES
ADVANCE & POST-PUBLICATION SALES
FREE GIVE AWAY CANVAS SECTION
FEES FOR CUSTOMIZED VERSIONS
ROYALTIES FROM PUBLISHERS

Alex Osterwalder, Author

Dr. Osterwalder is an author, speaker, and adviser on the topic of business model innovation. His practical approach to designing innovative business models, developed together with Dr. Yves Pigneur, is practiced in multiple industries throughout the world by companies including 3M, Ericsson, Capgemini, Deloitte, Telenor, and many others. Previously he helped build and sell a strategic consulting firm, participated in the development of a Thailand-based global nonprofit organization combating HIV/AIDS and malaria, and did research at the University of Lausanne, Switzerland.

Yves Pigneur, Co-Author

Dr. Pigneur has been a Professor of Management Information Systems at the University of Lausanne since 1984, and has held visiting professorships at Georgia State University in Atlanta and at the University of British Columbia in Vancouver. He has served as the principal investigator for many research projects involving information system design, requirements engineering, information technology management, innovation, and e-business.

Alan Smith, Creative Director

Alan is a big scale thinker who loves the details just as much. He's a co-founder at the aptly named change agency: The Movement. There he works with inspired clients to blend community knowledge, business logic, and design thinking. The resulting strategy, communications, and interactive projects feel like artifacts from the future but always connect to the people of today. Why? Because he designs like he gives a damn—every project, every day.

Tim Clark, Editor and Contributing Co-Author

A teacher, writer, and speaker in the field of entrepreneurship, Tim's perspective is informed by his experience founding and selling a marketing research consultancy that served firms such as Amazon.com, Bertelsmann, General Motors, LVMH, and PeopleSoft. Business model thinking is key to his *Entrepreneurship for Everyone* approach to personal and professional learning, and central to his doctoral work on international business model portability. *Business Model Generation* is his fourth book.

Patrick van der Pijl, Producer

Patrick van der Pijl is the founder of Business Models, Inc., an international business model consultancy. Patrick helps organizations, entrepreneurs, and management teams discover new ways of doing business by envisioning, evaluating, and implementing new business models. Patrick helps clients succeed through intensive workshops, training courses, and coaching.